ADVANCES IN INTERNATIONAL MARKETING

Volume 8 • 1996

ADVANCES IN INTERNATIONAL MARKETING

Series Editor: S. TAMER CAVUSGIL
The Eli Broad Graduate
School of Management
Michigan State University

Volume Editor: TAGE KOED MADSEN
Department of Marketing
Odense University

VOLUME 8 • 1996

 JAI PRESS INC.

Greenwich, Connecticut   London, England

Copyright © 1996 JAI PRESS INC.
55 Old Post Road No. 2
Greenwich, Connecticut 06836

JAI PRESS LTD.
38 Tavistock Street
Covent Garden
London WC2E 7PB
England

ISBN: 0-7623-0164-3

Manufactured in the United States of America

CONTENTS

LIST OF CONTRIBUTORS

Catherine N. Axinn

Department of Marketing
Ohio University

S. Tamer Cavusgil

Department of Marketing
and Supply Chain Management
Michigan State University

Adamantios Diamantopoulos

University of Wales,
Swansea

Nicholas M. Didow

The Kenan-Flagler Business
School
The University of North Carolina
at Chapel Hill

Felicitas Evangelista

University of Western
Sydney Nepean

Gary A. Knight

Department of Marketing
and Supply Chain Management
Michigan State University

Tage Koed Madsen

Department of Marketing
Odense University, Denmark

Paul Matthyssens

Limburgs Universitair Centrum
Belgium

George R. Milne

School of Management
University of Massachusetts

Matthew B. Myers

Department of Marketing
and Supply Chain Management
Michigan State University

Michael R. Mullen   Florida Atlantic University

Thomas Noordewier   The University of Vermont

Pieter Pauwels   Limburgs Universitair Centrum
                                                        Belgium

James M. Sinkula   School of Business
                                                        University of Vermont

Anne L. Souchon   European Business Management
                                                             School
                                                        University of Wales, Swansea

Lothar Weinland   Center for European Economic
                                                             Research
                                                        Germany

PREFACE

This special volume of *Advances in International Marketing* is guest-edited by Tage Koed Madsen of Odense University and reports on the 1995 meeting of the Consortium for International Marketing Research (CIMaR).

CIMaR was established by Michigan State University CIBER as a way of fostering collaborative research among colleagues from distant parts of the world. CIMaR researchers, now numbering two dozen colleagues from ten countries, meet annually. The purpose of the meeting is to report on past research and plan future collaboration.

Dr. Madsen hosted the 1995 meetings at Odense University, which resulted in the volume you are holding. Our thanks go to him for this timely professional contribution. Finally, we express our appreciation to Gayle Jerman and Danielle Shaban-Turner at JAI Press, who saw the volume through the production process.

S. Tamer Cavusgil
Series Editor

INTRODUCTION: EXPORT AND INTERNATIONALIZATION RESEARCH— ENRICHMENT AND CHALLENGES

Tage Koed Madsen

I. THE EVOLUTION OF EXPORT AND INTERNATIONALIZATION RESEARCH

During the past 30 years researchers as well as practitioners have shown an increasing interest in the field of export and internationalization. This is a logical consequence of the increasing internationalization and globalization of most markets.

In the 1970s comparable research streams could be identified in Europe and North America. In these early days of research the main point was to describe the evolution of firms' international activities. Often exporters were compared to non-exporters in an attempt to understand why some firms would start exporting where others did not. The European/Swedish approach (see e.g., Johanson & Wiedersheim-Paul, 1975; Johanson & Vahlne, 1977) as well as the

Advances in International Marketing, Volume 8, pages 1-8.
Copyright © 1996 by JAI Press Inc.
All rights of reproduction in any form reserved.
ISBN: 0-7623-0164-3

North American approach (see e.g., Bilkey, 1978; Cavusgil & Nevin, 1981) identified internationalization processes as being slow and incremental in nature. Often researchers would point out that their empirical results demonstrated that management support and internal processes are of critical importance when trying to explain why some firms become international—and others do not. The approach as well as the empirical findings were contrasted to the predominant microeconomic and neo-classical views of international trade.

After showing and describing actual internationalization processes of firms, academic researchers became interested in going one step further in their understanding of export and internationalization; in the late 1970s many empirical export performance studies were conducted, trying to identify the best export management practices (for a review, see Madsen, 1987; Aaby & Slater, 1989). The motivation was an aspiration to be able to demonstrate causal relationships between the export environment, firm characteristics, export (marketing) decisions and export performance. The intention was to be able to guide management in decision making by building normative models concerning export decisions (Madsen, 1989). Another aim was to assist public policy decisions makers in their efforts to establish effective export support and promotion programs (see e.g., Czinkota & Tesar, 1982).

In the 1990s both of these research streams are being developed further. Theoretical and methodological inadequacies of earlier approaches are discussed and highlighted. New conceptualizations of the substancial issues are advanced—some of them due to weaknesses of earlier approaches (e.g., Langhoff, 1994; Yeoh, 1994), others due to changing international environments (see e.g., Johanson & Vahlne, 1990). Nowadays empirical studies often have a narrow sample of quite homogeneous firms/export ventures whereas the very broad samples of earlier export performance studies are often rejected because generalizations at such an aggregate level are found to be less fruitful—and sometimes impossible in today's more specialized markets.

The present volume of *Advances in International Marketing* contains articles pertaining to these streams of research and attempts to bring academic research in the area one step further. Some of the articles challenge the existing body of research either by pointing out that new conceptualizations might be necessary (e.g., models of internationalization processes or measurements of export performance) or by drawing the attention to underresearched areas (such as export pricing policies and the use of export information). Other articles enrich the existing body of research by adding new aspects to conventional models or empirical research, for example, by explicitly combining a strategic view or a relationship marketing approach with empirical export performance research.

Sections II and III briefly introduce the contributions of the volume, which is organized in two sections: "Internationalization and Export Performance" and "Researching and Adapting to Export Conditions."

II. INTERNATIONALIZATION AND EXPORT PERFORMANCE

Four chapters focus on the internationalization process of firms or more specifically on their export performance. Knight and Cavusgil challenge the traditional internationalization theory as a result of a review of several publications which have demonstrated that the process of moving from being a purely domestically oriented firm to becoming a global firm is not always slow and incremental. Firms do not always become international like 'rings in the water.' The chapter especially stresses that newly established firms in today's market often have an international outlook from their birth and start exporting almost immediately, perhaps even to geographically and culturally distant markets. Oftentimes such firms also set up sales and production facilities abroad right away. Knight and Cavusgil discuss factors explaining this type of internationalization behavior, as well as the implications for management and international marketing research.

In a study that enhances previous approaches, Axinn, Noordewier and Sinkula empirically examine the relationship between export strategy (market spreading versus concentration and product adaptation versus non-adaptation) and export performance. They find significant support for the hypothesis that 'customized focused exporters' are more profitable than 'standardized focused exporters'; otherwise they conclude that export strategy must depend on the core competencies of the firm in question and the market conditions in which it operates. They conclude that their results for broad based exporters suggest that the "it depends" rationale seems more relevant than the the standardization argument supported by Levitt (1983). Furthermore, they find that the firm's commitment to exporting is an overall important factor regardless of the strategy chosen.

Evangelista contributes to the area of export performance reasearch by trying to integrate some of the reasoning of the interaction/network approach to industrial markets into an export performance study framework. Reviewing the latter type of studies she concludes that they are mainly following a traditional marketing mix approach to studying the associations between strategy and performance. Evangelista formulates an alternative export performance model building on the assumption that close and long-lasting relationships are the reality for many firms exporting industrial products. She formulates some propositions and discusses operationalization issues as well as the adaptations of research methodology following from the proposed view.

In the final chapter in this section, Matthyssens and Pauwels review the export performance literature published since 1989. They assess different authors' conceptualizations and operational-izations of performance by means of a model, which they formulate after reviewing the literature focusing on performance in the areas of strategic management and new product development. Their conclusion is that there is no agreement in the export performance literature about these issues, which leads to difficulties in comparing empirical research results. Matthyssens and Pauwels plea for more explicitness in future studies; it is important to discuss and clearly state the choices made when studying export performance. They propose that export performance measurement should take its starting point in both objective measures and subjective judgements such as managers' perception of their unit's own performance. The reason for the latter measures is that decisions about the future depend on such perceptions rather than on performance in absolute terms.

Research on internationalization and export performance must be very broad when conceptualizing the problems to be studied. The remaining part of this volume explores some more narrow issues pertaining to firms' marketing conditions and marketing decision making.

III. RESEARCHING AND ADAPTING
TO EXPORT CONDITIONS

The first two chapters in this part of the volume focus on the input side of decision making, namely the collection, analysis, interpretation, and use of export market information. It is well known that firms often do not research their markets very well before entering them. The first steps into international activities are characterized especially by a very low level of research and planning (Cavusgil, 1980). It is therefore very important to identify better methodologies for dealing with export market information as well as to capture a better understanding of present industry practices.

Diamantopoulos and Souchon do the latter by studying how and why firms gather, analyze, interpret, and use information about export markets. These issues have been widely researched in a domestic setting, but our knowledge about such practices on foreign markets is limited. Since the study is exploratory no firm conclusions can be drawn, but their findings indicate that managers find internal information sources (sales people, etc.) more accurate and reliable than external sources (research institutes, etc.). Therefore, information from internal sources often seems to go directly into the decision making process (instrumental use), whereas information bought from an outside agency tends to be used more conceptually, that is, as a sort of 'background' information.

Mullen, Milne and Didow's article attempts to improve the techniques that can be used when researching international markets; they discuss the methodological problems inherent in trying to apply the same questionnaire items in different cultural settings. More specifically they propose a test, which can be used to examine one of the measurement problems inherent in cross-cultural research— namely the question of metric equivalence. Their empirical study shows that respondents in different demographic/cultural groups do not always have the same underlying metrics when responding to questionnaire items. Also, they propose a procedure that proves its usefulness in exploring such differences in underlying metrics. The procedure is relevant for researchers as well as practitioners analyzing markets across cultures or nations.

The study by Mullen, Milne, and Didow focuses on brand loyalty, which is of course a very important concept when decisions have to be made concerning the pricing of a product on a foreign market.

The pricing issues are dealt with in detail in the article by Myers and Cavusgil. They call for more research on export pricing and its impact on export performance, after asserting that very little research has been done in the area, perhaps because managers are reluctant to discuss their pricing policies and practices, since these decisions are so important. Another reason may be that neo-classical economic thinking has been so strong that a more behavioralistic approach has been difficult to introduce. Myers and Cavusgil offer a conceptual model which attempts to capture the most important aspects of setting prices on international markets. Given the complexity of the matter they only cover some aspects more deeply, and they set up some propositions, which they recommned to be enlightened by future research.

In the final chapter of the volume, Weinland takes up an issue that is very important for the export performance of many countries and firms, namely export controls. Traditionally the arms and weapons industries have been subject to export control; but the export of many other so-called dual-use products are restricted also in many countries. Weinland analyses and discusses the harmonization of such export controls in the European Union after the disappearence of the Soviet Union and the Eastern Bloc. He concludes that export controls nowadays are more North-South controls than East-West controls. He also demonstrates that only very little harmonization has taken place within the European Union, leading to very different competitive conditions for different firms and nations.

IV. SOME SUGGESTIONS FOR FUTURE RESEARCH

Some of the papers in this volume of *Advances in International Marketing* enrich our understanding of exporting and internation-alization processes by refining existing models and theories. Other contributions challenge the past literature. Both are necessary. Since the business world is changing all the time it is very important that the scientific community is able to both reflect these changes as well as enhance our understanding of the present and future export conditions, and finally to govern managers in their decision making, so that they are able to take better decisions. The benefit for individuals, firms and society should be evident.

In order to meet these challenges, academia in the area of export and internationalization research must conduct empirical as well as theoretical research. Empirical work contributes with a description of the changing conditions for doing business on an international scale and has the potential, also, to counter some key success factors that may govern managers in their decision making. However, only by incorporating theoretical reflections and building more clear theoretical models can academic research give a more long-lasting contribution to the understanding, explanation and prediction of export and internationalization processes.

This area of research has a long tradition for being very empirically oriented, however. Theoretical constructs have been 'borrowed' from different sources in an eclectic way and oftentimes only implicitly. Therefore, the theoretical foundations of many empirical findings have been weak. So, a plea for more theoretical contributions seems to be justified. Attempts are made within the Consortium for International Marketing Research (CIMaR) collaboration to formulate a general model of export performance which may be shared by all researchers in the area. This is a diffucult task, however. Probably, in the future, researchers should much more conciously delimit the populations of their studies, and hence the range of validity of their theoretical models. Clearly, we should not build an export performance model for each single firm, but it might be necessary to build different models for different groups of firms or for different export conditions/environments. Many articles in this volume of *Advances in International Marketing* represent attempts in this direction.

REFERENCES

Aaby, N.E., & Slater, N.F. (1989). Management influences on export performance: A review of the empirical literature 1978-1988. *International Marketing Review, 6*(4), 7-26.

Bilkey, W.J. (1978). An attempted integration of the literature on the export behavior of firms. *Journal of International Business Studies, 9*(Spring/Summer), 33-46.

Cavusgil, S.T. (1980). On the internationalization process of firms. *European Research*, (November), 273-281.

Cavusgil, S.T., & Nevin, J.R. (1981). Internal determinants of export marketing behavior: An empirical investigation. *Journal of Marketing Research, 18*(February), 114-119.

Czinkota, M., & Tesar, G. (Eds.) (1982). *Export policy: A global assessment*. New York: Praeger.

Johanson, J., & Wiedersheim-Paul, F. (1975). The internationalization of the firm—four Swedish cases. *Journal of Management Studies*, (October), 305-322.

Johanson, J., & Vahlne, J.-E. (1977). The internationalization process of the firm—a model of knowledge development and increasing foreign commitments. *Journal of International Business Studies, 8*(1), 23-32.

Johanson, J., & Vahlne, J.-E. (1990). The mechanisms of internationalization. *International Marketing Review, 7*(4) 11-24.

Langhoff, T. (1994). The internationalization of the firm in an intercultural perspective. MAPP Working Paper, The Aarhus Business School, Denmark.

Levitt, T. (1983). The globalization of markets. *Harvard Business Review, 61*(May-June), 92-102.

Madsen, T.K. (1987). Empirical export performance studies: A review of conceptualizations and findings. *Advances in International Marketing, 2*, 177-198.

Madsen, T.K. (1989). Successful export marketing management: Some empirical evidence. *International Marketing Review, 6*(4), 41-57.

Yeoh, P.-L. (1994). Entrepreneurship and export performance: A proposed conceptual model. *Advances in International Marketing, 6*, 43-68.

PART   I

INTERNATIONALIZATION AND
EXPORT PERFORMANCE

THE BORN GLOBAL FIRM:
A CHALLENGE TO TRADITIONAL INTERNATIONALIZATION THEORY

Gary A. Knight and S. Tamer Cavusgil

ABSTRACT

This study investigates the widespread emergence in recent years of a relatively new type of firm: the "Born Global." Born Globals are small, technology-oriented companies that operate in international markets from the earliest days of their establishment. There is growing evidence of the emergence of Born Globals in numerous countries of the developed world. The Born Global phenomenon suggests a new challenge to traditional theories of internationalization. The study describes these firms, the critical factors and implications associated with their arrival, and the associated limitations posed for internationalization theory.

Advances in International Marketing, Volume 8, pages 11-26.
Copyright © 1996 by JAI Press Inc.
All rights of reproduction in any form reserved.
ISBN: 0-7623-0164-3

I. INTRODUCTION

This study attempts to explain the recent emergence in large numbers of a relatively new type of firm: the "Born Global". Born global firms are characterized by small size—typically less than 500 employees and annual sales under $100 million—and reliance on cutting edge technology in the development of relatively unique product or process innovations. But the most distinguishing feature of Born Global firms is that they tend to be managed by entrepreneurial visionaries who view the world as a single, borderless marketplace from the time of the firm's founding. Unlike traditional companies, management at Born Globals does not see foreign markets as simple adjuncts to the domestic market: they begin exporting one or several products within a few years of their establishment and tend to export at least a quarter of total production (McKinsey & Co., 1993).

There is increasing evidence from Australia/Asia, Europe, the United States, and other developed regions that, over the last decade or so, Born Global firms have begun to appear on the world business scene in large numbers (e.g., *The Economist*, 1993; Holstein, 1992; McKinsey & Co., 1993; Nordstrom, 1991; Oviatt & McDougall, 1994). The phenomenon presents an important new challenge to traditional theories of firm internationalization. Internationalization describes a process in which the firm gradually becomes involved in international business and enters foreign markets. The internationalization process has been the subject of widespread empirical research (e.g., Cavusgil, 1980; Johanson & Vahlne, 1977, 1990; Reid, 1981) and seems to enjoy general acceptance among most international business scholars.

The present study seeks to offer contemporary insights, which challenge and shed light on possible limitations to traditional internationalization models. Accordingly, the research objectives are to: (1) review traditional internationalization theory and criticisms thereof; (2) describe the emergence and characteristics of a relatively new type of enterprise—the Born Global firm (advancing, in the process, a substantive challenge to internationalization theory); (3) propose factors that may have given rise to the emergence of Born Global firms; (4) suggest implications that Born Globals may hold for management at smaller companies; and finally, (5) offer possible approaches for conducting research on these firms.

II. TRADITIONAL INTERNATIONALIZATION THEORY: HOW FIRMS ARE SUPPOSED TO GO GLOBAL

Historically, the internationalization process has been identified with two major models: the Uppsala model and the Innovation model. The Uppsala model was developed by Johanson and Wiedersheim-Paul (1975) and Johanson and Vahlne (1977, 1990), and has received considerable attention over the last two decades. Johanson and Wiedersheim-Paul (1975) delineated four distinctive stages of gradually increasing foreign involvement that firms follow on their way to becoming fully internationalized:

Stage 1: No regular export activities.
Stage 2: Export via independent representatives.
Stage 3: Establishment of an overseas sales subsidiary.
Stage 4: Foreign production/manufacturing.

The Uppsala model emphasizes incremental internationalization of firms' through the acquisition, integration, and use of knowledge concerning foreign markets as well as successively increasing commitment to those markets. The process begins with two existing state aspects--market knowledge possessed by the firm about specific foreign markets and market commitment of firm resources to those markets. Internationalization proceeds by means of two change aspects—commitment decisions taken by the firm regarding foreign markets and current activities performed in connection with those markets. In the Uppsala model, it is assumed that learning about a foreign market occurs primarily through personal, on-site experience, that management will not commit higher levels of resources to the market until it has acquired increasing levels of experiential knowledge, that such learning is time-consuming, and that, as a result, internationalization evolves stepwise at a relatively slow pace. Johanson and Vahlne (1977) emphasize that the slowness of the whole process is a consequence of incremental adaptations to changing firm and environmental conditions rather than the result of deliberate strategy.

The Uppsala model predicts that internationalization, once started, will tend to proceed even in the absence of strategic decisions taken regarding the market. Furthermore, the model assumes that internationalization evolves systematically from a situation of no involvement, through exporting, and ultimately to local manufacturing. The sequence entails a continuously growing commitment of resources to the market. Additionally, the firm will tend to enter new markets with increasingly greater psychic distance, where psychic distance is defined as aspects of language, culture, business practices, and industrial development, which tend to reduce the efficiency of information flows between the firm and the market (Johanson & Vahlne, 1977). Therefore, the model assumes that companies first target markets they understand best (Johanson & Vahlne, 1977, 1990).

In a similar vein, Johanson and Mattsson (1986) suggest that some firms may make an early start in internationalization by utilizing already-established agents in nearby markets. Such an approach is possible because use of the agent minimizes the need for investment and risk-taking as well as the need to develop special knowledge of the foreign market. As Johanson and Mattsson (1986) note, initiatives in early internationalization are often undertaken by counterparts, such as distributors in the foreign market.

The second major model describing firm internationalization—the Innovation model—derives mainly from the work of Bilkey and Tesar (1977), Cavusgil (1980), Czinkota (1982), and Reid (1981). It is similar to the Uppsala model except regarding internationalization's initiating mechanism. The model suggests that internationalization results from a series of management innovations that occur within the firm. In the original Bilkey and Tesar (1977) conceptualization, internationalization was also viewed as evolving in a series of learning stages. Exporting is usually the first major step to foreign expansion.

Cavusgil's (1980) review of various internationalization studies suggested that firms tend to internationalize without much rational analysis or deliberate planning. Furthermore, internationalization is seen as a gradual process, progressing in incremental stages, over a relatively long period of time. Each stage reflects increasing commitments of resources and managerial talent. The slowness of the process may be an indication of management's aversion to risk-taking and their inability to acquire relevant knowledge and information.

Both the Uppsala and Innovation models imply that internationalization occurs as a succession of incremental stages. In his excellent critique, Anderson (1993) noted that the two approaches are closely related. Both are behaviorally oriented and attribute the slow, incremental nature of internationalization to two factors: (1) lack of market knowledge by the firm, especially regarding experiential knowledge; and (2) uncertainty associated with successive decisions to internationalize.

III. CRITICISMS OF TRADITIONAL INTERNATIONALIZATION THEORY

Since the Uppsala and Innovation models were developed, numerous scholars have advanced various criticisms of the models' validity and assumptions. Some have said the models are too deterministic and neglect to consider that firms may not follow a consistent path to internationalization. While the Uppsala model assumes that internationalization evolves systematically, almost ceaselessly, from a situation of no involvement, to exporting, and finally to local manufacturing, it is likely that many firms rely instead on careful strategy-making, which accounts for a potentially wide array of product-market conditions and firm options (Reid, 1983; Rosson, 1987; Turnbull, 1987). Furthermore, the decision to go international may be carefully mapped out and based on consideration of a number of factors such as the nature of the foreign market opportunity, the firm's resources, the type of product, product life cycles, and anticipated demand in the domestic market (Cavusgil & Zou, 1994; Reid & Rosson, 1987; Welch & Luostarinen, 1988).

The first step in the process may not be exporting, but may be one of several other international expansion modes (e.g., Nordstrom, 1991). For example, the first international sales of many businesses these days may come through a foreign joint venture or a network relationship with companies abroad. For industrial firms, involvement in international networks provides a low risk conduit for foreign sales (Hakansson, 1982). Furthermore, there is substantial research indicating that companies may enter directly into foreign licensing, manufacturing, or assembly arrangements without ever engaging in exports (Carstairs & Welch, 1982/1983; Nordstrom, 1991; Reid, 1984; Root, 1987).

As further evidence of the inherent weakness of a deterministic, incremental approach to internationalization, Reid (1984) notes:

The empirical evidence for a stages approach to international expansion rests primarily on two empirical studies, a case analysis of four Swedish firms expanding internationally and an Australian investigation that treats domestic geographic expansion as analogous to export expansion. Although their position that firm expansion is incremental in character seems defensible, the authors pay little attention to market- and firm-specific characteristics that can account for the behaviors they observe. Thus the leap toward a general theory that implies that firm foreign expansion is deterministic is highly speculative (p. 200).

In an empirical study in the United Kingdom, Turnbull (1987) found that marine diesel engines, vehicle components, and telecommunications were industries, which did not follow an incremental, stages path to internationalization. Indeed, Turnbull's survey revealed that many highly internationalized firms relied on agents and distributors, while other companies, with less international experience, had already established sales offices on the continent. Turnbull (1987) concluded that a firm's stage of internationalization "is largely determined by the operating environment, industry structure, and its own marketing strategy" (p. 37). Other evidence supports the existence of companies in Italy (Varaldo, 1987), France (Roux, 1979), Norway (Garnier, 1982), Taiwan (Chang & Grub, 1992), the United Kingdom (Buckley et al., 1979), and Europe in general (Buckley, 1982) which similarly have not followed the traditional path to internationalization.

As Douglas and Craig (1989) note, the Uppsala theory focuses on the relationship between information acquisition and market commitment, rather than on the critical issue of strategy formulation. However, many small- and medium-sized firms may internationalize only after careful crafting of an international marketing plan (e.g., Douglas et al., 1982; Welch & Luostarinen, 1988). Numerous studies have found that management at internationalizing firms frequently consider a variety of strategic approaches (e.g., Buckley, 1982; Root, 1987). Each decision taken, in the face of a multiplicity of possible product-market combinations, is likely to pose differing implications for advancing the internationalization process. Reid (1983, 1984) views the internationalization process as contingency-based and consistent with the writings of Penrose (1959) who argued that firms strategically and deliberately adapt to evolving circumstances in their market environment. Therefore, it may not be entirely accurate to argue, as the Uppsala model does, that any particular foreign expansion mode, once started, is either terminal or irreversible (Reid, 1984).

Much emphasis is given in the traditional theories to an incremental character of internationalization, which Johanson and Vahlne (1977, 1990) believe is occasioned by lack of market information and resulting uncertainty about how to proceed in foreign markets. They state that "large increases in the scale of operations in the market will only take place in firms with large total resources or in firms that feel no uncertainty about the market" (emphasis added, 1977, p. 30). The notion of incremental expansion is logical given that information obtained from foreign markets is often incomplete or ambiguous. Risk-averse managers, especially those lacking direct experience in the target market, will be unwilling to take bold decisions on matters in which relevant data are deficient (March & Simon, 1958).

Reid (1984) points to factors such as government regulation regarding tariffs and other trade barriers, market access, and channel controls, which may permanently inhibit many companies from entering certain foreign markets. For example, Welch and Luostarinen (1988) note that foreign investment by Japanese companies in recent years has been partly stimulated by government-imposed protectionism. Indeed, they suggest that the success of firms in exporting to some countries is sometimes an impetus for local governments to erect import barriers, thereby encouraging firms to shift to some other type of entry strategy. Moreover, when government-imposed barriers are suddenly removed, it is reasonable to expect that some companies may enter markets at a speed and degree of commitment much greater than that implied by the traditional internationalization models.

Another criticism of the traditional internationalization models concerns the case of firms based in countries where there is already widespread internationalization of industry and marketing activities. Johanson and Vahlne (1990) cite the development patterns of firms in Japan whose access to foreign market information is such that internationalization can proceed in a more deliberate, non-incremental pattern, contrary to that proposed by the models. Their study suggests that establishment and growth strategies in foreign markets are evolving towards faster and more direct entry modes. Moreover, the world may be considered a good deal more complex than it was when the theories were first advanced.

In addition to the criticisms noted above, the Born Global phenomenon presents an important new challenge to traditional internationalization theory.

IV. CHARACTERISTICS OF THE BORN GLOBAL FIRM

The major objective of this study is to highlight the widespread emergence, in developed countries at least, of a relatively new type of international company. Such firms, which are referred to as "Born Globals," have emerged over the last decade or so in Australia, and there is increasing evidence that they have appeared in large numbers in the United States and Europe as well. Based on a major study conducted in Australia by McKinsey and Company (1993), the Born Global firm is said to possess the following characteristics:

- Management views the world as its marketplace from the outset of the firm's founding; unlike traditional companies, they do not see foreign markets as simple adjuncts to the domestic market.
- Born Globals begin exporting one or several products within two years of their establishment and tend to export at least a quarter of total production.
- They tend to be small manufacturers, with average annual sales usually not exceeding $100 million.
- The majority of Born Globals are formed by active entrepreneurs and tend to emerge as a result of a significant breakthrough in some process or technology.
- They may apply cutting edge technology to developing a unique product idea or to a new way of doing business.
- The products that Born Globals sell typically involve substantial value adding; the majority of such products may be intended for industrial uses.

In addition, others have reported recently on the increasing emergence of globalizing firms possessing similar characteristics (e.g., *The Economist*, 1993; Gupta, 1989; Jolly, Alahuhta, & Jeannet, 1992; Oviatt & McDougall, 1994). In the case of Australia's Born Globals, the McKinsey study found that the firms are growing rapidly, with average growth rates exceeding 14 percent per year. Most have been exporting for 12 or more years. Some 25 percent of newly emerging Australian exporters are seen as fitting the Born Global criteria. The Australian firms are truly global--they export an average of 76 percent of total production. They tend to compete on value, strongly emphasizing product quality, high technology, and differentiated product design (McKinsey & Co. 1993).

In the United States, Holstein (1992) reported in *Business Week* on recent, new global initiatives of thousands of small firms which possess numerous characteristics like those of Australia's Born Globals. Experts claim that at least 10 percent of U.S. exporters have annual revenues of less than $300 million and fully 87 percent of such firms employ fewer than 500 workers (Holstein, 1992). Trade forecasters note that recent growth in U.S. exports has come in large part from small firms. Major growth has occurred among small firms specializing in medical products, scientific instruments, environmental systems, computer-related products, and consumer goods. These products represent narrow market niches in which small firms may be able to avoid or minimize competitive pressures posed by larger, more efficient operators. In 1989, just 7.5 percent of America's gross domestic product came from exports, whereas, in 1994, the figure had risen to 12.2 percent, largely reflecting the foreign expansion activities of firms new to exporting (*The Economist*, 1993; Holstein, 1992; Norton, 1994; U.S. Department of Commerce, 1995)

V. HISTORICAL PRECEDENTS: PRIOR STUDIES ON BORN GLOBALS

The literature offers a number of examples of studies that support the existence of the Born Global firm. In relevant research of the past 20 years, there are numerous precedents of companies resembling in many respects the Born Global firm of this study. For example, Buckley et al. (1979) investigated foreign direct investment as the initial foreign entry mode of small firms from the United Kingdom. The authors noted that, out of 43 firms in various industries in their sample, numerous companies had set up overseas manufacturing facilities while still small. The majority of the firms had established operations in countries such as South Africa, West Germany, Australia, and Belgium—lands which in psychic and/or geographic terms are significantly separated from the home country.

In France, Roux (1979) reported on a sample of 19 firms of less than 500 employees each in five different industries. Interestingly, while nearly all had been in existence ten or more years, 12 companies had started exporting within three years of their founding. Six companies had begun exporting concurrently with their establishment, including one chemical manufacturer that had been started at the turn of the century. In a study in Canada, Garnier (1982) similarly found that some of the businesses in his sample of 39 firms had followed the traditional path to internationalization, whereas others began exporting within a year of their creation. In firms that went international early, there was generally a proactive entrepreneur at the helm possessing a positive outlook toward exporting and insisting on a multinational presence. Studies by Denis and Depelteau (1985) and Litvak and Maule (1971) provided additional evidence supporting the existence of Born Global firms in Canada. Their research revealed that new, smaller Canadian firms have long exported to the United States, among other foreign markets.

In Taiwan, Chang and Grub (1992) described how 76 percent out of a total sample of 54 small firms in the Taiwanese information technology industries had expanded operations overseas by pursuing narrow market niches. They found that "like their American competitors in the computer industry, small and relatively new Taiwanese firms have been remarkably active in (foreign) markets that more established firms left unattended" (p. 20). The Taiwanese firms began selling abroad shortly after their founding and emphasized distinctive competence in R&D, product innovativeness, and specialized manufacturing to target markets as psychically diverse as Scandinavia, Spain, and the former Soviet Union.

Most recently, Oviatt and McDougall (1994) reported on the emergence of what they term "international new ventures"—firms having "an international vision ... from inception, an innovative product or service marketed through a strong network, and a tightly managed organization focused on international sales growth" (p. 47). In an attempt to cast such companies within a traditional conceptual framework, the stages theory of MNE evolution was found to be wanting. Their research suggests that contemporary theories of international business cannot fully explain the occurrence of Born Global firms. Oviatt and McDougall (1994) emphasized that, lacking resources and power, new ventures must rely on governance structures less involving than foreign direct investment, in order to extend their activities abroad. Furthermore, in the tradition of Dunning (1988), such businesses must possess some countervailing assets that provide an advantage over local firms in foreign markets.

FACTORS GIVING RISE TO THE EMERGENCE
OF BORN GLOBAL FIRMS

Several recent trends have given rise to the emergence of Born Global firms and help explain why such companies can successfully cultivate export markets. First is the increasing role of niche markets, especially in countries of the developed world (Holstein, 1992; Robinson, 1986). There is growing demand among consumers in mature economies for specialized or customized products. With the globalization of markets and increasing worldwide competition from large multinationals, many smaller firms may have no choice but to specialize in the supplying of products that occupy a relatively narrow global niche.

A second important trend is recent advances in process technology. Improvements in microprocessor-based technology imply that low-scale, batch-type production can be economical. New machine tools now permit the manufacture of complex, non-standard parts and components with relative ease. New technologies allow small companies to achieve comparable footing with large multinationals in the production of sophisticated products for sale around the world. Holstein (1992) notes that technology is allowing American small exporters to streamline production in ways that make their products highly competitive in the global marketplace. Furthermore, technology is facilitating the production of widely diverse products on an ever smaller scale (Robinson, 1986). The consequence of this is increasing specialization in many industries— more and more consumer goods will likely be tailor-made to fit ever diverse preferences.

A third trend in favor of Born Globals is recent advances in communications technology. Gone are the days of large, vertically-integrated firms where information flows were expensive and took considerable time to be shared. With the invention of telecommun-ications aids such as the fax machine, voice mail, and computer-supported technology such as electronic data interchange and electronic mail, managers even at small firms can efficiently manage operations across borders. Information is now readily and more quickly accessible to everyone. Holstein (1992) notes that small American exporters are using "fax machines, (toll free) 800 numbers, and overnight air express services to shave the once formidable costs of going global" (p. 70). Pundits suggest that, thanks to advances in communications technology, it is now substantially less expensive for small enterprise to go international than it was just 10 years ago (Holstein, 1992).

A fourth trend is the inherent advantages of small companies—quicker response time, flexibility, adaptability, and so on—which facilitate the international endeavors of Born Globals. Small American exporters are more flexible and quicker to adapt to foreign tastes and international standards. The McKinsey study (1993) found that Born Global Australian firms have a strong customer orientation and are quick to tailor their products to meet specific customer requirements.

A fifth factor concerns the means of internationalization—knowledge, technology, tools, facilitating institutions, and so forth—which have become more accessible to all firms (Czinkota & Ronkainen, 1995; Nordstrom, 1991). For example, since the early 1970s, the integration of world financial markets has become a driving force in the global economy. Now more than ever, smaller firms can access funding for new projects and for overseas introductions. Another important trend is the globalization of technology. Joint research and development platforms, international technology transfers, and the cross-border education of students in science and engineering have all exploded in recent years. As such, new and better approaches to manufacturing, product innovation, and general operations have become much more readily available to smaller firms.

Finally, a sixth important phenomenon promoting Born Globals is the trend to global networks (Hakansson, 1982; Thorelli, 1990). Successful international commerce today is increasingly facilitated through partnerships with foreign businesses—distributors, trading companies, subcontractors, as well as more traditional buyers and sellers. Inexperienced managers can improve their chances for succeeding in international business if they take the time to build mutually-beneficial, long-term alliances with foreign partners.

VI. IMPLICATIONS FOR PRACTITIONERS AND SCHOLARS

The rise of small- and medium-size enterprises that achieve considerable success in export markets is exciting. The phenomenon suggests that, in spite of small size and inexperience in international transactions, high value-adding manufacturing firms can outperform their larger, more resourceful counterparts in foreign markets. The key element of success appears to be genuine customer orientation and value, coupled with commitment to selling in international markets by firm's management. Such firms are well advised to identify their distinctive competencies and nourish them constantly— whether it is a unique process or product, quicker response time, intimate knowledge of customer, or other. Synergistic partnerships with carefully selected foreign business also can take the mystery and complexity out of international business transactions.

Managers also should tap into formal and informal information networks in order to position themselves as proactive players in international business. Smaller firms lack the resources to compete on equal terms with large MNEs. They must rely on their knowledge of specialized, relatively narrow product niches in order to succeed. Additionally, these companies must internalize the right combination of facilitating technologies, international business know-how, and access to appropriate contacts abroad. Much of the learning associated with this process results from being linked into information networks both at home and abroad. To the extent that small firms can be the engine of growth for innovation and economic development, the advent of the Born Global firm bodes well for the progress of world trade and global prosperity.

Clearly, additional research is needed on the Born Global phenomenon. As a first step, a framework for studying Born Global firms should be developed. The framework should be a roadmap, capable of assisting scholars in a systematic study of the Born Global firm. The framework should account for those factors in the internal and external environment of the firm that can potentially engender and mediate the Born Global's development and progress.

Next, a causal model that can explain and validate the existence of Born Globals needs to be developed. For greatest utility, the key research objective should be to elucidate those factors associated with Born Globals that account for superior performance. Once developed, the explanatory model should be tested in an empirical study, with actual Born Global firms, to ensure that theory corresponds with outcomes and actual practice. As possible, the model should be developed and tested in a variety of national and cultural settings. As usual with such studies, in order to assess the Born Global firm across time, longitudinal research will be preferred.

Finally, once the nature and success factors of the Born Global are reasonably well understood, research that explores appropriate public policy needs to be pursued. The objective should be to suggest public policy initiatives that can facilitate and promote the development and progress of the Born Global firm.

REFERENCES

Anderson, O. (1993). On the internationalization process of firms: A critical analysis. *Journal of International Business Studies 24* (2), 209-231.

Bilkey, W. J., & Tesar, G. (1977). The export behavior of smaller Wisconsin manufacturing firms. *Journal of International Business Studies, 9* (Spring/ Summer), 93-98.

Buckley, P. (1982). The role of exporting in the market servicing policies of multinational manufacturing enterprises. In M.R. Czinkota & G. Tesar (Eds.), *Export management*. New York: Praeger.

Buckley, P., Newbould, G.D., & Thurwell, J. (1979). Going international—The foreign direct investment behavior of smaller UK firms. In L.G. Mattsson & F. Wiedersheim-Paul (Eds.), *Recent research on the internationalization of business*. Uppsala, Sweden: Proceedings of the Annual Meeting of the European International Business Association.

Carstairs, R.T., & Welch, L.S. (1982/1983). Licensing and internationalization of smaller companies: Some Australian evidence. *Management International Review, 22*, 33-44.

Cavusgil, S. T. (1980). On the internationalization process of firms. *European Research 8*(6), 273-281.

Cavusgil, S.T., & Zou, S. (1994). Marketing strategy—performance relationship: An investigation of the empirical link in export market ventures. *Journal of Marketing, 58*(January), 1-24.

Chang, T., & Grub, P.D. (1992). Competitive strategies of Taiwanese PC firms in their internationalization process. *Journal of Global Marketing 6*(3), 5-27.

Czinkota, M. R. (1982). *Export development strategies: U.S. promotion policies*. New York: Praeger Publishers.

Czinkota, M.R., & Ronkainen, I. (1995). *International Marketing*, 4th ed. Fort Worth, TX: The Dryden Press.

Denis, J., & Depelteau, D. (1985). Market knowledge, diversification, and export expansion. *Journal of International Business Studies 16*(3), 77-89.

Douglas, S., & Craig, S. (1989). Evolution of global marketing strategy: Scale, scope, and synergy. *Columbia Journal of World Business, 24*(3), 47-59.

Douglas, S., Craig, S.,& Keegan, W.J. (1982). Approaches to assessing international marketing opportunities for small and medium-sized companies. *Columbia Journal of World Business, 17*(3), 26-32.

Dunning, J. (1988). The eclectic paradigm of international production: A restatement and some possible extensions. *Journal of International Business Studies, 19*, 1-31.

The Economist. (1993). America's little fellows surge ahead, (July 3), 59-60.

Garnier, G. (1982). Comparative export behavior of small Canadian firms in the printing and electrical industries. In R. Czinkota & G. Tesar (Eds.), *Export management.* New York: Praeger.

Gupta, U. (1989). Small firms aren't waiting to grow up to go global. *Wall Street Journal,* December 5, p. 2.

Hakansson, H. (1982). *International marketing and purchasing of industrial goods: An interaction approach.* New York: John Wiley.

Holstein, W. J. (1992). Little companies, big exports. *Business Week* (April 13), pp. 70-72.

Johanson, J., & Mattsson, L.G. (1986). International marketing and internationalization processes: A network approach. In S. Paliwoda & P. Turnbull (Eds.), *Research in international marketing.* London: Croom Helm.

Johanson J., & Vahlne, J. (1977). The internationalization process of the firm— a model of knowledge development and increasing foreign market commitments. *Journal of International Business Studies, 8*(1), 23-32.

Johanson, J., & Vahlne, J. (1990). The mechanism of internationalization. *International Marketing Review 7* (4), 11-24.

Johanson, J., & Wiedersheim-Paul, F. (1975). The internationalization of the firm: Four Swedish cases. *Journal of Management Studies 12*(3), 305-322.

Jolly, V., Alahuhta, M., & Jeannet, J. (1992). Challenging the incumbents: How high technology start-ups compete globally. *Journal of Strategic Change 1,* 71-82.

Litvak, I., & Maule, C. (1971). *Canadian entrepreneurship: A study by small newly established firms.* Ottawa: Technological Innovation Studies Program, Department of Industry, Trade and Commerce.

March, J., & Simon, H. (1958). *Organizations.* New York: Wiley.

McKinsey & Co. (1993). *Emerging exporters: Australia's high value-added manufacturing exporters. Melbourne: Australian Manufacturing Council.*

Nordstrom, K. A. (1991). *The internationalization process of the firm.* Doctoral dissertation. Stockholm: Institute of International Business, Stockholm School of Economics.

Norton, R. (1994). Strategies for the new export boom. *Fortune* (August 22), 124-132.

Oviatt, B., & McDougall, P. (1994). Toward a theory of international new ventures. *Journal of International Business Studies, 25*(1): 45-64.

Penrose, E. (1959). *The theory of the growth of the firm.* London: Basil Blackwell.

Reid, S. (1981). The decision-maker and export entry and expansion. *Journal of International Business Studies, 12*(Fall), 101-111.

Reid, S. (1983). Firm internationalization, transaction costs and strategic choice. *International Marketing Review 1*(2), 44-56.

Reid, S. (1984). Market expansion and firm internationalization. In E. Kaynak (Ed.), *International marketing management.* New York: Praeger.

Reid, S., & Rosson, P.J. (1987). Managing export entry and expansion: An overview. In P. Rosson & S. Reid (Eds.), *Managing export entry and expansion.* New York: Praeger.

Robinson, R. (1986). Some new competitive factors in international marketing. In S. T. Cavusgil (Ed.), *Advances in international marketing* (Vol 1). Greenwich, CT: JAI Press.

Root, F. (1987). *Entry strategies for international markets.* Lexington, MA: Lexington Books.

Rosson, P. J. (1987). The overseas distributor method: Performance and change in a harsh environment. In P. Rosson & S. Reid (Eds.), *Managing export entry and expansion.* New York: Praeger.

Roux, E. (1979). The export behavior of small and medium size French firms. In L.G. Mattsson & F. Wiedersheim-Paul (Eds.), *Recent research on the internationalization of business.* Uppsala, Sweden: Proceedings of the Annual Meeting of the European International Business Association.

Thorelli, H. (1990). Networks: The gay 90s in international marketing. In H. Thorelli & S.T. Cavusgil (Eds.), *International marketing strategy*, 3rd ed. New York: Pergamon Press.

Turnbull, P. (1987). A challenge to the stages theory of the internationalization process. In P. Rosson & S. Reid (Eds.), *Managing export entry and expansion.* New York: Praeger.

U.S. Department of Commerce. (1995). Merchandise trade: Exports by commodity. *National trade data bank* (July), Disk 1.

Varaldo, R. (1987). The internationalization of small- and medium-sized Italian manufacturing firms. In P. Rosson & S. Reid (Eds.), *Managing export entry and expansion.* New York: Praeger.

Welch, L., & Luostarinen, R. (1988). Internationalization: Evolution of a concept. *Journal of General Management 14*(2), 34-55.

EXPORT STRATEGIES AND EXPORT PERFORMANCE:

AN EMPIRICAL INVESTIGATION OF A PRODUCTS/MARKETS TYPOLOGY

Catherine N. Axinn, Thomas Noordewier and
J. M. J. Sinkula

ABSTRACT

Our understanding of the relationship between export strategy and export performance can be advanced substantially by utilizing a typology based upon products and markets. Drawing upon the work of Ansoff (1957, 1965, 1969), Kleinschmidt and Cooper (1984), Levitt (1983), and Porter (1980, 1985), this paper develops a products/ markets typology of export strategy, and empirically tests propositions relating specific strategy choices to performance outcomes. Findings indicate that a standardized broad-based strategy, such as advocated by Levitt, does not produce better sales or profit performance than

Advances in International Marketing, Volume 8, pages 27-58.
Copyright © 1996 by JAI Press Inc.
All rights of reproduction in any form reserved.
ISBN: 0-7623-0164-3

an adaptive, customized broad-based strategy. In addition, placing a higher priority on exporting is significantly linked with higher export performance, while having higher expectations of future exports is significantly associated with lower levels of current export performance. The authors also take advantage of their longitudinal sample to examine the issue of export performance stability over time. Results suggest that organizational learning does take place with respect to exporting and there is a significant carryover effect in the export performance of firms.

> *Strategic decisions are primarily concerned with external, rather than internal, problems of the firm and specifically with selection of the product mix which the firm will produce and the markets to which it will sell.*
>
> —H. Igor Ansoff (1965)

A fundamental way of thinking about marketing strategy is in terms of products and markets (Ansoff, 1957, 1965, 1969). Specifically, which products shall we market, and where? Usually, we think about these two factors jointly rather than independently. This is particularly so in international marketing and in export decision making (Piercy, 1982). Consider the firm that decides to target only one of its existing domestic products to one foreign market. Contrast this with the firm that pursues a strategy of adapting most of its products for export to many foreign countries. These two organizations are apt to have drastically different business philosophies, levels of export commitment, export intentions and behaviors, and marketing mix strategies. But the rudimentary question is, which of these two strategies will lead to better performance?

One well-accepted paradigm would fit the two firms contrasted above into one of the so-called stages-of-export involvement (Bilkey & Tesar, 1977; Bilkey, 1978; Cavusgil, 1980, 1984; Czinkota & Johnston, 1981; Joynt & Welch, 1985; Kotabe & Czinkota, 1992). This is typically done by examining the percent of total sales exported in conjunction with the amount of experience the firm has in exporting. Firms are then classified based upon their degree of dedication to exporting. Unfortunately, even though success is implicit as firms move from stage to stage, specific strategies leading to such success are typically not included in the paradigm. That is, the paradigm does not explicitly link together export strategy and export success. Fortunately, several interconnected lines of reasoning from the export and strategic planning literatures have recently begun to emerge, suggesting the basis for a framework explicitly tying together export strategy and export success.

First, the export literature increasingly reflects the importance of strategy (Kleinschmidt & Cooper, 1984; Möller, 1984; Piercy, 1982; Turnbull & Valla, 1986; Yaprak, Sorek, & Parameswaran, 1984). In general, a shift has taken place in recent years from studies which center on firms which export versus those which do not (Bilkey, 1978; Bilkey & Tesar, 1977; Cavusgil, Bilkey, & Tesar, 1979) to studies which center on export success (Axinn, 1988; Christensen, da Rocha, & Gertner, 1987; Kleinschmidt & Cooper, 1984; Edmunds & Khoury, 1986). This, of course, still begs the proverbial strategy question, "*how* have successful exporters *become* successful exporters?"

Second, there is growing recognition that export strategy must be grounded squarely in an understanding of the marketing mix (Bilkey, 1985; Kacker, 1975; Kirpalani & MacIntosh, 1980; McGuinness & Little, 1981; O'Rourke, 1985, Piercy, 1982; Weinrauch & Rao, 1974). Research has recently focused on issues like product adaptation (Kleinschmidt & Cooper, 1984), channels of distribution (Seely & Inglarsh, 1981), export promotion (Albaum, 1983; Axinn & Thach, 1990; Czinkota, 1979; Cavusgil, 1984), and pricing (Czinkota, 1979; Delacroix, 1984; Thach & Axinn, 1991). Almost out of necessity, firms are learning, the decision of whether to standardize international marketing revolves around marketing mix strategies (Bartels, 1968; Buzzell, 1968; Keegan, 1969; Levitt, 1983; Ricks, 1983).

Third, the broader literature on strategic planning argues for a process beginning with a product/market opportunity analysis before setting down the marketing mix strategy (cf. Kotler, 1980). Unfortunately, research on exporting has not embraced this perspective with any degree of consistency. Hence, much of the export literature fails to integrate the lessons taught in the marketing management and strategy literature. Consequently, relatively few *broad* typologies exist for framing export strategy (Kleinschmidt & Cooper, 1984). Moreover, although there has been considerable speculation about the performance implications of alternative marketing strategies abroad (Levitt, 1983; Porter, 1985), there remains, as yet, little "hard" empirical evidence to recommend one strategy over another. Clearly, both conceptually sound typologies and statistically-based empirical evidence are necessary if we are to understand the consequences of pursuing specific strategies from among the multitude of strategies available.

We empirically examine the relationship between export strategy choice and export performance. Based upon a products/markets (P/M) approach to strategic planning, and drawing upon the work of Kleinschmidt and Cooper (1984), Levitt (1983), Porter (1980, 1985) and others, we propose a framework for classifying export strategy alternatives. The framework is then used to develop empirically testable propositions relating specific export strategy decisions to export performance outcomes. The propositions are tested utilizing a longitudinal sample of firms which export.

I. EXPORT STRATEGY TYPOLOGY

Examination of the export performance effects of product and market variables *independent* of each other presents nothing new to the export literature. *Product* variables frequently revolve around the degree to which firms adapt products for export and their subsequent export success (Fenwick & Amine, 1979; Kleinschmidt & Cooper, 1984; Tookey, 1964). Most studies reveal a positive relationship between product adaptation and export performance. Product sophistication has also been found to be heightened among firms which export versus those that do not (Cavusgil & Nevin, 1981). Additionally, the technological effort exerted by industries has been shown to be significantly related to their proportion of exported output (Lowinger, 1975).

Markets in the export literature are often synonymous with countries. Some writers look at the number of countries to which a firm exports. For example, Piercy (1982) argues that the choice between market concentration and market spreading is the fundamental strategy choice which could have lasting consequences to the firm. On the one hand, exporters may focus their efforts on a small number of target markets (Piercy, 1982). On the other hand, they may choose to spread products across a large number of export markets (Ayal & Zif, 1979).

To date, Kleinschmidt and Cooper (1984) have been the only researchers who have looked *jointly* at product and market variables to build a typology which is then used to explain export performance. Out of their work comes a typology of six strategies, based on where the firm exports (only to its nearest neighbor or world-wide), the degree to which the firm adapts its products and the degree of within-country segmentation. For example, a firm exporting only to its nearest neighbor and conducting no product adaptation is classified differently from a firm exporting to markets around the world and adapting its products. Significant differences in export growth and in export level were shown to exist across the six levels of the typology.

There are obviously an infinite number of ways in which export strategies could be categorized. But a products/markets (P/M) approach is so fundamental to the way that executives think and to the way that marketing scholars since Ansoff (1957) have conceptualized strategy, that it is surprising the approach has not been used more widely. Hence, we propose a products/markets (P/M) typology of export strategy as depicted in Figure 1.

	Adapt Products for Export	Do Not Adapt Products for Export
Export to Many Countries	**Cell 2** **CUSTOMIZED BROAD-BASED EXPORTERS** n=16 (22.5%) *Analogous Frameworks:* *Buzzell (1968)* *Multinational Strategy (Levitt 1983)* *Flexible Global Strategy (Kotler 1991)* *Differentiation Strategy (Porter 1985)*	**Cell 1** **STANDARDIZED BROAD-BASED EXPORTERS** n=17 (23.9%) *Analogous Frameworks:* *Global Strategy (Levitt 1983)* *Overall Cost Leadership Strategy* *Porter (1985)*
Export to Few Countries	**Cell 3** **CUSTOMIZED FOCUSED EXPORTERS** n=11 (15.6%) *Analogous Framework:* *Differentiation Focus (Porter 1985)*	**Cell 4** **STANDARDIZED FOCUSED EXPORTERS** n=27 (38%) *Analogous Framework:* *Cost Focus (Porter 1985)*

Figure 1. Export Strategy

Like Kleinschmidt and Cooper's (1984) conceptualization, the present typology employs the notion of product adaptation as one dimension. This dimension is grounded in Ansoff's (1957) notion of "newness" (i.e., in his product/market matrix he classified a modified product as "new") and in Porter's (1985) "differentiation" versus "low cost" strategy paradigm. However, unlike other conceptualizations (including Kleinschmidt and Cooper's), product adaptation as employed here is purposefully far more encompassing. Since observers often disagree over what constitutes a "product" and hence "product adaptation," we do not attempt to distinguish between notions such as "minimal" (Kleinschmidt & Cooper, 1984), "minor," "fundamental," "required," or "voluntary" product adaptation (cf. Kacker, 1975). Instead, our interest focuses on whether the firm engages in *any* adaptation, where adaptation is defined by the firm, not an outside observer. While we discuss the sample in detail below, we note here that nearly 62 percent of the firms in our sample indicate that they *do not* engage in any product adaptation. These firms are not necessarily unsophisticated, small, young, or non-market oriented. They may merely have chosen to grow in other ways; ways which do not require product modification. Hence, a fundamental strategy choice for the firm lies in the ultimate decision of whether even minor modifications are worth the effort to gain entry into certain markets. It is this fundamental choice which we attempt to capture in the strategy typology.

Like many others, this study conceptualizes markets as countries. However, rather than basing our classification of markets on the notion of proximity (real or psychological) we base it on the number of markets served (many or few). This view is partially drawn from Ayal and Zif (1979) and partly from collective observation of the behavior of managers in designing strategy. The strategic options which are meaningful to managers marketing their products in only a few markets are likely to vary in character, number and degree from the strategic options which are meaningful to managers who are simultaneously juggling marketing activities in numerous markets. Thus, the second dimension of the typology divides firms into those which export to relatively few countries (4 or fewer) versus those which export to relatively many countries (5 or more).

The four strategy alternatives in the new typology include the following: firms which do not adapt their products and export to many countries (standardized broad-based exporters: Cell 1 firms),

firms which adapt their products and export to many countries (customized broad-based exporters: Cell 2 firms), firms which adapt their products but export to few countries (customized-focused exporters: Cell 3 firms) and, finally, firms which do not adapt their products and export to few countries (standardized-focused exporters: Cell 4 firms). These export strategies represent common, but fundamentally different approaches to exporting.

II. STRATEGY-PERFORMANCE HYPOTHESES

Much of the literature on global marketing management focuses on the distinction between adapting and standardizing products and other elements of the mix for markets worldwide. Since the issue was first raised by Buzzell (1968), one of the most noted proponents of standardization has been Levitt (1983), whose distinction between multinational and global corporations is particularly noteworthy here. According to Levitt, the *multinational* corporation adjusts its products to each country served in an effort to satisfy what amount to often superficial preferences. The *global* company, on the other hand, "sells the same things in the same way everywhere," offering standardized products which capitalize on the increasingly homogeneous wants of world markets. In contrast to the relatively high cost and hence self-limiting strategy of adaptation, Levitt argues, the strategy of global standardization offers companies "vastly expanded markets and profits" (Levitt, 1983, p. 102). Recent research by Szymanski, Bharadwaj and Varadarajan (1993) examines the influence of standardization in strategy/resource allocation on the performance of multinational corporations serving Western markets. Their "findings suggest that a...business that employs a similar pattern of resource allocation among marketing mix variables when serving the U.S., U. K., Canadian, and Western European markets would find that, on average, the standardized approach evokes similar performance responses..." (Szymanski, Bharadwaj, & Varadarajan, 1993, p. 11). They go on to state, however, that "further research directed at the nature of the underlying relationship between a .... business's strategic orientation and its market share/ performance is required to illuminate fully this relationship" (p. 11).

A counter-argument to Levitt's global markets thesis is found in Buzzell (1968), who nearly three decades ago made the point that, while standardization may permit significant cost savings, the final decision (on standardization versus adaptation) should balance "the pros and cons ... based on estimated overall revenues and costs" (p. 113). Kotler (1991), similarly, criticizes Levitt's argument, noting that global standardization "is not an all-or-nothing proposition but a matter of degree" (p. 419). Specifically, he challenges Levitt's assumption that standardization will always simultaneously increase sales and profits by virtue of lowering costs and appealing to price-conscious buyers, observing that "rather than assuming that the company's product can be introduced as is in another country, the company should review all possible adaptation elements and determine which adaptations would add more revenue than cost" (Kotler, 1991, p. 419). Quelch and Hoff (1986, p. 60) also reject the concept of global marketing as "an either-or proposition—either full standardization or local control." What is needed, they point out, is flexibility. In common, Kotler (1991), Buzzell (1968) and Quelch and Hoff (1986) acknowledge the need for a global marketing outlook, but argue that this does not preclude the need to consider adaptation to accommodate country differences. Similarly, Douglas and Wind (1987) contend that:

> [W]hile global products may be appropriate for certain markets and in certain product segments, adopting such an approach as a universal strategy in relation to all markets may not be desirable and may lead to major strategic blunders. Furthermore, it implies a product orientation, and a product-driven strategy, rather than a strategy grounded in a systematic analysis of customer behavior and response patterns and market characteristics (p. 19).

Translated in terms of our proposed four-cell strategy framework, Levitt's argument would lead to the expectation of a contrast in performance between standardized and customized broad-based exporters (Cell 1 and Cell 2 firms, respectively). Cell 1 firms, logically, would be expected to exhibit higher levels of sales and profit performance than Cell 2 firms. In contrast, Buzzell, Kotler, Douglas and Wind, and Quelch and Hoff's "it depends" line of reasoning would suggest that the difference in sales and profits between the two cells will depend upon the specific revenue/cost-based adaptations made by firms. Thus, *either adaptation or lack of adaptation could, depending upon the situation, produce the highest performance outcome, and neither Cell 1 nor Cell 2 strategies would be preferred, a priori.*

We concur with the perspective that adaptation *may* be needed to accommodate country/market differences, noting that such a view is also consistent with the marketing concept. On the basis of this discussion, therefore, we propose to empirically test the following proposition:

H₁ Sales and profit export performance will not be higher for those firms which adapt their products and export to many markets (customized broad-based exporters) than for those which do not adapt their products and export to many markets (standardized broad-based exporters).

In terms of Figure 1, this is equivalent to the hypothesis that there will not be a significant difference in sales and profit performance between firms in Cell 2 and firms in Cell 1.

An analogous question to the one examined above is whether export performance differs between standardized and customized focused exporters (Cell 4 and Cell 3 firms, respectively). Although writers in the standardization/adaptation literature do not directly address this issue, Michael Porter (1980, 1985) does. In drawing on Porter's (1985) framework for "generic strategies," we suggest that his competitive scope dimension is analogous to number of countries served. Thus, his "broad target/narrow target" dichotomization becomes many countries/few countries in our framework. Second, we note the parallel between Porter's "competitive advantage" dimension and product adaptation in Figure 1. We suggest that firms adapting their products are doing what Porter would call "differentiation" and that not adapting products is closely allied to following a "lower cost" strategy. More specifically, looking within the cells of Porter's matrix, his "cost leadership" strategy (broad target-lower cost) translates reasonably well to what we refer to as standardized broad-based exporting (Cell 1). His "differentiation" strategy (broad target-differentiation) is analogous to what we call customized broad-based exporting (Cell 2). Porter's "differentiation focus" strategy (narrow target-differentiation) is similar to our customized-focused exporting strategy (Cell 3). Last, his "cost focus" strategy (narrow target-lower cost) can be likened to our standardized-focused exporting strategy (Cell 4).

Porter (1985) persuasively argues that both differentiation focus and cost focus are viable strategic alternatives, since the focuser "...

exploits differences in cost behavior in some segments ... [and] the special needs of buyers in certain segments" (p. 15). Thus, both strategies *can*, at least potentially, be successful approaches. Drawing a parallel between Porter's work and our own proposed typology, we propose the following empirically testable proposition:

H_2 Sales and profit export performance will not be any higher for those firms which adapt their products and export to few countries (customized-focused exporters) than for those which do not adapt their products and export to few countries (standardized-focused exporters).

In terms of Figure 1, this is represented by the hypothesis that there will not be a significant difference in sales and profit performance between firms in Cell 3 and firms in Cell 4.

Finally, in addition to testing the two formal hypotheses above, we believe it is possible and meaningful to examine the remaining pairwise contrasts in the framework. Since firms seem to follow all four strategies in Figure 1, it seems reasonable to assume that managers believe in the merits of their chosen strategy. Thus it should be meaningful to determine empirically whether or not performance outcomes differ significantly, depending on strategy, regardless of the availability of *theoretical* support for such differences.

The value of the present typology is that it reflects an initial framework for thinking about *joint* product/market involvement, a framework which can then be related to the general nature of the firm and its export performance. More importantly, its discrete operationalization of key dimensions of strategy allows for an empirical test of disparate theories and arguments which have dominated the strategy and international marketing literature for some time.

A. Nonfocal Variables

Although our interest in H_1 and H_2 centers on the relationship between export strategy and export performance, the influence of other variables potentially affecting performance must be considered in any empirical test of a strategy-performance linkage. So, beyond categorizing P/M strategy types and associating them with export performance, we also consider (control for) the following nonfocal variables: the priority firms attach to exporting (international marketing primacy), their export intentions, the frequency with which they conduct foreign market information searches, and firm size (see Table 2 for the actual measures).

International marketing primacy is best thought of as the priority an organization places on the conduct of business in the domestic arena vis-a-vis the world arena. While primacy, *per se*, has not been assessed in other export studies, the closely analogous construct of commitment has consistently been linked with performance (Axinn & Thach, 1990; Cavusgil, 1984; Fenwick & Amine, 1979; Kirpalani & MacIntosh, 1980; Thach & Axinn, 1991). It therefore seems plausible that the primacy organizations attach to exporting will exert an influence on export performance, irrespective of the particular export strategy chosen.

Measures of export intention, market information search, and size have been proposed before, and are straightforward in concept (Reid, 1983, 1984). Export intention concerns actual near-term plans to export to new markets, introduce new products abroad, increase export sales to current markets, and so on. Perhaps a more tangible indicator of export orientedness than marketing primacy, export intention is obviously implicated in any assessment of export performance. Market information search concerns the frequency with which foreign market opportunities are formally analyzed. Logically, more frequent search may affect performance. Finally, although evidence has been mixed, another potentially important nonfocal performance-influencing variable is firm size (Axinn, 1988; Reid, 1983). Specific measures of the variables proposed above, both focal and nonfocal, are presented in a later section.

III. EXPORT PERFORMANCE STABILITY HYPOTHESIS

Hypotheses H_1 and H_2 focus on how strategy choices at a given point in time may influence export performance at a given point in time. As a separate issue, we also propose to examine whether export performance in one time period is predictable based on the level of previous export performance. That is, taking as given the strategies adopted by firms, do firms that exhibit good (poor) performance in time period one tend to exhibit good (poor) performance in time period two?

Although the export literature attests to the growing interest in and emphasis on exporting, little general information is available about the issue of export performance carryover. It is possible, of course, to cite specific examples of firms which have displayed great skill and consistency in exporting, performing at a high level year after year. It may be that these firms are the beneficiaries of a resident export "champion," a uniquely fostering corporate culture, some form of organizational learning, or some combination of these (and perhaps other) factors. However, the question we pose is, *to what extent do firms, in general, exhibit export performance stability over time*? Does performance carryover exist over modest time intervals of, say, three or four years? If so, what is the magnitude of this carryover effect? Even Christensen, da Rocha and Gertner's (1987) panel study of the performance of Brazilian exporters did not directly examine this issue.

The issue is critical, since if there is carryover—whether a persistence of good performance over time or poor performance across periods—then it clearly makes sense to continue research into the nature of its causes (or sources) and attempt to formulate appropriate managerial prescriptions. If, on the other hand, there is little or no evidence of export performance stability over time, then the normative implications to be drawn from research on export strategy options and other putative drivers of performance are not clear.

In the absence of positive evidence on the issue of carryover, it seems logical that factors such as organizational learning and culture, which are fairly enduring factors, influence not just domestic operations but export activities as well. Therefore, we hypothesize that export performance will exhibit significant carryover over modest time intervals, spanning periods of three to five years. Fortunately, the longitudinal performance data available in this study allow us to empirically test for carryover. Stated formally, we propose to examine the following exploratory hypothesis:

H₃ Export performance will exhibit moderate to high carryover (i.e., stability) over short time intervals. That is, over modest time intervals, high (low) levels of export performance at the beginning of a period will be associated with high (low) levels of export performance at the end of a period.

A latent variable approach to empirically testing this hypothesis is outlined below.

IV. METHOD

A. Sample and Data Collection

Organizations entering foreign markets do so in stages (Bilkey & Tesar, 1977; Cavusgil, 1984; Czinkota & Johnston, 1981; Kotabe & Czinkota, 1992; Joynt & Welch, 1985; Reid, 1983). But few studies track firms which export over time (Bilkey, 1985; Buatsi, 1986; Christensen, da Rocha, & Gertner, 1987). One aim of this study was to do so. Hence, data were collected in a New England state over a period of three and one half years. A panel design was employed, the objective of which was to develop longitudinal measures of performance which facilitate tracking specific firms. Two separate questionnaires were used, one sent in 1988 and one in 1991. The questionnaires were mailed to firms which had been identified as having exported product(s) at least once. The frame was obtained from the state's Department of Economic Development.

Some of the measures in the second survey were identical to those in the first, a number were similar, but refined, measures, and others were totally new. Hence, elements of a traditional panel were combined with elements of an omnibus panel (Kinnear & Taylor, 1991). Using the same case identification numbers in each survey allows examination of each company across two points in time. Figure 2 illustrates the overall response rates and data sets involved in the study.

Both instruments were lengthy (15 pages) and complex. Hence, prior to the mailing of each survey, subjects were telephoned and asked to participate. In the first survey, questionnaires were mailed to 206 firms in three waves over a period of approximately three months, each wave including a new questionnaire to non-responding firms. After each mailing, a reminder post card was sent to each non-respondent. This process resulted in 161 returned questionnaires for an overall response rate of approximately 78 percent.

The same process was utilized three years later in the second survey. However, only 182 of the questionnaires were deliverable in 1991, indicating that 24 companies had either gone out of business or

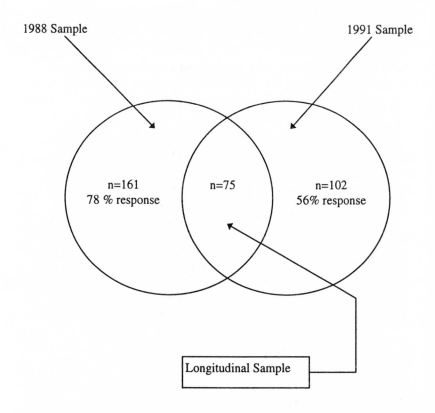

Figure 2.   The Samples

moved from the state. The return of 102 usable questionnaires represents a response rate of 56 percent for the 1991 study. Twenty-seven of the 1991 respondents had not participated in the 1988 study. Therefore, as shown in Figure 2, only 75 firms participated in both studies. These firms provide the data used to test all three hypotheses. Unfortunately, because 4 did not answer the product adaptation question, the analysis sample for H_1 and H_2 is reduced to 71 firms. We turn now to a characterization of the organizations in this longitudinal sample.

Responding organizations are quite heterogeneous, representing industries such as Electrical (11%), Machinery (8%), Publishing and Printing (8%), Food Products (7%), Mining/Stone Products (5%), Woodworking (5%), Sporting Goods (5%), Forestry and Lumber (4%), and others.[1] Fifty percent of the firms are closely held

Table 1. Selected Sample Summary Statistics

Variable	Mean
Company Age in Years	44.75 years
Sales Revenues in Dollars	$8.46 million
Number of Employees	92.42 people
Years Exporting	16.45 years
Export Sales as a Percentage of Total Sales Volume	16.1%
Export Profit as a Percentage of Total Profit	16.8%
Firm Type:	
Consumer Goods Manufacturer	49.3%
Industrial Goods Manufacturer	50.6%
Export Department Type:	
No employees formally assigned to handle exporting	36.8%
No formal export department, but at least one assigned employee	52.9%
Formal export department	10.3%
Product Life Cycle Stage of Main Product Line[a]	
Introduction/Growth Stage	41.3%
Maturity/Decline State	58.7%
Manager Characteristics:	
Percent of managers with college degrees	67.1%
Percent of managers with foreign experience	13.9%
Percent of managers who can speak $\geq$ foreign language	19.6%

Notes: [a]question phrasing, "Which of the following best describes the stage of market development of your firm's major product line?

1=Introductory Stage: Primary demand for product line is just starting to grow, product line is still unfamiliar to many potential users.

2=Growth Stage: Demand is growing at 10 percent or more usually; technology and/or competitive structure is still changing.

3=Maturity Stage: Product line is familiar to the vast majority of potential users; technology and/or competitive structure is reasonably stable.

4=Decline Stage: Product line is viewed as a commodity; weaker competitors are beginning to exit the market."

corporations, with 16 percent family owned, 12 percent individually owned, 9 percent partnerships, 7 percent cooperatives, 4 percent publicly-traded corporations, and 2 percent having other forms of ownership. Sixty-two percent of the firms describe themselves as somewhat to very diversified.

The average age of the organizations is approximately 45 years, with a mean sales volume of 8.46 million dollars and an average of 92 employees. The firms have been involved in exporting for 16.5 years on average, while a mean of 1.6 people per firm are assigned responsibilities directly related to exporting. Table 1 provides summary statistics for these and other sample characteristics.

B. Measures

A number of measures were used in the study, and are briefly described below. To test hypotheses H_1 and H_2, the measures used were those obtained from the 1991 instrument. For hypothesis H_3, the relevant 1991 measures were paired with their counterparts from the 1988 instrument. As mentioned earlier, for purposes of consistency, all hypotheses were tested with data from the longitudinal sample.

Product Adaptation

As noted previously, an intentionally all-encompassing measure is used to assess the product adaptation dimension of the P/M strategy matrix. Product adaptation (ADAPT) is operationalized with the question "We adapt our products for about _____ percent of our foreign markets." Firms were then grouped as adapters if their answer was greater than zero (a median split) and non-adapters if they answered zero. Typically, firms which answered greater than zero answered much greater than zero, adapting for an average of 73.33 percent of their foreign markets.

Number of Export Countries

The second dimension of the P/M typology, number of export countries (NUMBER), reflects the conceptualization of markets as countries. Operationally, the median number of countries to which firms exported is used as the cut-off point for this measure. Thus, firms exporting to five or more countries were placed in the "many" category and firms exporting to four or fewer were assigned to the "few" category.

Sales from Exports

This measure (PCTSALES) of export performance captures export sales as a percentage of a firm's total sales volume. It is operationalized with the question "Approximately what percentage (%) of your firm's total 1990 sales volume came from export sales? _____ %." This measure has been commonly used in the international marketing literature to operationalize export performance (cf. Kotabe & Czinkota, 1992).

Profits from Exports

This measure (PCTPROFIT) consists of the percentage of a firm's total profits attributed to export activities. It is operationalized with the question "Approximately what percentage (%) of your firm's total 1990 profits would you attribute to its export activities? _____ %." There is, again, ample evidence from the international marketing literature to support such a measure (Kotabe & Czinkota, 1992).

International Marketing Primacy

In contrast to the above measures, the marketing primacy construct (PRIMACY) is assessed with a multi-item measure. The construct is operationalized in terms of eight items, measured on a 5-point "strongly agree/strongly disagree" continuum. The initial (unpurified) set of items is listed in Table 2. Since the construct is a new one, one-on-one personal interviews were conducted with thirty practicing managers to craft appropriate language for the items in the measure.

Export Intention

Export intention (INTENT), which concerns an organization's near-term plans to export to new markets, expand export sales by introducing new products, and so on, is operationalized using four items adapted from Reid (1983, 1984) and measured on a 5-point "very likely/very unlikely" continuum (see Table 2).

Market Information Search

This measure (SEARCH) describes the frequency with which firms look at published materials for information about foreign versus U.S. markets (see Table 2). It is a four-item measure adapted from Reid (1983). Three of the items are scaled on a 5-point "at least once per week/never" continuum, and one is scaled on a 5-point "strongly agree/strongly disagree" continuum. In contrast to Reid (1983), our measure does not include an "export program" utilization indicant since the state in which the data were collected conducts very few export stimulation programs.

Table 2.   Hypothesized Construct Configuration

Scale and Corresponding Items	Mean	Std	Item-total Correlation
International Marketing Primacy (PRIMACY)[a] α=.89			
1. Our export business is not a high priority for us.	3.04	1.28	.69
2. What sets us apart from our compentition is that we are probably the most serious in our export efforts.[b]	2.57	1.05	.62
3. We look at our exporting as being secondary.[c]	2.84	1.24	.56
4. There is still a lot to do in the domestic area before we turn our major efforts to the international.	2.96	1.07	.69
5. We must take care of current needs before we can really devote the time necessary for exports.	3.36	1.09	.67
6. We have not really set up any formal marketing attempts at this point to go outside the U.S.	3.32	1.34	.70
7. We have made a clear decision to expand the export part of our business.[b]	3.29	1.11	.66
8. Our overseas business is really just incidental. We don't actively go after the overseas business.	3.04	1.30	.77
Export Intention (INTENT) α=.75			
Over the next 12 months, how likely[d] are you to			
1. ...export to new foreign markets?	3.19	1.45	.59
2. ...introduce new products into foreign markets?	3.15	1.57	.57
3. ...increase the proportion of export sales to current markets?	3.66	1.14	.60
4. Over the next 12 months, do you expect export sales to...[e][c]	3.90	.76	53
Market Information Search (SEARCH) α=.87			
About how often[f] do you look at published materials for inormation about...			
1. ...current U.S. markets?	3.62	1.43	.72
2. ...current foreignn markets?	3.00	1.33	.90
3. ...potential foreign markets?	2.84	1.34	.86
4. Analyzing foreign market opportunities is a frequent task.[a][b]	2.87	1.30	.45

Notes: [a]5=strongly disagree; 1=strongly agree. [b] reverse coded item. [c] when examined via confirmatory factor analysis, this item was eliminated from subsequent analysis. [d] 5=very likely; 1=very unlikely.
[a]5=increase greatly; 4=increase slightly; 3=stay the same; 2=decrease slightly; 1=decrease greatly.
[f]5=at least once per week; 4=monthly; 3=several times per year; 2=annually or less; 1=never.

Company Size

Company size (SIZE) is operationalized in terms of sales revenues (in actual dollars).

V. ANALYSIS AND RESULTS

A. Measure Validation

The multi-item measures (PRIMACY, INTENT, and SEARCH) in the study were subjected to a two-step purification process (cf.

Churchill, 1979). First, item analysis procedures, including calculation of item-total correlations and coefficient alpha, were conducted to assess the quality and unidimensionality of the constructs. Second, the sets of items were subjected to confirmatory factor analyses.[2] This step allows for a more rigorous assessment of the hypothesized factor structure of a construct (cf. Bagozzi, 1980; Long, 1983; Noordewier, John, & Nevin, 1990).

In the case of PRIMACY, coefficient alpha for the eight items is a relatively high .89 (cf. Nunnally, 1967). However, a single factor measurement model consisting of all eight items does not produce an adequate fit to the data $\chi^2(20) = 32.78, p = .036$). Based upon its low multiple correlation with the construct, item 3 was deleted. This resulted in a revised model consisting of seven items and providing an acceptable fit to the data ($\chi^2(14) = 20.31, p = .12$), with all seven of the loadings on the construct both large in magnitude and statistically significant.

In the case of INTENT, coefficient alpha appears reasonable (.75), but a confirmatory factor model reveals a poor fit to the data ($\chi^2(2) = 6.71, p = .035$). Subsequently, item 4 was deleted based upon its relatively low squared multiple correlation with the hypothesized factor, resulting in a three item factor model. Analysis of these factor loadings revealed that the coefficients were similar in magnitude. Hence, we constrainted the loadings on the items to be equal. The hypothesis of equal loadings cannot be rejected ($\chi^2(2) = 3.46, p = .18$). Accordingly, a single factor representation of the INTENT construct is used.

For the market information search construct (SEARCH), no unidimensional (confirmatory) model could be found which fit the data, despite the high coefficient alpha (.87). Failure to confirm the hypothesized domain of SEARCH reaffirms the value of covariance structure analysis when employing multi-item measures, highlighting in particular the inherent limitations of conventional tools applied to measure purification. Further work involving the hypothesized SEARCH construct was abandoned at this time since it could not be verified empirically. Therefore, there is no further analysis of this construct in this report.

B. Export Strategy-Performance Tests

The hypothesized contrasts, H_1 and H_2, were tested using a regression modeling approach. Models of the following form were fit to the data for both of the dependent variables, PCTSALES and PCTPROFIT:

$$Y_i = \beta_0 + \beta_1 C_{1i} + \beta_2 C_{2i} + \beta_3 C_{3i} + \beta_4 SIZE_i + \beta_5 PRIMACY_i + \beta_6 INTENT_i + \epsilon_i$$

where:

Y_i	is the value of the dependent variable (PCTSALES or PCTPROFIT).
$\beta_0, \beta_1, \ldots \beta_6$	are unknown regression parameters (intercept and slope terms, respectively).
C_{1i}, C_{2i}, C_{3i}	are the indicator (dummy) variables for Cell 1, 2, and 3 strategies, respectively (the dummy variable for C_{4i} was omitted to avoid singularity).
$SIZE_i$	is the company size, in sales dollars.
$PRIMACY_i$	is the mean score of the items comprising the international marketing primacy measure.
$INTENT_i$	is the mean score of the items comprising the export intent measure.
ϵ_i	is a random (stochastic) error term.
$i = 1,2,\ldots,n$	observations.

The theoretical rationale for this type of model, in which strategic combinations (cells) of NUMBER and ADAPT are represented as indicator (dummy) variables, can be found in Marascuilo and Levin (1976). These authors point out that a "cell means"-type model in a "two-way layout is functionally like viewing the design as a one-way layout, with 'treatment effects' defined as the combination of [the two factors comprising it]" (Marascuilo & Levin, 1976, p. 63). Using this model, one can investigate both nested and interaction-like comparisons. In a regression formulation of the cell means model, a test statistic for the simple pairwise contrasts embodied in H_1 and H_2 can be formed by taking the (estimated) contrast and dividing it by its (estimated) standard deviation. The t-value obtained is then compared to the tabled critical value for significance. We illustrate the process and report our findings below.

The results of the regressions are reported in Table 3. For both regressions, overall F-tests indicate that statistically significant amounts of variation in the data have been explained. The adjusted R_2 values are 24.7 percent and 29.8 percent for PCTSALES and PCTPROFIT, respectively.

Table 3. Regression Results

| Independent Variable | Dependent Variable | | | |
| | PCTSALES | | PCTPROFIT | |
	Parameter Estimate	Standard Error	Parameter Estimate	Standard Error
Constant	-7.07	8.08	-4.97	8.05
C_1	9.58	5.98	9.49	5.96
C_2	3.51	7.14	4.22	7.11
C_3	10.57	6.85	14.45^a	6.83
SIZE	-6.76^{E-8}	1.3^{E-7}	7.67^{E-8}	1.3^{E-7}
PRIMACY	11.42^a	3.24	11.70^a	3.22
INTENT	-4.97^a	2.21	-6.22^a	2.20
R^2 adj	24.7%		29.8%	
$F_{(6,64)}$	4.835		5.962	
	$(p<.001)$		$(p<.001)$	

Note: [a] Indicates significant at $p<.05$.

In terms of the hypothesized contrasts, consider first H_1, and possible performance differences between customized broad-based and standardized broad-based exporters (Cell 2 and Cell 1 firms, respectively). For the dependent variable PCTSALES, the actual performance difference between Cell 2 and Cell 1 firms is estimated to be-6.07, calculated from the estimated coefficients $b_2-b_1 = 3.51-9.58$. This difference, divided by its estimated standard deviation, yields a t-value which is not significant at the .10 level. For the dependent variable PCTPROFIT, the Cell 2 versus Cell 1 performance difference is estimated by-5.27 ($b_2-b_1 = 4.22-9.49 =-5.27$). Comparing the calculated t-value to the tabled t-value reveals that the contrast is not significant at the .10 level. Summarizing, the contrasts involving customized broad-based and standardized broad-based exporters are not significantly different from zero, for either of the dependent variables: PCTSALES and PCTPROFIT . Hence, H_1 is *not rejected*.

Consider now H_2, and possible performance differences between customized-focused and standardized-focused exporters (Cell 3 and Cell 4 firms, respectively). For the dependent variable PCTSALES, the actual performance difference between Cell 3 and Cell 4 firms is estimated to be 10.57 (given by $b_3-0.0 = 10.57-0.0$, since C_{4i} was the omitted, baseline, indicator variable). This difference, divided by its estimated standard deviation, gives a t-value which is not significant at the .10 level. For the dependent variable PCTPROFIT, the Cell 3 versus Cell 4 performance difference is estimated by 14.45 (b_3-0.0 = 14.45). This difference, divided by it estimated standard deviation, gives a t-value which *is* significant at the .05 level. Summarizing, the contrast involving customized-focused and standardized-focused exporters is not significantly different from zero for PCTSALES, but is significantly different from zero (p =.05) for PCTPROFIT. Hence, H_2 is *not rejected* for *PCTSALES,* but *is rejected* for *PCTPROFIT.*[3]

Although we did not offer formal hypotheses involving the remaining four pairwise contrasts, tests like those performed for H_1 and H_2 were conducted for the two vertical and two diagonal contrasts. None of the contrasts were significantly different from zero.

The influence of the nonfocal variables on performance must be considered in any empirical test of a strategy-performance linkage. Accordingly, the control variables included in the regression models were SIZE, PRIMACY, and INTENT (recall that the domain of the hypothesized information search construct, SEARCH, could not be confirmed empirically, resulting in its elimination from further analyses).

Both PCTSALES and PCTPROFIT increase significantly as the priority (PRIMACY) attached to exporting by an organization increases. That PRIMACY influences performance even after controlling for the effects of strategy suggests that selecting and pursuing an export strategy in a mechanistic way, without attaching any real priority to it, is unlikely to result in an optimal level of performance.

PCTSALES and PCTPROFIT both significantly decrease as the likelihood of near-term export intentions increases (INTENT). This result makes sense since the expectation of expanded exports in the near future is more likely to occur in firms which have been lacking in past export performance.

Firm size (SIZE), measured in terms of sales revenues, is not significantly related to either dependent variable (PCTSALES or PCTPROFIT).

C. Test of Export Stability

In addition to assessing the relationship between specific P/M strategy cells and performance, we also examined the possibility of stability in the export performance of firms over time, referred to previously as export carryover. This issue is addressed irrespective of the strategy choices made by firms.

In order to examine this issue empirically, we tested a model in which export performance is assumed to have the same measurement model over time and is allowed to covary (correlate) across occasions of measurement. For both PCTSALES and PCTPROFIT, 1988 and 1991 levels are assessed.

Since we are dealing with a two-period longitudinal design, it makes sense both substantively and statistically to allow for correlated residuals in the model. Specifically, we hypothesize a model in which the loadings on the specific indicators are assumed (constrained) to be equal (so, e.g., the magnitude and direction of the loading of PCTSALES on the performance construct is the same between 1988 and 1991), the residual (specific) variances are identical, and the covariances of residuals are the same (for extended treatment of the logic of such constraints, see Joreskog & Sorbom, 1989; Loehlin, 1987; Bentler, 1989). These restrictions serve both to identify the model and to allow for a rigorous test of the hypothesis of stability over time in the factor structure. The proposed model, shown in Figure 3, has six free parameters, all of which are identified.

Since we parameterize the model by setting the variances of the export performance factors at 1.0, the covariance between the factors can be interpreted as a correlation (Bentler, 1989). In fitting this model to the data, our interest centers on the correlation between the latent export performance factors, EXP88 and EXP91. If this correlation is significantly greater than zero, then there is evidence of performance carryover, or stability over time.

SAS's CALIS procedure was used to implement the model and estimate the relevant parameters. Overall, the fit of the model to the data is poor ($\chi^2(4) = 40.73$, $p = .0001$), leading to rejection of the composite (overall model) hypothesis. We note, however, that all of the model's estimated loadings are significant at the .05 probability level and, of particular interest, that the export performance factor correlation coefficient is significant ($\phi = .534$, $s.e. = .09$, $t = 5.91$). The latter finding implies that the null hypothesis of zero correlation is rejected at the .05 level (cf. Long, 1983), and that the two performance factors are not unrelated over time. Specifically, a correlation of .534 implies that $(.534)^2$, or 28.5 percent, of the variance of EXP91 can be predicted from EXP88 (Bentler, 1989).

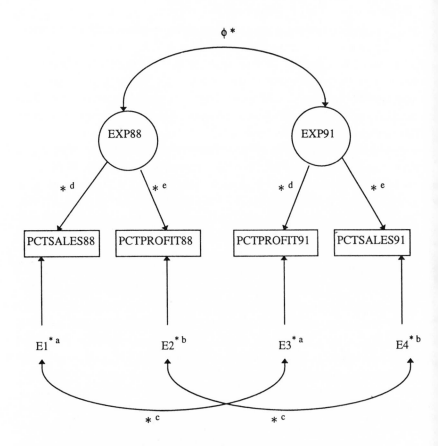

Note: 1 Parameters indicated by a,b,c,d or e are equal.
      2 Following Bentler and Weeks, a * indicates a free parameter.
      3 The variances of the factors EXP88 and EXP91 are fixed at 1.0.

Figure 3. Performance Factor Model

However, we emphasize that the overall chi-square is small compared to its degrees of freedom, implying that the composite model is inadequate. It is therefore more appropriate to regard the finding of a significant factor correlation as *suggestive* rather than conclusive (Bentler, 1989).

VI. DISCUSSION AND CONCLUSIONS

Our purpose in this paper was to empirically examine the relationship between export strategy choice and export performance. Although the marketing management literature is rich with speculation about performance implications of international strategy alternatives similar to those presented here, little empirical work has been done. Moreover, to the best of our knowledge, no work has been done which examines export performance stability over time. Hence, our sample of exporting firms was carefully examined across two time periods, utilizing both survey and personal interview techniques to acquire the necessary information.

Operationalizing our objectives required development of a framework (typology) for classifying strategy alternatives. We believe that our framework is plausible, sensible and well grounded in previous scholarship (Ansoff, 1957, 1965, 1969; Buzzell, 1968; Douglas & Wind, 1987; Kotler, 1991; Kleinschmidt & Cooper, 1985; Levitt, 1983; Quelch & Hoff, 1986). Moreover, we believe it to be isomorphic with the way international marketing managers think.

While our sample of firms populates all quadrants of the P/M typology, it is notable that only a little more than one-third of them have chosen to adapt products for export. Clearly, then, a measure of product adaptation (*any* product adaptation) serves as a major differentiating factor when classifying our sample. We argue that firms consciously make this choice by balancing the benefits of gaining entry into foreign markets via an adaptation strategy against the costs of doing so (i.e., managers "believe" in the merits of the chosen strategies).

Failure to reject the hypothesized null relationship (H_1) between export performance and export strategy alternatives for *broad-based* exporters suggests that the "it depends" rationale of Buzzell (1968), Douglas and Wind (1987) Kotler (1991), and Quelch and Hoff (1986) may be more applicable to the export scenario than Levitt's (1983) standardization argument. That is, our results suggest that a standardized approach to *broad-based* exporting (controlling for firm size, international marketing primacy, and export intention) will not produce universally superior export sales or export profit performance. Hence, our findings indicate that a standardized broad-based strategy, such as advocated by Levitt, does not produce better sales or profit performance than the more adaptive, customized broad-based strategy. In our sample, the *broad-based* exporters, which populate the "adapt/do not adapt" cells almost equally, do equally well (poorly) in their export endeavors. Presumably, the performance of firms following the customized broad-based strategy is obtained because their managers systematically assess customers' behavior and response patterns to their varied market offerings (Douglas & Wind, 1987).

Mixed results for our second hypothesis (H₂) suggest that the "standardization/performance" question for *focused* exporters is more complex. For instance, if one bases performance on sales (market share), we cannot reject the null hypothesis of no difference in performance between customized-focused and standardized-focused strategies. Hence, this result supports Porter's (1985) argument that "If a firm can achieve sustainable cost leadership (cost focus) *or* differentiation (differentiation focus)... then the focuser will be an above-average performer in its industry" (p. 16, emphasis added). However, if one bases performance on profit, our results suggest that customized-focused exporters out-perform standardized-focused exporters. While this discrepancy may seem puzzling, Porter's (1985) work does suggest an explanation. He notes that "cost focus [standardized-focused] exploits differences in *cost* behavior in some segments, while differentiation focus [customized-focused] exploits the needs of buyers in certain segments" (Porter, 1985, p. 15, italics added). If a focused exporter adopts a standardization (cost-based) strategy, then lowering costs (and revenue if demand does not offset the cost reduction) to gain international market entry could affect profit. Thus, a performance measure based upon profit may show differences between customized-and standardized-focused exporters when a performance measure based upon sales would not. One could argue that this does not happen for broad-based exporters because they reap economies of scale by standardizing in many markets (countries).

Results concerning the nonfocal variables also provoke thought. Analyses indicate significant, though opposite, associations between the independent variables, PRIMACY and INTENT, and *both* dependent performance measures. Our data show that placing a higher priority on exporting is significantly linked with higher export performance in terms of both sales and profits. This result supports previous research linking commitment and performance, given the conceptual similarity between PRIMACY and commitment. On the other hand, our findings illustrate that having good intentions, or higher expectations of *future* exports, is significantly associated with lower levels of *current/past* export performance. Thus the INTENT measure seems to captured the hopes of firms which may not yet have reached their full potential.

With respect to H_3, recent arguments suggest that as organizations become successful the successes become inculcated into an "organizational memory" through organizational learning (cf. Sinkula, 1994). The argument for organization learning appears to be supported by our findings. Our results suggest that organizational learning *does* take place with respect to exporting and that there is a significant carryover effect in the export performance of firms. Therefore, it would be a natural next step to carefully examine organizations that have negative performance carryover in an attempt to help them "unlearn" those organizational behaviors which inhibit performance.

It is in this regard that government agencies may play a key role. When a firm has ventured into exporting, but experienced deteriorating performance, it is possible that an outsider (a government trade specialist) may be able to step in and provide a critical perspective. Analysis by a trade specialist could reveal counter productive behaviors which may have become habitual to the firm, fostering performance decline.

While we believe these findings add substantively to our knowledge about the export strategy/performance linkage, the study is not without its limitations. Perhaps most notably, the sample size was relatively small, thereby limiting the power to statistically discern the effects of interest. Also, a significant percentage of the firms included in the study were rather small, so that our findings may not be as readily generalizable to a population of larger firms (we note, however, that SIZE was not a significant control variable). The sample was also regional, with all respondent firms derived from a single state. Moreover, the state in question was beginning to experience economic difficulties over the time interval in which the data were collected. Hence, research examining the strategy/performance relationship and export stability hypothesis under different macroeconomic conditions would augment the findings of this study.

A. Future Directions

In order for future research in international marketing to progress, general models which explain performance must be more fully developed. The prime tenet of this paper is that strategy models show the best promise of doing so. In particular, models which begin with broad conceptualizations of strategy as they relate to more "micro" (e.g., marketing mix) strategies are more like what occurs in practice. Product/market models are especially powerful, warranting further research for a number of reasons.

First, there is ample literature which effectively frames strategic market planning issues from a product and/or market perspective. From Ansoff (1957) to the present, over thirty years of research suggests that products and markets are the cornerstones of marketing strategy and performance. Scholars interested in exporting issues would do well to use more of this literature in framing their research.

Second, placing the appropriate product into the appropriate market is what talented international marketers do. It is surprising that research in international marketing has more often looked independently at products and markets than it has looked at them jointly. Studies following this one might develop or refine paradigms for exploring joint product/market strategies.

Third, while they can be improved on, the measures of products and markets used in this study are quite straightforward. That is, they do not pose problematic or complex measurement issues. Thus, product/market models constitute an area of marketing inquiry in which substantial agreement may emerge fairly quickly on the measures of the central constructs. Certainly, we do not claim to have developed the ultimate measures here. Later work should attempt improvements.

Finally, P/M typologies appear to be generalizable across industries and company types. Conclusions presented in this paper do not derive from only one or two industries or from only industrial (versus consumer) goods manufacturers. A purposefully broad sample of firms was utilized, in part, to encourage others to utilize such samples. Indeed, the time has come to emphasize longitudinal methodologies, where appropriate, and to augment the generalizability of findings by utilizing across-industry studies.

Adopting these goals holds tremendous promise for expanding the usefulness of our collective findings while at the same time focusing and refining our thinking about exporting and international marketing.

ACKNOWLEDGMENT

The authors wish to thank Bill Baker and Ron Savitt (both of the University of Vermont), two anonymous reviewers, and the editor of this volume, Tage Koed Madsen, for their helpful comments on previous versions of this chapter. We also wish to acknowledge the financial assistance of the State of Vermont in facilitating the collection of the data presented here.

NOTES

1. While firms were able to categorize themselves generally as consumer versus industrial goods marketers, presumably because of diversification efforts, a good many firms (36.8%) could not fit themselves into one specific industry. Hence, they are categorized as "other."

2. Covariance, not correlation, matrices are used in all of the models analyzed in this paper. As detailed by Cudek (1989), the use of correlation matrices can actually change the form of the structure under examination, result in different values of the test statistic, and produce incorrect estimated standard errors.

3. A variety of regression diagnostics were performed to check the assumptions underlying the models. In particular, we checked for the influence of outliers, collinearity problems, and the distribution of the residuals. No problems were evident.

REFERENCES

Albaum, G. (1983). Effectiveness of government export assistance for U.S. smaller-sized manufacturers: Some further evidence. *International Marketing Review, 1*(1), 68-75.

Ansoff, I. H. (1957). Strategies for diversification. *Harvard Business Review, 35* (September-October), 113-124.

Ansoff, I. H. (1965). *Corporate strategy.* New York: McGraw-Hill.

Ansoff, I. H. (1969). *Business strategy.* Baltimore, MD: Penguin Books.

Axinn, C. N. (1988). Export performance: Do managerial perceptions make a difference?. *International Marketing Review, 5*(2), 61-71.

Axinn, C.N., & Thach, S.V. (1990). Linking export performance to the marketing practices of machine tool exporters. In S. T. Cavusgil (Ed.), *Advances in international marketing* (Vol. 4, pp. 117-139). Greenwich, CT: JAI Press.

Ayal, I., & Zif, J. (1979). Market expansion strategies in multinational marketing. *Journal of Marketing 43*(Spring), 84-94.

Bagozzi, R. P. (1980). *Causal models in marketing.* New York: Wiley.

Bartels, R. (1968). Are domestic and international marketing dissimilar? *Journal of Marketing, 32* (July), 56-61.

Bentler, P. M. (1989). *EQS structural equations program manual [Version 3.0].* Los Angeles: BMDP Statistical Software.

Bilkey, W. J. (1978). An attempted integration of the literature on the export behavior of firms. *Journal of International Business Studies, 9*(Spring-Summer), 33-46.

Bilkey, W. J. (1985). Development of export marketing guidelines. *International Marketing Review, 2*(1), 31-40.

Bilkey, W. J., & Tesar, G. (1977). The export behavior of smaller sized Wisconsin manufacturing firms. *Journal of International Business Studies, 8*(Spring-Summer), 93-98.

Buatsi, S. N. (1986). Organizational adaptation to international marketing. *International Marketing Review, 3*(4), 17-26.

Buzzell, R. D. (1968). Can you standardize multinational marketing? *Harvard Business Review, 46*(November-December), 102-113.

Cavusgil, S. T. (1980). On the internationalization process of firms. *European Research, 8*(November), 273-281.

Cavusgil, S. T. (1984). Organizational characteristics associated with export activity. *Journal of Management Studies, 21*(January), 3-22.

Cavusgil, S. T., Bilkey, W.J., & Tesar, G. (1979). A note on the export behavior of firms: Exporter profiles. *Journal of International Business Studies, 10* (Spring-Summer), 91-97.

Cavusgil, S. T., & Nevin, J. R. (1981). Internal determinants of export marketing behavior: An empirical investigation. *Journal of Marketing Research, 18*(February), 114-119.

Christensen, C. H., da Rocha, A., & Gertner, R.K. (1987). An empirical investigation of the factors influencing exporting success of Brazilian firms. *Journal of International Business Studies, 18*(Fall), 61-77.

Churchill, G.A. Jr. (1979). A paradigm for developing better measures of marketing constructs. *Journal of Marketing Research, 16*(February), 64-73.

Cudek, R. (1989). Analysis of correlation matrices using ccovariance structure models. *Psychological Bulletin, 105* (2), 317-327.

Czinkota, M. R. (1979). An analysis of export development strategies in selected U.S. industries. Dissertation. Ohio State University.

Czinkota, M. R., & Johnston, W.J. (1981). Segmenting U.S. firms for export development. *Journal of Business Research, 9* (December), 353-365.

Delacroix, J. (1984). Export strategies for small American firms. *California Management Review, 26*(Spring), 138-153.

Douglas, S. P., & Wind, Y. (1987). The myth of globalization. *Columbia Journal of World Business, 22*(Winter), 19-29.

Edmunds, S. E., & Khoury, S. J. (1986). Exports: A necessary ingredient in the growth of small business firms. *Journal of Small Business Management, 24*(October), 54-65.

Fenwick, I., & Amine, L. (1979). Export performance and export policy: Evidence from the U.K. clothing industry. *Journal of the Operational Research Society, 30*(8), 747-754.

Joreskog, K.G., & Sorbom, D. (1989). *LISREL VII: Users guide*. Mooresville, IN: Scientific Software, Inc.

Joynt P., & Welch, L. (1985). A strategy for small business internationalization. *International Marketing Review, 2*(3), 64-73.

Kacker, M. P. (1975). Export oriented product adaptation: Its patterns and problems. *Management International Review, 14*(6), 61-70.

Keegan, W. J. (1969). Multinational product planning: Strategic alternatives. *Journal of Marketing, 33*(January), 58-62.

Kinnear, T. C., & Taylor, J.R. (1991). *Marketing research: An applied approach.* New York: McGraw-Hill.

Kirpalani V. H., & MacIntosh, N. B. (1980). International marketing effectiveness in technology-oriented small firms. *Journal of International Business Studies, 11*(3), 81-90.

Kleinschmidt, E. J., & Cooper, R.G. (1984). A typology of export strategies applied to the export performance of industrial firms. In E. Kaynak (Ed.), *International marketing management* (pp. 217-231). New York: Praeger.

Kotabe M., & Czinkota, M.R. (1992). State government promotion of manufacturing exports: A gap analysis. *Journal of International Business Studies, 23*(4), 637-658.

Kotler, P. (1980). *Marketing management: Analysis, planning, and control.* Englewood-Cliffs, NJ: Prentice-Hall.

Kotler, P. (1991). *Marketing management: Analysis, planning, implementation, and control.* Englewood Cliffs, NJ: Prentice-Hall.

Levitt, T. (1983). The globalization of markets. *Harvard Business Review, 61*(May-June), 92-102.

Loehlin, J. C. (1987). *Latent variable models: An introduction to factor, path, and structural analysis.* Hillsdale, NJ: Lawrence Erlbaum Associates, Publishers.

Long, J. S. (1983). *Confirmatory factor analysis.* Beverly Hills: Sage Publications.

Lowinger, T. C. (1975). The technology factor and the export performance of U.S. manufacturing industries. *Economic Inquiry, 13*(June), 221-236.

Marascuilo, L. A., & Levin, J.R. (1976). The simultaneous investigation of interaction and nested hypotheses in two-factor analysis of variance designs. *American Educational Research Journal, 13* (1), 61-65.

McGuinness, N. W., & Little, B. (1981). The influence of product characteristics on the export performance of new industrial products. *Journal of Marketing, 45*(Spring), 110-122.

Möller, K. (1984). Role of promotional management in exporting to the Soviet Union and OECD countries. In E. Kaynak (Ed.), *International marketing management* (pp. 318-334). New York: Praeger.

Noordewier, T. G., John, G. & Nevin, J.R. (1990). Performance outcomes of purchasing arrangements in industrial buyer-vendor relationships. *Journal of Marketing, 54*(October), 80-93.

Nunnally, J.C. (1967). *Psychometric theory.* New York: McGraw-Hill.

O'Rourke, A. D. (1985). Differences in exporting practices, attitudes and problems by size of firm. *American Journal of Small Business, 9*(Winter), 25-29.

Piercy, N. (1982). *Export strategy: Markets and competition.* London: George Allen & Unwin.

Porter, M. E. (1980). *Competitive strategy: Techniques for analyzing industries and competitors.* New York: The Free Press.

Porter, M. E. (1985). *Competitive advantage: Creating and sustaining superior performance.* New York: The Free Press.

Quelch, J. A., & Hoff, E.J. (1986). Customizing global marketing. *Harvard Business Review, 64*(May-June), 59-68.

Reid, S. D. (1983). Managerial and firm influences on export behavior. *Journal of the Academy of Marketing Science, 11*(Summer), 323-332.

Reid, S. D. (1984). Information acquisition and export entry decisions in small firms. *Journal of Business Research, 12*(April), 141-157.

Ricks, D. A. (1983). *Big business blunders: Mistakes in multinational marketing.* Homewood, IL: Irwin.

Seely, R., & Inglarsh, H.J. (1981). International marketing in the context of the small business. *American Journal of Small Business, 6*(October-December), 33-37.

Sinkula, J. M. (1994). Market information processing and organizational learning. *Journal of Marketing, 58*(January), 35-45.

Szymanski, D. M., Bharadwaj, S.G., & Varadarajan, P.R. (1993). Standardization versus adaptation of international marketing strategy: An empirical investigation. *Journal of Marketing, 57*(October), 1-17.

Thach, S.V., & Axinn, C.N. (1991). Pricing and financing practices in industrial exporting firms. *International Marketing Review, 8*(1), 32-46.

Tookey, D. A. (1964). Factors associated with success in exporting. *Journal of Management Studies, 1*(March), 48-66.

Turnbull, P. W., & Valla, J-P. (1986). *Strategies for international industrial marketing.* London: Croom Helm.

Weinrauch, D. J., & Rao, C.P. (1974). The export marketing mix: An examination of company experiences and perceptions. *Journal of Business Research, 2*(October), 447-452.

Yaprak, A., Sorek, C., & Parameswaran, R. (1984). Competitive strategy in multinational oligopolies. In E. Kaynak (Ed.), *International marketing management* (pp. 232-255). New York: Praeger.

LINKING BUSINESS RELATIONSHIPS TO MARKETING STRATEGY AND EXPORT PERFORMANCE:
A PROPOSED CONCEPTUAL FRAMEWORK

Felicitas U. Evangelista

ABSTRACT

While it is common knowledge that business relationships play an important role in marketing, very little has been done to empirically determine their impact on export performance. This article provides some evidence of this defficiency through a review of a number of relevant empirical studies. Based on the interaction theory, it analyzes the links between close and lasting relationships and export performance, and suggests that relationship management become a component of a firm's marketing strategy in addition to the traditional marketing mix variables.

Advances in International Marketing, Volume 8, pages 59-83.
Copyright © 1996 by JAI Press Inc.
All rights of reproduction in any form reserved.
ISBN: 0-7623-0164-3

I. INTRODUCTION

Industrial products are a major export of many countries. Studies have shown that industrial marketing involves buyer seller relationships which tend to be close, complex and lasting (IMP Project Group, 1982). The literature on buyer-seller relationships which has grown rapidly in the last two decades, clearly shows that significant theoretical advances have been achieved in this area. More sophisticated studies have been undertaken and the focus of both conceptual and empirical studies has progressed from the simple dyadic, two party model to the more complex network theory. Leading marketing scholars notably Hunt and Webster have acknowledged the role of exchange relationships in marketing (Dwyer, Schurr, & Oh, 1987) and industrial marketing (Hallen, Johanson, & Mohamed, 1987), respectively.

Export marketing research, however, has given the relationship aspect of export marketing very limited attention. Major reviews of empirical export performance studies (Aaby & Slater, 1988; Madsen, 1989; Gemunden, 1991; Chetty & Hamilton, 1993; see also Appendix) provide concrete evidence to this effect. The trend in the literature on international marketing as a whole, also shows that there is a need for more behavioral studies on buyer-seller relationships in export markets (Ford & Leonidou, 1991).

The aim of this paper is thus, to develop a framework for analyzing: (1) the role of business relationships in export marketing, (2) how relationships impinge on export marketing strategy, and (3) the impact of both on export performance. Based on the interaction approach to industrial marketing, the proposed framework incorporates a number of constructs, most of which have not been empirically tested before in the context of export marketing. Also, unlike the IMP methodology which strictly adheres to a relationship based analysis, the proposed conceptual framework may be empirically tested from the standpoint of just a single entity that is, the exporting firm.

II. MARKETING STRATEGY: TWO DIFFERENT VIEWS

The influence that marketing strategy exerts on export performance can be analyzed from at least two perspectives namely, the marketing mix management view and the interaction approach.

A. The Marketing Mix View

According to the simplified model adopted by CIMaR (Axinn, 1994) and the reviews of empirical research conducted by Aaby and Slater (1988) and Chetty and Hamilton (1993), strategy is a major determinant of export performance. A comprehensive review of 12 major empirical researches devoted to strategy and export performance from 1982-1994 which is presented in the Appendix, shows that the framework adopted by most of these studies was based on the marketing mix management view. The strategy components that were investigated could be categorized according to those defined by Hofer and Schendel (1978) and which appears in many textbooks (e.g., Boyd & Walker, 1990) namely scope, pattern of resource deployment or strategy content, competitive advantage and synergy. Of these components, the first three have received considerable attention in export marketing research. While scope refers to the number and location of markets, market segments and regions, and the extent by which these are diversified, strategy content focuses on the marketing mix variables with the standardization or adaptation issue being the common thread among these studies. Finally, competitive advantage deals with the firm's marketing mix strategy as they stand relative to those of competitors. Although different measures were adopted, many of the studies reviewed, found these strategy components to have a significant effect on export performance.

B. The Interaction Approach

Another way of conceptualizing marketing strategy is by viewing industrial marketing as an interaction process. In its simplest form, the interaction approach views the marketing and purchasing of goods and services as a continuous exchange of not only goods or services for financial returns, but also the exchange of information and social elements. Through time this exchange process may become routinized leading to the establishment of clear roles or responsibilities, standard operating procedures, trust and norms of conduct for each party. Through communication or exchange of information, contact patterns among individuals or groups of individuals in different functional departments are developed. Contributing to the building of this relationship are the adaptations that both buyers and sellers undertake to accommodate each other's requirements. On the supplier's side, these adaptations could be in the form of modifications of products, pricing, delivery, information routines while buyers can consider adaptations in its own product requirements, production methods and prices it is willing to accept. These adaptations indicate that both parties invest time and resources in the relationship (Hakansson, 1982).

The relationship between supplier and customer as shown in Figure 1 is influenced by the characteristics of the organizations and individuals involved, the environment within which the interaction takes place and the atmosphere surrounding the interaction. The organization factors include the production technology of both parties, organization size, structure and strategy, organizational experience and characteristics of the individuals representing the organizations (Hakansson, 1982).

The interaction theory may be extended to cover multi-party relationships. Besides its customers, a supplier's activities may be influenced by its customer's customers, its customer's other suppliers, intermediaries and other parties all of which constitute an industrial network. A schematic diagram of an industrial network involving an exporter is shown in Figure 2. Note that the specific entities comprising the network and their interconnections are not predetermined nor known, but rather they emerge from the interactions among exchange partners (Axelsson, 1992).

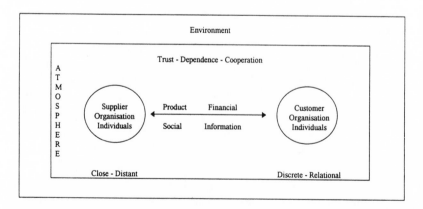

Figure 1.   Supplier-Customer Interaction
(Adapted from IMP, 1982, p. 20)

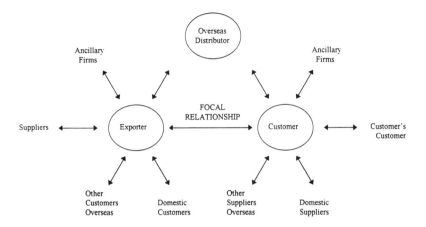

Figure 2.   Relationships in a Network

Through time, firms in the network develop their own strategic identities and positions which reflect the perceived attractiveness of the firm as a partner (Anderson et al., 1994) as well as its role in the network (Hakansson & Snehota, 1989). Network position could also be viewed as a structural concept of location of power to create or influence networks (Thorelli, 1986). The strategies a firm adopts would frequently aim to enhance its identity or strengthen its network position.

The interaction theory thus, presents the view that relationship management is the essence of industrial marketing management. Although there are those who advocate that it should replace the marketing mix approach as the mainstream paradigm in marketing (Gronroos, 1993), it appears that if one approach is taken as a supplement to the other following the suggestion of Thorelli (1986), a more comprehensive world view of industrial marketing could be achieved. This paper will thus proceed to analyze the role of business relationships in export marketing with insights drawn from both the interaction theory and the literature in industrial marketing.

III. RELATIONSHIPS AND NETWORK POSITION

International business relationships emanate mainly from the parties that comprise the focal relationship namely, the exporter, its distributor and the customer.

A. Exporter-Customer Relationship

Buyer-seller relationships have often been described as either transactional/discrete or relational/long term; and close or distant. Traditionally, the exchange between buyer and seller has been viewed as adversarial and transactional in nature. Buyers relied on a large number of suppliers who can be played off against each other to gain price concessions and ensure a continuity of supply. Buyers also assumed an arms length posture and used only short-term contracts. (Spekman, 1988). In more recent times however, more and more manufacturing companies are reducing their supplier base and are moving towards developing closer relationships with them as well as buying under longer term contracts (Spekman, 1988; Kalwani & Narayandas, 1994).

Close and Lasting Relationships

The trend towards closer ties between seller and buyer has been increasingly reported in both the popular business literature (Spekman 1988; Ganesan 1994) and academic publications (Ford 1978; Hakansson 1982; Turnbull & Valla, 1986; Hallen et al., 1987). In the IMP study involving 1000 business relationships within and between five European countries, the reported average age of the relationships was 15 years (Johanson & Hallen, 1989). Based on the same study, analysis of a smaller subsample of 300 relationships showed an average age of 10 years for export relationships and 22 years for domestic relationships. Although domestic relationships turned out to be longer on the average, the age of export relationships in absolute terms is nevertheless a considerable figure. In terms of closeness or friendliness of relationships, the proportion of respondents who considered their domestic relationships to be so ranged from 60-100 percent while for export relationships, the range was from 30-100 percent (Johanson & Hallen, 1989).

The explanations given to support the existence of close and long term relationships between buyers and sellers include : (1) that suppliers and customers in industrial markets need extensive knowledge about each other. In order to conduct important business deals, information about products, ability to fulfill commitments, resources, organization and strategies are needed by both parties. The process of obtaining these information is both time consuming and costly; and (2) that the customers' needs may have to be matched with the supplier's capability. This matching process may involve adaptations from both sides and may take time (Johanson & Hallen, 1989). The need for lasting and close relationships is particularly felt in industrial markets as this could lead to cost savings or avoidance of problems associated with changing suppliers/customers, switching costs, cost reduction or increased revenues (Ford, 1980), product differentiation, competitive advantage and barriers to entry (Day & Wensley, 1988; Mintzberg & Quinn, 1991).

Benefits to Buyer

The benefits of long term and close relationships to buyer firms are quite well established in the literature. By working closely with suppliers, buyer firms are able to effect design changes that facilitate manufacturing operations, minimize scrap and reduce costs. Supplier's expertise and resources can be used to contribute substantially to the buyer's value analysis programs which can reduce cost and lower purchase prices (Landeros & Monczka, 1989). Buyers can also benefit in terms of technical development and cost rationalization (Gadde & Hakansson, 1994).

Benefits to Suppliers

On the other hand, the net effect of long term relationships to suppliers has long been considered as suspect. On the positive end, supplier firms can obtain higher sales and earn greater returns from resources invested to enhance customer relationships through: (1) higher repeat sales and cross selling opportunities (Kotler & Armstrong, 1991), and (2) lower likelihood of supplier switching if effective product differentiation is in place. Existing customers can also be the source of new product ideas and market information and they also can serve as testing grounds for new products and/or processes (Jackson, 1985). On the other side of the equation however, a small customer base could mean higher pressures for price concessions in the short term, reduced gross margins or even recurrent losses as experienced in the automobile industry in the United States (Kalwani & Narayandas, 1994). These plus the observation that customers who are willing to engage in long term relationships are also the most difficult to serve satisfactorily because of their intolerance to any inadequacies of the few select vendors they rely on, reinforce the popular view that suppliers tend to lose out in these relationships (Ramsay, 1990).

The empirical findings regarding the impact of long term relationships on the supplier although limited, has been very encouraging. In a study conducted by Kalwani and Narayandas (1994) it was found that suppliers do benefit from adopting a strategy of maintaining long term relationships as compared to employing a transactional approach with their customers. Suppliers maintaining long term relationships with their customers were found to have been able to reduce their inventory and holding costs as well as their selling, general and administrative expenses that were tied to such factors as lower customer turnover, higher customer satisfaction and lower service costs, and higher effectiveness of selling expenditures. On the whole, firms that have maintained long term relationships with their customers were found to have higher average ROI compared to those that adopted a transactional approach (Kalwani & Narayandas, 1994).

Impact on Export Performance

The impact of long term relationships on the supplier would thus be in terms of the level of sales, cost, price structures and profits. Long term relationships will enable the supplier to know, understand and anticipate better the needs of their customers as well as their customer's customers. Suppliers could then develop products that have a better fit with the customer's requirements compared to those of competitors and with enhanced customer loyalty that tend to develop over time, suppliers would have better opportunities for higher sales in the long run.

This scenario becomes more meaningful in an international setting because of the physical distance and cultural gap (Madsen, 1994) between the exporter and its overseas customers. With distance comes the need for more time and resources to develop a fruitful relationship and exporters would stand a better chance of reaping more benefits if the exchange relationship is for a longer period of time. Selling and customer servicing cost on the other hand, can be reduced as a result of long term relationships as exporters need not be constantly looking for new customers. Selecting the strategic partner then becomes a crucial undertaking. A small customer base can be risky especially if the customers face reduced demand over time as in the case of the defense industry in the United States (Kalwani & Narayandas, 1994), and if servicing the needs of a few select customers would make it difficult for suppliers to compete in other markets (Miles & Snow, 1992).

Long term relationships can affect the closeness of the relationship between or among exchange partners. Heide and John (1990) find that close relationships emerge in response to the need for protecting relationship specific assets. They also suggest that closeness in a relationship is affected by joint action, expected continuity and verification efforts. Joint action can take the form of cooperation between supplier and buyer. Cooperative buyer-seller relationships are said to have five attributes (Landeros & Monczka, 1989) namely, a supply pool consisting of one or a preferred few suppliers, an alliance between buying and selling firms, joint problem solving activities, exchange of information and joint adjustments to marketplace conditions. Cooperative buying and selling relationships have contributed to the ability of buying firms to take on strategic postures in the marketplace. With the support of few preferred suppliers, buyer manufacturers are in a better position to pursue a more strategic orientation be it based on cost, differentiation or a focused market (Landeros & Monczka, 1989).

With derived demand and the network view of marketing, it is logical to expect that suppliers would benefit from the strategic postures their customers and their customers' customers are able to achieve. On the whole, close and lasting relationships with buyers would yield either higher level of sales or a lower level of cost which in the long run will lead to higher profits.

B. Relationship with Distributors

For many industrial manufacturers, overseas distributors are "an important fact of life" (Rosson & Ford, 1982, p. 57). Their importance in exporting has been established in a number of studies (see Appendix). In most of these studies however, the contributions of distributors to export performance were mainly in terms of support provided to them by the manufacturer and their own performance and attributes. The onus has always been on the exporter to find reliable, energetic and successful distributors and provide them with adequate incentives in the form of attractive profit margins and other types of support.

Based on the interaction approach, the relationship between manufacturer and distributor is viewed as one of exchange between two independent entities that have their own goals. As these goals do not always match perfectly, the possibility of tension and conflict exists. Although the negative consequences of conflict on domestic marketing channels are well established in the literature (Rosson & Ford, 1982), in international marketing, the evidence is rather limited.

Two studies cited in the Appendix namely those by Rosson and Ford (1982) and Madsen (1989) are among the few that provide some strongly supported insights into this issue. The first study which involved 21 dyadic relationships between Canadian manufacturers and their U.K. distributors found a significant link between performance and conflict while the second, reported some indications of positive effects of good personal contacts, joint decision making and better relations on performance. Increased personal contacts were thought to cause an exporter to understand better the needs and behaviors of its customers and channel members (Madsen, 1989). A third study, that of Bello and Williamson (1985), examined the impact of contractual agreements between suppliers and export management companies on such relationship variables as dependency, power, conflict and export performance. Although limited, these findings strongly suggest the need to incorporate the relationship aspects of an exporter's distribution strategy or program in determining export performance.

C. Relationship Dimensions

Thus far, the concept of relationship has been discussed in the context of two major dimensions namely close-distant and discrete-relational while mention have also been made of other atmosphere variables such as conflict, dependence, power, trust, and cooperation. A number of other dimensions can be found in the literature (see Rosson & Ford, 1982; Hallen, Johanson, & Mohamed, 1987; Hallen & Sandstrom, 1991) but are not covered in this paper. If all these dimensions are aggregated into a single construct called "Quality of Relationship" the general proposition that export performance is influenced by the quality of relationship between exporter and customer; exporter and distributor as well as distributor and customer could be made.

D. Network Position

Network position refers to the role and importance of the firm in the network as well as the strength of its relationships with those firms with which it has direct or indirect relationships (Johanson & Mattson, 1988). Under the network model, the boundaries of business organizations are regarded as arbitrary and would cover the resources and activities belonging to other entities in the network which the organization can control (Hakansson & Snehota, 1989). This control may be exercised through power, influence and trust (Thorelli, 1986) or the power and dependence structures of the network (Cunningham & Culligan, 1988). The basic assumption is that a firm can gain access to external resources or to another firm's internal assets to supplement its own resources, competencies and capabilities. A simple example is that of an industrial exporter's relationship with a technologically innovative customer in one country enhancing the former's capability and network position with respect to customers in other countries.

Unlike in the traditional marketing mix management view of marketing wherein a firm's position is determined mainly by its resources that is, size, skills, reputation, being a market leader and the like (Mintzberg & Quinn, 1991), under the interaction approach, position is the product of a firm's interactions, adaptations, and relationships with other entities in the network. These relationships with other parties and the position of these other parties, then determine how a firm and its potential as a trading partner is perceived and evaluated. The perceived position of the firm which in the literature is referred to as strategic identity, determines the attractiveness of the firm as a supplier, customer or distributor. The performance of a firm is therefore affected by its strategic identity, the identity of its partners and by how well it is able to harness the resources of others, to influence their activities, and be dependent on them to achieve organizational goals. In addition, the business relationships that establish a firm's network position could also be viewed as a source of advantage that would not be available to competitors.

The concepts of strategic identity and network position are particularly relevant in international marketing. The geographical and cultural distance between supplier and buyer makes the tasks of establishing, developing, maintaining and defending a network position much more challenging. The choice of a trading partner by an exporter becomes a very strategic decision which is linked to its market selection and entry strategies. Based on three in-depth case studies, Axelsson and Johanson (1992) identified positioning as one of the three critical issues in foreign market entry. Some of the relevant observations made were: (1) positions in the domestic market or in third markets may be important stepping stones into the entry market, (2) the relationship with a specific prestigious customer may be a necessary condition for the development of relationships with other customers although in some cases it could be an obstacle to the development of positions with respect to other competing customers, and (3) the position of a firm could be undermined by the actions of other entities in the network. The impact of an exporter's network position on export performance would thus be in terms of how good the exporter is perceived to be as a supplier by potential and current buyer firms and how well it can utilize its relationships with its current customers and other third parties to attract other customers either in the same market or in other markets.

IV. THE ROLE OF MARKETING STRATEGY

Marketing strategy from the marketing mix management view, involves the traditional 4Ps which in industrial marketing consist mainly of product, price, delivery and service. The interaction approach on the other hand, focuses on the primacy of relationships as the basis of marketing strategy. This section analyzes how both can operate hand in hand in influencing the marketing strategy of an exporter. This section also reviews the popular international marketing issue of standardization and adaptation with the aim of unravelling the relationship dimension involved.

A. Relationship Management Strategy

Unlike in the current marketing mix approach where the market is viewed as a total, faceless, uncontrollable environmental factor, the interaction model views customers as identifiable entities that are oftentimes limited in number (Hakansson & Snehota, 1990). From the viewpoint of an industrial exporter, this assumption appears to be realistic especially now that industrial buyers are moving towards having a smaller supplier base. Under such a situation, the role of marketing is to establish, develop and maintain relationships with a portfolio of customers at both the strategic and tactical levels.

At the strategic level, customer management involves segmenting current and potential customers according to some viable basis such as (1) stage in the life cycle of the relationship or stage or phase in the development process of the relationship (Ford, 1980; Dwyer, Schurr, & Oh, 1987), (2) the importance of the customer to the seller, or (3) the nature of the relationship, that is, discrete or relational (Dwyer, Schurr, & Oh, 1987). In addition, customer management would include a strategy for deploying scarce technical and marketing resources among different customers (Campbell & Cunningham, 1983) and developing an appropriate strategy for interacting with each group.

Developing an appropriate strategy requires a good understanding of the interaction processes that take place between supplier and customer including those that involve information and social exchanges (see Figure 1). Information exchange is particularly important in industrial marketing because of the nature of the products involved. The more complex the product, the more information exchange is required to ensure a proper match between the sellers' offer and the customer's requirements.

Social exchange is another element that needs to be incorporated in a relationship management strategy. The importance of interpersonal communication and interaction in industrial markets has long been recognized by academics and practitioners alike. Studies have shown the importance of personal contacts in developing technical confidence, trust, loyalty and the free flow of information between supplier and customer (Cunningham & Homse, 1986). The importance placed by firms on social exchanges to some extent determines the interaction strategies they adopt. While some firms operate on the basis of an "open friendly" mode, others prefer to remain "strictly business" (Hakansson, 1982). The need for interpersonal contacts may in fact be greater when the firm is dealing with foreign customers (Turnbull, 1979). More comprehensive interaction strategies categorized as competitive, cooperative, command and coordinative may also be adopted (Campbell, 1985; Dabholkar et al., 1994). While competitive and command behavior would tend to increase role conflict and reduce performance, cooperative and coordinative behavior would have the opposite effects (Dabholkar et al., 1994).

Developing and implementing a strategic relationship management program involves the allocation of financial resources for this purpose. Organization support in the form of employing a client or customer relationship manager or setting up a relationship management department may also be necessary (Ford, 1980). Although the discussion thus far has focused on customer relationship management, it is anticipated that similar propositions would apply to exporter-distributor relationships. The justification for this is that both firms are participants in the same exchange relationship and symmetry in the behavioral constructs underlying the relationship is expected (Anderson & Narus, 1990).

B. Marketing Mix Strategy

Traditionally, the industrial marketing process consists of market segmentation, targeting and positioning followed by the development of the marketing mix strategy. The resulting product, pricing, distribution and promotion strategies would then influence the performance, ie. sales and profits of the supplier firm. The focus of this approach is placed on the design of a suitable bundle of offerings for the selected target market without necessarily paying particular attention to the relationship aspect of the exchange.

In terms of the marketing process, both approaches appear to adhere to the concepts of market segmentation and targeting although the bases for segmenting markets vary. With the interaction approach, the suggested criteria for market segmentation as earlier mentioned, are relationship based whereas, the traditional factors would include company size, geographical location, S.I.C. category, intended use of product, type of buying situation, stage in the decision process, and type of problem being solved (Webster, 1991). The other major difference between the two approaches lies in the focus of the marketing strategy. While the first emphasizes relationship management, the latter builds on the optimum marketing mix principle. In practice, the latter neglects relationship management at the strategy level and instead relegates it to the salespeople who are in direct contact with the buyers. In this situation, resources are not usually allocated specifically for relationship enhancement programs.

C. Marketing Strategy: An Augmented View

From the previous discussion, it is obvious that both approaches do complement each other. It is clear that relationship management is a logical addition to the marketing mix strategy of a firm. In practice, this is not an unreasonable proposition especially because there is empirical evidence that both are interrelated. In a study of 196 European buyers, Ford (1984) found that "buyers' judgments of suppliers' technical and commercial skills are not made "in isolation" but are closely associated with the buyers' assessment of the quality of the relationships that have been established by the suppliers". The impact of business relationships on export performance could thus be both direct and indirect, the latter being one that is embedded within the marketing mix component of strategy.

Both the relationship management and marketing mix strategies would also have an impact on the network position of the firm mainly because network position is determined by the cumulative effects of the interactions that occur through time. The manner by which these interactions is managed and carried out will influence the nature or quality of its relationships with other relevant parties which in turn affects the firm's network position.

D. Standardization vs. Adaptation

The lack of attention accorded to relationships is very clear in the case of the commonly discussed issue of standardization vs. adaptation. The main arguments for standardization of the marketing program have been reduced cost, development of worldwide products and achievement of better marketing performance (Jain, 1993). The argument for adaptation on the other hand relies mainly on the differences prevailing across markets. The degree of product and promotion adaptation is affected by the characteristics of the firm, product, industry and export market. Based on this marketing mix perspective, a large number of studies (Aaby & Slater, 1988; see also Appendix) have empirically tested the relationship between degree of adaptation of product and promotion with such variables as international competence of the firm, product uniqueness, cultural specificity, export market competitiveness, firm's experience, technology orientation and brand familiarity (Cavusgil & Zou, 1994).

Under the interaction approach, adaptation is viewed as a behavior that either seller or buyer or both may initiate to accommodate each others requirements. "When companies adapt to each other they become tied to each other, which strengthen the relationship" (Hallen et al., 1987, p. 25). Although the need to adapt is still affected by the nature of the product and other factors, cultural affinity of the supplier with the buyer has been found to play a significant role. Suppliers who are culturally close to their customers tend to adapt their marketing offer more because of their better understanding of the customers needs (Hallen & Johanson, 1985). Adaptations in effect would tend to increase the bonding between exporter and customer through both the tangible benefits of having in the extreme case, a custom made product and delivery cum financing package for the customer and a stronger and probably more lasting relationship. Both dimensions obviously would have an impact on the performance of the exporter. Moreover, because adaptations can lead to resource interdependencies between exporter and customer, it is anticipated that it will also have an effect on the network position of the exporting firm.

V. THE PROPOSED FRAMEWORK

The general proposition being advanced in this paper is that there is a relationship aspect to an exporter's marketing strategy. Relationship based variables could be used together with other variables to segment an export market in the same way that relationship management could go hand in hand with the marketing mix strategy of a firm. The role of business relationships and marketing strategy in determining the performance of an exporting firm may thus be analyzed in terms of the framework presented in Figure 3.

As shown in Figure 3, a firms' export performance is influenced by its business relationships, network position and marketing strategy. Its relationships with its exchange partners that is, customers, distributors and other relevant entities may be close or distant, transactional/discrete or relational/lasting. Other dimensions for example, conflict, dependence, power and trust although not covered in detail in this paper could also come into play. The firm's business relationships and network position are in

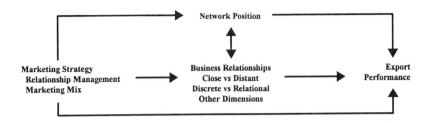

Figure 3. Strategy, Relationships and Export Performance

turn determined by its marketing strategy which now refers to both the marketing mix and relationship management components. Export performance here is viewed in the general context of organizational goals which is akin with such commonly used measures as export sales, profits, satisfaction, or success.

VI. CONCLUDING REMARKS

The proposed conceptual framework establishes the links among business relationships, marketing strategy and export performance. Although this framework appears to be versatile in that it could apply to any firm whether it is an exporter or not, this paper shows that the variables comprising the model do have some unique dimensions if the firm is internationally oriented. The proposed framework however is limited in the sense that antecedent factors for example, firms, managers, countries and the environment are excluded. Empirical testing of this framework will make new inroads into areas that up to the present time remain under explored in the field of export marketing.

APPENDIX

A. Review of Selected Empirical Research on Strategy and Export Performance

Author (Year)	Type of Product	Unit of Analysis	Strategy Components			Relationship Variables
			Scope	Content	Comp Adv	
Bello & Williamson (1985)	Unspecified	Exp Mgt Company		x		x
Bodur (1994)	Food and Textile	Firm	x	x		
Cavusgil & Zou (1994)	Consumer and Industrial	Product market venture		x		
Cooper & Kleinschmidt (1985)	Electronics		x	x	x	
Diamantopoulos & Inglis (1988)			x	x	x	
Dominquez & Sequeira (1993)	Consumer and Industrial	Firm	x	x	x	
Gronhaug & Lorentzen (1982)	Industrial	Firm	x	x		
Koh (1991)	Industrial	Firm		x		x
Madsen (1989)	Consumer and Industrial	Product Market Venture		x	x	x
Namiki (1989)	Industrial	Firm	x	x		
Rosson & Ford (1982)	Industrial	Relationship		x		x
Sriram (1989)	Industrial	Firm		x		

B. Strategy Components and Measures Adopted by Export Marketing Researchers

Component/Variable/Measure	Researcher (Year)
Scope	
Number of Markets (Countries)	Diamantopoulos & Inglis (1988) Gronhaug & Lorentzen (1982)
Countries exported to: * neighbor vs. world	Cooper & Kleinschmidt (1985)

(continued)

Appendix   (*Continued*)

No. of market segments * single vs. multi segments	Cooper & Kleinschmidt (1985)
No. of regions *	Diamantopoulos & Inglis (1988)
Degree of worldwide orientation * nearest neighbouring countries exporting to 2-3 regions worldwide	Namiki (1989)
Market Diversification *	Bodur (1993)
Product Market Diversification *	Dominquez & Sequeira (1993)
Product Strategy Degree of product adaptation * Initial and subsequent to entry Labelling in local language	Cavusgil & Zou (1994)
Degree of adaptation of packaging	Cavusgil & Zou (1994)
Quality Adaptation	Bodur (1993)
Product adaptors vs. non adaptors *	Cooper & Kleinschmidt (1985) Diamantopoulos & Inglis (1988)
Level of Product Modification (relative to domestic)	Koh (1991)
Product Adaptation (Scale 1-7) *	Namiki (1989)
Brand Adaptation	Bodur (1993)
Product labelling (own brand, not own brand)	Koh (1991)
Product/Service Quality	Dominquez & Sequeira (1993) Cooper & Kleinschmidt (1985)
Product Strength (relative to domestic market)	Madsen (1989)
Type of product consumer, industrial	Cavusgil & Zou (1994)
Product diversification	Bodur (1993)
Importance of product strategy	Bodur (1993)
Product Base full or limited range	Diamantapoulos & Inglis (1988)
Percent of Sales by New Products *	Cooper & Kleinschmidt (1985)
Number of Patents	Cooper & Kleinschmidt (1985)
R & D Expenditures	Cooper & Kleinschmidt (1985)
Distribution Contractual Agreement * formal, informal, no agreement	Bello & Williamson (1985)

(continued)

Appendix (Continued)

Support to Foreign Distributor/Subsidiary*
  overall support
  training of sales force
  promotion support
	Cavusgil & Zou (1994)

Distribution Strategy *
  Type of Distribution Channel
    (Independent local distributor,
    Independent local distributor with
    company office, company-owned
    subsidiary)
  Number of export customers
  Sales goal of the venture
	Cavusgil & Zou (1994)

Sole importer, wholesaler-retailer own dist office	Gronhaug & Lorentzen (1982)
Direct to final user vs. import intermediaries *	Dominquez & Sequeira (1993)
Operate own overseas sales office or national*	Dominquez & Sequeira (1993)
Final user, Foreign middlemen, US export agent*	Koh (1991)
Level of dealer support none, moderate, strong	Koh (1991)

Export channel *
  separate export department, own domestic
  marketing department, US export agent
	Koh (1991)

Importance of Physical Distribution *	Bodur (1993)

Channel support (relative to domestic market)*
  amount of sales support to channel member
  equality in relationship with channel member
  stabilities in deliveries
  size of profits given to channel members
	Madsen (1989)

Degree of Adaptation (Scale 1-7) *	Namiki (1989)
Formalization of Agreement	Rosson & Ford (1982)
Standardization (Stability of Roles) *	Rosson & Ford (1982)
Reciprocity	Rosson & Ford (1982)
Contact Intensity *	Rosson & Ford (1982)
Conflict Frequency *	Rosson & Ford (1982)

Price
Pricing Strategy
  Degree of Price Competitiveness
  Degree of target market specification
	Cavusgil & Zou (1994)

Export Pricing Relative to Domestic Price * Lower, equal, higher	Koh (1991) Bodur (1993)

(continued)

Appendix (*Continued*)

Determination of Export Price Strategy domestic price list, cost plus or competitive pricing	Koh (1991)
Price Quotation (FAS, CIF)	Koh (1991)
Degree of adaptation (Scale 1-7) *	Namiki (1989)
Importance of Price *	Bodur (1993)
Promotion Degree of Adaptation (positioning, packaging, promo approach, market coverage)	Cavusgil & Zou (1994)
Degree of Adaptation(Scale 1-7) *	Namiki (1989)
Frequency of face to face contact	Koh (1991)
Participation in international trade fairs	Bodur (1993)
Communication intensity (relative to that in domestic market)* relative size of promotion campaigns amount of contact with end users magnitude of personal contact with middleman	Madsen (1989)
Importance of Promotion *	Bodur (1993)
Personal Visits to Foreign Markets *	Bodur (1993)
Competitive Advantage Differential advantages ie. product, price, distribution, advertising advantages	Cooper & Kleinschmidt (1985)
Proportion of items that described firms strategy low price, low labor cost, raw material cost advantage	Dominquez & Sequeira (1993)
Perceived relative product quality, price, distribution and technology	Sriram (1989)
Technological/product advantage *	Cooper & Kleinschmidt (1985)
Perceived Competitiveness of Price *	Madsen(1989)

Note: *Relationship with export performance significant at different alpha levels (highest reported < 0.10)

ACKNOWLEDGMENT

The author gratefully acknowledges the comments and suggestions of an anonymous reviewer and Dr. T. Madsen, Odense University, Denmark.

REFERENCES

Aaby, N.E., & Slater, S.F. (1988). Management influences on export performance: A review of the empirical literature 1978-88. *International Marketing Review, 6*(4), 7-26.

Anderson J.C., & Narus, J. A. (1990), A model of distribution firm and manufacturing firm working partnership. *Journal of Marketing, 54*(January), 42-58.

Anderson, J.C., Hakansson, H., & Johanson, J. (1994). Dyadic business relationships within a business network context. *Journal of Marketing, 58*(October), 1-15.

Axelsson, B. (1992). Corporate strategy models and networks—diverging perspectives. In B. Axelsson & G. Easton (Eds), *Industrial networks: A new view of reality* (pp. 184-204). London: Routledge, Chapman and Hall Inc.

Axelsson, B., & Johanson, J. (1992). Foreign market entry—the textbook vs the network view. In B. Axelsson and G. Easton (Eds), *Industrial networks: A new view of reality* (pp. 218-231). London: Routledge, Chapman and Hall Inc.

Axinn, C. (1994). International perspectives on export marketing. In S.T. Cavusgil & C. Axinn (Eds.), *Advances in international marketing* (Vol. 6, pp. xi-xvi). Greenwich, CT: JAI Press.

Bello, D.C., & Williamson, N.C. (1985). Contractual arrangements and marketing practices in the indirect export channel, *Journal of International Business Studies*, (Summer), 65-82.

Bodur, M. (1994). Foreign market indicators, structural resources and marketing strategies as determinants of export performance. In S.T. Cavusgil & C. Axinn (Eds.), *Advances in international marketing, 6*, 183-206

Boyd, H.W., & Walker, O.C. (1990). *Marketing management: A strategic approach.* Homewood, IL: Irwin.

Campbell, N.C.G. (1985). An interaction approach to organisational buying behaviour. *Journal of Business Research, 13*, 35-48.

Campbell, N.C.G., & Cunningham, M.T. (1983). Customer analysis for strategy development in industrial markets. *Strategic Management Journal, 4*, 369-380.

Cavusgil, S.T., & Zou, S. (1994). Marketing strategy—performance relationships: An investigation of the empirical link in export market ventures. *Journal of Marketing, 58*(1), 1-21.

Chetty, S.K., & Hamilton, R.T. (1993). Firm level determinants of export performance: A meta-analysis. *International Marketing Review, 10*(3), 26-34.

Cooper, R.G., & Kleinschmidt, E.J. (1985). The impact of export strategy on export sales performance. *Journal of International Business Studies*, Spring, 37-55.

Cunningham, M.T., & Homse, E. (1986). Controlling the marketing-purchasing interface: Resource development and organisational implications. *Industrial Marketing and Purchasing, 1*(2), 3-27.

Cunningham, M.T., & Culligan, K. (1988). Competitiveness through networks of relationships in information technology product markets. In *Proceedings of 4th IMP Conference*, Manchester.

Dabholkar, P.A., Johnston, W.J., & Cathey, A.S. (1994). The dynamics of long term business to business exchange relationships. *Journal of the Academy of Marketing Science, 22*(2), 130-145.

Day, G., & Wensley, R. (1988). Assessing advantage: A framework for diagnosing competitive superiority. *Journal of Marketing, 52*(April), 1-20.

Diamantopoulos, A., & Inglis, K. (1988). Identifying differences between high and low involvement exporters. *International Marketing Review, 5* (Summer), 52-60.

Dominquez, L.V., & Sequeira, C.G. (1993). Determinants of LDC exporters' performance: A cross national study. *Journal of International Business Studies*, 19-40.

Dwyer, F.R., Schurr, P.H., & Oh, S. (1987). Developing buyer-seller relationships. *Journal of Marketing, 51*(April), 11-27.

Emshwiller, J.R. (1991). Suppliers struggle to improve quality as big firms slash their vendor rolls. *Wall Street Journal*, August 16, B1-B2.

Ford, D. (1980). The development of buyer-seller relationships in industrial markets. *European Journal of Marketing, 14*(5), 339-354.

Ford, D. (1984). Buyer/seller relationship in international industrial markets. *Industrial Marketing Management, 13*(2), 101-113.

Ford, D., & Leonidou, L. (1991). Research developments in international marketing: A european perspective. In S.J. Paliwoda (Ed.), *New perspectives on international marketing* (pp. 3-32). London: Routledge, Chapman and Hall Inc.

Gadde, L.E., & Hakansson, H. (1994). The changing roles of purchasing: Reconsidering three strategic issues. *European Journal of Purchasing, 1*(1), 27-36.

Ganesan, S. (1994). Determinants of long-term orientation in buyer-seller relationships. *Journal of Marketing, 58*(April), 1-19

Gemunden, H.G. (1991). Success factors of export marketing: A meta analysis critique of the empirical studies. In S.J. Paliwoda (Ed.), *New perspective on international marketing* (pp. 33-62). London: Routledge, Chapman and Hall Inc.

Gronroos, C. (1993). From marketing mix to relationship marketing: Toward a paradigm shift in marketing. *Monash Colloquium in Relationship Marketing*, Melbourne (August).

Gronhaug, K., & Lorentzen, T. (1982). Exploring industrial export strategies, in an assessment of marketing thought and practice. *American Marketing Association Proceedings, 48*, 294-298.

Hakansson, H. (Ed). (1982). *International marketing and purchasing of industrial goods: An interaction approach*. New York: John Wiley and Son.

Hakansson, H., & Snehota, I. (1989). No business is an island: The network concept of business strategy. *Scandinavian Journal of Management, 5*(3), 187-200.

Hallen, L., & Johanson, J. (1985). Industrial marketing strategies and different national environments. *Journal of Business Research, 13*, 495-509.

Hallen, L., & Sandstrom, M. (1991). Relationship atmosphere in international business. In S. J. Paliwoda (Ed.), *New perspectives on international marketing* (pp. 108-125). London: Routledge.

Hallen, L., Johanson, J., & Mohamed, N.S. (1987). Relationship strength and stability in international and domestic industrial marketing. *Industrial Marketing and Purchasing, 2*(3), 22-37.

Heide, J.B., & John, G. (1990). Alliances in industrial purchasing: The determinants of joint action in buyer-supplier relationships. *Journal of Marketing Research, 27*(Feb.), 24-36.

Hofer, C.W., & Schendel, D. (1978). *Strategy formulation: Analytical concepts.* New York: West Publishing Co.

IMP Project Group. (1982). An interaction approach. In D. Ford (Ed.), *Understanding business markets* (pp. 7-26). London: Harcourt Brace & Co.

Jackson, B. B. (1985). *Winning and keeping industrial customers: The dynamics of customer relationships.* Lexington, MA: Lexington Books.

Jain, S.C. (1993). *International marketing management.* California: Wadsworth Publishing Co.

Johanson, J., & Hallen, L. (1989). International business relationships and industrial networks. In S.T. Cavusgil, L. Hallen & J. Johanson (Eds.), *Advances In International Marketing, 3*, xiii-xxiii.

Johanson, J., & Mattson, L.G. (1988). Internationalisation in industrial systems: A network approach. In N. Hood & J.E. Vahlne (Eds.), *Strategies in global competition.* London: Croom Helm.

Kalwani, M., & Narayandas, N. (1994). Long term manufacturer-supplier relationship: Do they pay off for supplier firms. *Journal of Marketing, 59*(January), 1-16.

Koh, A.C. (1991). Relationship among organisational characteristics, marketing strategy and export performance. *International Marketing Review, 8*(3), 46-60.

Kotler, P., & Armstrong, G. (1991). *Principles of marketing*, 5th ed. Englewood Cliffs, NJ: Prentice-Hall.

Landeros, R., & Monczka, R.M. (1989). Cooperative buyer/seller relationships and a firm's competitive posture. *Journal of Purchasing & Materials Management, 25*(Fall), 9-18.

Madsen, T.K. (1989). Successful export marketing management: Some empirical evidence. *International Marketing Review, 6*(4), 41-57.

Madsen, T.K. (1994). A contingency approach to export performance research. In S.T. Cavusgil & C. Axinn (Ed.), *Advances in international marketing* (Vol. 6, pp. 25-42). Greenwich, CT: JAI Press.

Miles, R., & Snow, C.C. (1992). Causes of failure in network organizations. *California Management Review, 34*(Summer), 53-72.

Mintzberg, H., & Quinn, J.B. (1991). *The strategy process.* Englewood Cliffs, NJ: Prentice Hall.

Namiki, N. (1989). The impact of competitive strategy on export sales performance: An exploratory study. *The Mid Atlantic Journal, 25*(6), 21-37.

Ramsay, J. (1990). The myth of the cooperative single source. *Journal of Purchasing and Materials Management, 26*(Winter), 2-5.

Rosson, P.J., & Ford, L. (1982). Manufacturer-overseas distributor relations and export performance. *Journal of International Business Studies* (Fall), 57-72.

Spekman, R. E. (1988). Strategic supplier selection: Understanding long-term buyer relationships. *Business Horizons, 31*(July-August), 75-81.

Sriram, V., Neelankavil, J., & Moore, R. (1989). Export policy and strategy implications for small to medium sized firms. *Journal of Global Marketing,* *3*(2), 43-59.

Thorelli, H.B. (1986). Networks: Between markets and hierarchies. *Strategic Management Journal, 7,* 37-51.

Turnbull, P.W. (1979). Roles of personal contacts in industrial export marketing. *Scandinavian Journal of Management,* 325-337.

Turnbull, P.W., & Valla, J. P. (1986). *Strategies for international industrial marketing.* London: Croom Helm.

Webster F.E. (1991). *Industrial marketing strategy,* 3rd Ed. New York: John Wiley and Sons.

ASSESSING EXPORT
PERFORMANCE MEASUREMENT

Paul Matthyssens and Pieter Pauwels

ABSTRACT

This study compares and evaluates approaches to measure export performance. The review demonstrates that researchers use a variety of measures, most of them even without mentioning the rationale behind. An analytical framework containing five dimensions is used to categorize the measurement approaches. During the process, analogies with measuring problems in the associated fields of strategic marketing and new product development are drawn. The comparison leads to better insight into measurement problems. Recommendations for better measurement of export performance are formulated.

I. INTRODUCTION

When studying success determinants in export marketing, a valid and reliable measurement of export performance is critical. However, to

Advances in International Marketing, Volume 8, pages 85-114.
Copyright © 1996 by JAI Press Inc.
All rights of reproduction in any form reserved.
ISBN: 0-7623-0164-3

date no systematic research has been conducted on the performance measures themselves. This article concentrates on the dimensions of export performance measurement. In the next section, the importance of a valid and reliable measurement of (export) performance is highlighted. Drawing analogies with and borrowing concepts from strategic marketing and new product development research, the measurement issue is dealt with. In the third section, five dimensions of export performance measurement are examined: *level of analysis, frame of reference, time frame, the measures themselves* and *the data collection method.* These dimensions make it feasible to review and evaluate how the export performance measure was applied in some recent empirical publications in the field. This way, major points of doubt in export performance measurement are addressed by classifying and assessing measurement approaches. For each dimension, a comparison with the other business policy research approaches is undertaken. In the final section, implications for operationalizing export performance in future international marketing research are discussed.

II. THE CHALLENGE OF MEASURING PERFORMANCE

In 1981, Biggadike evaluated the contributions of marketing to the strategic management science. He concluded that marketing researchers did not succeed in formulating a set of propositions suggesting what kind of actions would lead to performance under a specific set of contextual conditions. Since then, some subfields of marketing have concentrated on identifying *key success factors*, notably the fields of strategic marketing (Grunert & Ellegaard, 1993, for an overview), new product development (Brown & Eisenhardt, 1995, for an overview) and export marketing strategy (Cavusgil & Zou, 1994, for an overview). A lot of progress has been made since Biggadike's article. However, all subfields cope with a similar problem which Grunert and Ellegaard (1993, p. 253) describe in clear terms: "Both success and factors leading to it are often difficult to operationalize, and many times little is known about the reliability and validity of the measurements."

To date no uniform definition of *export performance* exists in the export marketing strategy literature (Grabner-Kräuter, 1992). Moreover, no systematic research has been conducted on the performance measures themselves (Thach & Axinn, 1994). In this field of export marketing strategy, Cavusgil and Zou (1994) pinpointed the lack of a uniform approach. In an overview table they illustrated the variety of export performance measures adopted by previous researchers. Thach and Axinn (1994) expanded this table to demonstrate an even greater diversity in definition and operationalization.

These are certainly not the first calls for attention in the field of international marketing research. In their seminal review, Aaby and Slater (1989) stated that: "The two major areas for improvement are performance measurement and the use of longitudinal designs" (p. 22).

When studying success determinants in export marketing a valid and reliable measurement of the dependent variable is critical to the overall validity of the study. A poor conceptualization of export performance seems to be one of the reasons why researchers have made contradictory recommendations (Lee & Yang, 1991).

Researchers in export marketing strategy are confronted with this challenge in a similar vein as their colleagues from strategic marketing and new product development research. Therefore, it seems beneficial to review the measurement issues involved in studying export performance, while at the same time learning from the experiences of other business policy researchers.

In the remainder of this section, we demonstrate the importance and key aspects of this discussion by referring to these similar streams of research, respectively the strategic marketing and management area, and next, the new product development literature.

A. Strategic Marketing and Management

According to Snow and Hrebeniak (1980, p. 318), organizational performance or effectiveness is a "multifaceted phenomenon." They argue that the concept is hard to comprehend and measure, not in the least because the perspective on effective performance may vary according to whose viewpoint is taken (e.g., shareholders versus employees), the time period observed (e.g., long run versus short term), the criteria used (e.g., market share versus profit), and so on.

Eight years later, Zeithaml et al. (1988), in a discussion of the contingency approach to marketing science, argued in a similar way. They stress that the multiplicity in contingency frameworks associated with organizational effectiveness was due in part to the absence of consistent definitions of performance.

Ford and Schellenberg (1982), reviewing the perspectives on the assessment of organizational performance, proposed the *constituent approach* as an integrative measurement approach. They define performance "as the constituent's(s') evaluation, using efficiency, effectiveness, or social referent criteria as to how well the organization is meeting the constituent's(s') aspiration level" (Ford & Schellenberg, 1982, p. 50). As such, this approach recognizes that performance is both multidimensional and subject to multiple evaluations. Further, each evaluation is idiosyncratic to the evaluator. It is argued that differences in evaluation schemes by different constituents have led to inaccurate results in performance studies. They conclude that the use of any overall measure of performance equalizes ignorance of differences in constituents' expectations.

Chakravarthy (1986) puts forward that frequently used *financial performance criteria* are too limited. Such measures exclude certain stakeholders and merely signal the history of the firm. No single profitability measure is capable of discriminating excellence. Chakravarty proposes a multifactor function to gauge the multidimensionality of the construct. ROI and similar profitability measures have often been used by academics, for instance in the well-known PIMS-studies (Kerin, Mahajan, & Varadarajan, 1990). The reliance on ROI has often been criticized. Anderson and Pain (1978) judged the measure to be overly conservative and short-sighted.

Also Jacobson (1987) refers to many scholars labelling ROI inappropriate. His own study proves the limitations of ROI as a measure of performance, although his findings suggest that ROI does contain *some* information about economic rate of return. Practitioner-oriented publications suggest the use of composite measures of financial performance in combination with non-financial measures (Kaplan & Norton, 1992; Brown & Laverick, 1994). Eccles (1991, p. 137) speaks of "a new philosophy of performance measurement that regards it as an ongoing, evolving process."

In a similar vein, Venkatraman and Ramanujam (1986) have labelled the use of outcome-based financial performance indicators the 'narrowest conception of business performance.' They suggest to supplement such criteria with 'operational performance measures' (market share, product quality, etc.). The authors suggest that: "The inclusion of operational performance indicators takes us beyond the 'black box' approach that seems to characterize the exclusive use of financial indicators and focuses on those key operational success factors that might lead to financial performance" (Venkatraman & Ramanujam, 1986, p. 804).

In brief, the strategic marketing and management theory building has been wrestling with performance measurement issues such as: (a) the multidimensionality, (b) the subjectivity according to stakeholders' viewpoint and (c) the overreliance on financial criteria. In general, the use of composite measures is accepted but definite agreement on the criteria to be included has not been reached so far. As will be clarified these are important issues in the export marketing research as well.

B. New Product Development

In marketing a lot of effort has been invested to distinguish successful new products from failures. This research stream aims to 'predict a winner' and offers guidelines for an effective new product development (Cooper, 1979; Montoya-Weiss & Calantone, 1994 and Brown & Eisenhardt, 1995 for an overview).

Hart and Craig (1993) tried to uncover the underlying dimensions of *new product success measurement*. They notice that: "There is very little consensus among the major research studies on how best to define success, which dimensions of success to include and how to set about measuring these dimensions" (Hart & Craig, 1993, p. 208).

Due to the *resemblance*[1] between this research stream and the study of success factors in export marketing, it is important to learn from the experiences of new product researchers concerning performance measurement.

Griffin and Page (1993) compared the performance measures used in academic research studies with measures used by practitioners and came to the following conclusions. Academics and practitioners both use the following types of measures: *customer acceptance measures, firm-level measures, product-level measures* and *financial performance*. On average, academics use about three performance indicators covering one or two of the four categories of measures whereas practitioners use about four indicators from two different dimensions. Only a quarter of all identified measures are used by both practitioners and by academics. Practitioners tend to overstress profitability and sales revenue measures. However, if practitioners could select their own measures, the majority would use only customer acceptance measures.

Academics seem to be interested in performance at the *firm level*, whereas practitioners focus on measures associated with success and failure of individual *projects*. Hart and Craig (1993) argue that attention should be paid whether the study concentrates on the program level or on the project level.

Other scholars have formulated useful recommendations as well. Johne and Snelson (1988) come to the conclusion that striving for short-run performance is no guarantee for the long-run success of a business. When measuring performance, the academic and the practitioner should take the *time frame* of the measures into account.

Further, academics should be aware that strategies leading to good performance on one criterion could be quite different from strategies required for proficiency on another. In other words (Cooper, 1982): "trade-offs between different types of performances and their associated strategies become inevitable" (p. 12). Researchers should be aware of the *multidimensionality* of success.

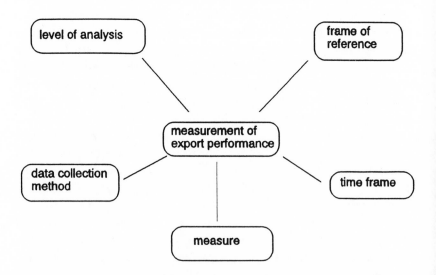

Figure 1.   A Framework for Considering the Measurement of
Success in Export Marketing Strategy

Although in new product development research no consensus exists on how to define and measure performance, contrary to international marketing scholars, most researchers have explicitly given attention to the underlying dimensions of program and project performance. Many use multiple measures (Page, 1993). However, the use of multiple measures brings two problems. First, the boundary between 'success' and 'failure' is difficult to delineate. Second, it is difficult to combine multiple measures in one overall index. Although some scarce trials are reported (McGrath & Romeri, 1994; Cooper & Kleinschmidt, 1987), until now, both topics are left unresolved.

C. Structure of the Discussion

Building on the frameworks implemented by Venkatraman and Ramanujam (1986), Hart and Craig (1993) and Griffin and Page (1993), the measurement approaches of the export performance literature will be discussed following the framework presented in Figure 1. It is argued that a deeper insight in each of these dimensions is necessary for defining export performance and implementing indicators to measure export performance. In this framework five dimensions are distinguished: the level of analysis, the frame of reference, the time frame, the measures themselves and the data collection method.

The *level of analysis* refers to the strategic level at which export performance is measured (e.g., corporate or SBU). This dimensions was suggested by Griffin and Page (1993) and Hart and Craig (1993) to organize the measures used in new product development research.

It is relevant for the assessment of export performance measurement to discuss the *frame of reference*. The strategic management researcher Piëst (1988) introduced this term to refer to the norm against which success is judged.

The *time frame* gives an answer to the non-static nature of success. The importance of using this evaluative dimension was recognized by Johne and Snelson (1988) in the new product development literature and by Brown and Laverick (1994) and Eccles (1991) in the strategic marketing literature.

The classification scheme implemented by Venkatraman and Ramanujam (1986), taking account of the source of data and the character of the measures (e.g., financial versus non-financial) fits into the data collection method and measures dimensions of the framework presented in Figure 1. The *data collection method* combines the sources of data and the data collection method used. Hart and Craig (1993) have shown that the source of the data very much determines the data collection method. The dimension *measures* refers to the criteria along which performance is judged. As must be clear from the preceding discussion, researchers in strategic marketing and in new product development research have spent a lot of attention on the type of criteria to be used.

In the next section, the different views of export performance measurement in the export marketing strategy literature will be confronted and analyzed along the five dimensions suggested in Figure 1.

III. OVERVIEW OF EXPORT PERFORMANCE MEASUREMENT IN PREVIOUS LITERATURE

Table 1 contains a selection of international publications studying export success factors. Publications that were eligible for this review had to meet the following criteria: (1) have a dependent variable measuring export performance (success and/or failure); (2) have one or more explanatory variables identified as determinants of export success or export failure; and (3) aim at discriminating successful exporters from less successful exporters.

According to these rules, valuable publications concentrating on exporters versus non-exporters (e.g., Burton & Schlegelmilch, 1987; Bodur, 1994) or studies aimed at the identification of potential exporters (e.g., Yang, Leone, & Alden, 1992) were excluded. Publications were traced following 'leads,' that is, citations in previously found articles. When a valuable article was found, all consultable volumes of the particular journal have been checked for more relevant studies. Because the seminal article by Aaby and Slater (1989) gave a state of the art at that time, no studies published before their review were included in the Table. Although the utmost effort has been devoted to discover the most relevant publications in this field, Table 1 will not be exhaustive. Nevertheless, the table gives a fair overview of measurement practices in the export marketing strategy literature.

As was shown in Figure 1, each study's performance measurement can be described along the five dimensions defined in the preceding section.

Table 1. Export Success: Selection of Literature 1989-1994

Author	Level of Analysis	Frame of Reference	Time Frame	Measures	Data Collection Method
Madsen (1989)	One product in one country	Relative to domestic market	Dynamic avg. 2 years back	-Export sales; -export growth; -export profitability (7-points semantic differentials)	Mail questionnaire (52%) Self-assessment
Fraser & Hite (1990)	Firm	Objective	Static	-Market share -ROI (absolute)	Mail questionnaire (18.3%) Researcher assessment
Louter et. al. (1991)	Firm	Relative to implicit goals and domestic market	Implicitly Dynamic	-Export/sales-ratio (absolute); -export profit./domestic profit (absolute) -degree in which export was sufficiently profitable (unidentified scale)	Mail questionnaire (54%) Self-assessment
Koh (1991)	Firm	Relative to domestic market	Static	-Perceived profitability of export (5-points scale)	Mail questionnaire (24.5%) Self-assessment
Lee & Yang (1991)	Firm	Relative to domestic market and industry avg.	Dynamic avg. 5 years back	-Export/sales-ratio -relative export growth -relative export profitability (7-points Likert scale)	Interview Self-assessment Interviewer assessment
Holzmüller & Kasper (1991)	Firm	Objective	Dynamic avg. 3 years back	-Export/sales-ratio -evolution of export/sales-ratio (absolute)	Mail questionnaire (93.63%) Researcher assessment
Samiee & Roth (1992)	Business-unit	Subjective, relative to industry avg., objective	Dynamic avg. 3 years back	-ROI; ROA; sales growth (objective, 7 points Likert scale) -ROI; ROA; sales growth (rel. to ind. avg., 5 points Likert scale) -int. profit/total profit-ratio (absolute) -total sales;-tot. int. sales (absolute)	Mail questionnaire (46%) Self-assessment

(continued)

93

Table 1. (Continued)

Chetty & Hamilton (1993)	Firm	Relative to industry avg.	Static	-Export/sales-ratio (absolute)	Structured in-depth interviews Self-assessment Interviewer assessment
Cavusgil & Kirpalani (1993)	Product	Relative to explicit goals	Dynamic L.R. profit oriented	-Expectations of managers met -achieved sales -achieved market share -contribution of export to company profitability (indicators leading to 3-points researcher evaluation)	Analysis of published cases Case writer assessment Researcher assessment
Kaynak & Kang-yen Kuan (1993)	Firm	Subjective	Static	-Export sales -export profit -internat. sales/total sales-ratio -internat. profit/total profit-ratio (7-points Likert scale)	Mail questionnaire (12.5%) Self-assessment
Zwart & Bijmolt (1993)	Firm	Subjective, relative to domestic market and implicit goals	Dynamic avg. 5 years back	-Export sales/total sales-ratio (6 categories) -export profit/domestic profit-ratio -avg. export result -degree of satisfaction (5-points Likert scale)	Mail questionnaire (31.7%) Self-assessment
Beamish et al. (1993)	Firm	Objective, Relative to domestic market	Static	-Export sales representing a large % of total sales -export profitability exceeding domestic profitability	Mail questionnaire Self-assessment Researcher assessment

(continued)

Table 1. (Continued)

Author	Level of Analysis	Frame of Reference	Time Frame	Measures	Data Collection Method
Cavusgil & Zou (1994)	P/M-ventures	Relative to explicit goals	Dynamic avg. 5 years back	-Initial strategic goals achieved -avg. annual growth rate of export sales of the venture (7-points scale) -overall export profitability of the venture -perceived success of the venture by management (10-points scale)	In-depth interview Self-assessment Interviewer assessment
Diamantopoulos & Schlegelmilch (1994)	Firm	Objective Subjective	Static Dynamic Next 3 years	-Export sales/total sales -export sales/number of employees -export sales/number of export managers -number of product groups exported/total number of product groups (absolute) -Management's projection of export involvement (5-point scale)	Mail questionnaire (13%) Self-assessment Researcher assessment
Evangelista (1994)	Firm	Subjective Relative to implicit goals	Static	-Satisfaction with the company's export performance (5-points scale)	Mail questionnaire (9.7%) Self-assessment

Table 1 shows a diversity of approaches, indicating that Aaby and Slater's (1989) call for improvement and consistency in the area of measurement, has only partially been realized. A lack of consensus remains, but some studies have increased the level of sophistication in their approach. We will now discuss the five columns of the table consecutively, thereby comparing different measurement approaches.

A. Level of Analysis

Various studies identifying success determinants in export marketing come to contradictory recommendations. Different perspectives regarding the level of analysis is one of the primary reasons.

By analogy with the *program* and *project* level distinguished in new product development literature (Hart & Craig, 1993; Johne & Snelson, 1988), a distinction can be made between research at the *corporate export* level and research at the *venture* level. A study at the corporate export level seeks for success determinants describing the overall export activity of a firm that generates various export ventures over time. A study at the venture level focuses on performance determinants of a particular product/market-combination.

Studies at the corporate export level are valuable because they can bring insight into how various export ventures are generated and managed within a company. Such studies can also learn how sustained export success is created. It is argued that focusing only on particular export ventures does not bring insight in the long-term export performance of a company. For instance, a failure can be considered as part of a learning process leading to overall corporate export success. Research at the corporate export level makes longitudinal research inevitable (Johne & Snelson, 1988). A firm is excellent only if it has in addition."... the ability to transform itself in response to changes in its environment" (Chakravarty, 1986, p. 455). Slack resources must be assessed to measure the 'adaptive ability.' When studying the corporate export activity, one should look at the long term management of the various export ventures a company is engaged in. At the corporate level, improvement of export performance should be measured using *corporate export performance measures*.

At the firm level, the influence of potential success determinants that are not directly related to a specific product/market venture (e.g.,

overall firm strategy, company culture, organizational structure, ...)
is examined. It can be argued that such corporate factors can be
considered as contextual conditions for the different ventures. The
influence of these factors on the export performance is hard to
understand, unless one studies different ventures within one
company. Investigating couples of ventures (e.g., one success case and
one failure case) in each company can bring a solution to this problem
(Madsen, 1989)

However, measuring export performance at a corporate export
level has some major drawbacks. Within a firm, 'success' and 'failure'
can live together. Performance shows variance across the different
export ventures. When studying individual export ventures,
corporate export level performance analysis is inappropriate
because of the heterogeneity of the corporation's operations
(Jacobson, 1987).

Twelve out of fifteen studies identified in Table 1 focus on the *firm*
level. Although Samiee and Roth (1992) contend that their analysis
is on the business level, they define this level in an aggregate way.
They consider a division or a profit unit of a company as a business
unit. This view, however, also implies that product/market ventures
will be combined into a whole as is the case at the firm level. Ten
of these twelve studies use performance indicators that try to capture
the performance of the corporate export activity within a company.
The majority of researchers use traditional indicators such as *export/
sales-ratio, export profitability, export sales* and more. Only Fraser
and Hite (1990) and Samiee and Roth (1992) use indicators as *ROI,
ROA, market share* and *sales growth*, that way considering export
performance a synonym of overall performance. The researcher,
however, can not control the influence of other intervening variables
on overall corporate performance. Performance in export is just one
aspect of overall corporate performance. Although most published
studies in export marketing literature try to capture success
determinants at the corporate export level, longitudinal studies in
export marketing research are still very scarce, a finding already
reported by Aaby and Slater (1989).

As can be read from Table 1, only three out of the fifteen
publications address export performance at the *venture* level. Due
to their concrete orientation on particular export ventures Madsen
(1989), Cavusgil and Kirpalani (1993) and Cavusgil and Zou (1994),
bring added value to the understanding of export management. When

the researcher is investigating at the business level, *export venture performance measures* should be used. Indicators such as *initial strategic goal achieved, perceived success by management, export profitability of the venture* or *achieved market share of venture* (Cavusgil & Kirpalani, 1993; Cavusgil & Zou, 1994) are suitable at the venture level. To the contrary, indicators such as *export growth, contribution of export to company profitability* or *overall export profitability* (Madsen, 1989; Cavusgil & Kirpalani, 1993) are suitable at the corporate level. We argue that performance variables should be implemented at the appropriate level.

The overreliance on corporate performance measures is also noticed in both the strategic marketing research (Venkatraman & Ramanujam, 1986) and in the new product development research (Griffin & Page, 1993). It is argued that most researchers measure performance at the corporate level because of availability of secondary data and because companies are more likely to reply when asked about aggregate performance than when researchers ask about performance of a particular venture. Moreover, research at the business level usually excludes the usage of published and objective data (Dess & Robinson, 1984).

B. Frame of Reference

Piëst (1988) argues that each inquiry in the domain of strategic key success factors should start from a frame of reference. We identified five different frames: an objective, a subjective, a goal-related, a domestic and an industry-related frame.

Fraser and Hite (1990), Holzmüller and Kasper (1991), Beamish, Craig, and McLellan (1993) and Diamantopoulos and Schlegelmilch (1994) adopt an *objective frame*. They try to grasp export performance by measuring objective indicators (e.g., *market share, export/sales-ratio*, etc.) in a direct way. By doing so, these scholars avoid the influence of any controllable or uncontrollable subjective reference point that might be used by the respondents. It can be argued, however, that the application of this frame has certain drawbacks. Asking for objective (financial) figures leaves the cutting-off problem to the researcher (Hart & Craig, 1993). In most studies, the researcher will use the sample average as cutting-off point between 'success' and 'failure.' However, most empirical studies concentrate on a rather heterogeneous population which makes that the cutting-off point becomes rather arbitrary. Finally, when the researcher focuses on the venture level, it will be very difficult to implement the objective frame.

A researcher who adopts a *subjective frame* (Kaynak & Kang-yen Kuan, 1993; Zwart & Bijmolt, 1993; Samiee & Roth, 1992; Diamantopoulos & Schlegelmilch, 1994; Evangelista, 1994), leaves the decision on which reference point to use to the individual respondent. With a 7-points Likert scale, Kaynak and Kang-yen Kuan (1993) ask for a subjective assessment of the performance criteria without indicating the frame of reference to be used by the respondent.

Implementing a subjective frame is possible on both the corporate export and the venture level, but the method has certain drawbacks. First, it will be impossible to use only secondary data. Furthermore, the reference point against which the actual performance is evaluated can not be controlled by the researcher. On the one hand, it can be stated that this approach is a valid one because in business life, every manager evaluates strategic performance against one's own standards. On the other hand, comparing the answers of the different respondents becomes very difficult. In fact, it is even possible that the same absolute result could be evaluated as a success by one respondent and as a failure by another.

In the objective frame *the researcher* assesses whether a case is a success or a failure, whereas in the subjective frame *the respondent* evaluates his case. Using the objective frame seems to bring a higher reliability.

When the researcher adopts a *goal-related frame* (e.g., Louter et al. 1991; Cavusgil & Kirpalani, 1993; Cavusgil & Zou, 1994; Evangelista, 1994), performance will be deliberately measured relative to the managers' implicit or explicit goals. Although this frame gives evidence of a certain degree of *competitor myopia* (Grabner-Kräuter, 1992), it remains fairly valid. In fact, when internal objectives are achieved, but the company or business unit is not doing as good as certain competitors, one should not conclude immediately that the objectives were set too low. The history of the company, the performance on the domestic market, or other determinants influence the formulation of objectives. Furthermore, in export markets, various companies set objectives in a broader context which makes comparison with competitors very difficult. For instance, several multinationals consider a small country such as Belgium as a test market for which financial results might be of minor importance.

Although in new product development various frames of reference are implemented (Johne & Snelson, 1988), the goal-related frame seems to be preferred over the other frames (Page, 1993).

Various export marketing strategy researchers use a *domestic frame* (Madsen, 1989; Louter et al., 1991; Koh, 1991; Lee & Yang, 1991; Zwart & Bijmolt, 1993; Beamish et al., 1993). In this frame the respondent evaluates his actual performance in an export market against his performance in the domestic market. Adopting a domestic frame is possible both at the corporate export level and at the venture level. At the former level, export performance can be compared to performance of other strategic options within the firm. Because this frame considers export as one alternative of strategic growth, it can be valid for various companies or business units (Thach & Axinn, 1994).

When the researcher takes the options of an *industry-related frame*, he implements external assessment of performance. The respondent evaluates his actual performance against the performance of his direct competitors (Lee & Yang, 1991; Samiee & Roth, 1992; Chetty & Hamilton, 1993). A company or business unit is successful when it can distinguish itself in a sustainable way from the competition and when the market appreciates this competitive advantage. To be able to evaluate the performance correctly, comparison should only be made with companies or business units in the same *strategic group* (Frazier & Howell, 1983).

Whereas researchers in new product development prefer internal frames (e.g., goal-related frame) above external frames, in the strategic marketing literature a strong preference for the industry-related frame exists. The argument for this is given by Eccles (1991, p. 133): "This externally oriented approach makes people aware of improvements that are orders of magnitude beyond what they would have thought possible. In contrast, internal yardsticks [...] rarely have such an eye-opening effect." Most researchers who apply the industry-related frame compare the performance for a particular case to the average performance of the direct competitors (Venkatraman & Ramanujam, 1986). From a managerial perspective, Eccles (1991) plead for benchmarking with the best in the strategic group.

In Table 1 it can be noticed that various researchers adopt more than one frame of reference *simultaneously*. In seven of the fifteen studies a multiple measurement of success brings along the adoption of various frames of reference. We argue it would be better to use one frame only. Although the multidimensional latent variable 'performance' requires more than one indicator to be operationalized, a unique norm for performance assessment is recommended. It is however valuable to do a parallel analysis using different frames separately. The *objective* frame is the most reliable frame because the researcher has full control over the cutting-off point between success and failure. The *subjective* frame, however, is a more valid frame. Researchers have to accept that a project or an export program is a success (or a failure) when the responsible manager, using his own criteria, comes to this conclusion. In that sense, *perceived* performance is more important than real performance. Because the researcher has no control over the criteria used by the respondent, the reliability of this frame is very low.

Both the *domestic* and the *goal-related* frame are internal frames. The policy orientation of this research stream in mind, we argue that an external frame that takes account of the performance of the other strategic group members is more valid.

When the researcher adopts an *industry-related frame*, he will have to implement the measures that truly predict long-term financial success in this particular strategic group (Eccles, 1991; Frazier & Howell, 1983). This means that measures may change when different strategic groups are being investigated.

C. Time Frame

Most studies presented in Table 1 use performance measures reflecting how a business has dealt with the past. At best, measures like *export growth, evolution of export/sales-ratio*, and so on grasp actual export performance. It is often implicitly assumed that past and current success can be extrapolated into the future. Both in strategic marketing as in new product development research this lack of orientation towards the future is recognized. As Brown and Laverick (1994, p. 96) put it: "Instead of yesterday's performance measuring yesterday's decisions, what are needed are measures that provide today's decisions which will benefit tomorrow's performance."

In pure economic terms, performance is defined as *sustained profitability* (Aaby & Slater, 1989). Six out of fifteen studies identified in Table 1 measure success in a *static* way. However, taking for granted the growth perspective of a firm and the necessity of creation of shareholder value, time becomes a reference point.

Nine out of fifteen publications adopt a *dynamic* orientation. Some researchers (e.g., Madsen, 1989; Lee & Yang, 1991; Holzmüller & Kasper, 1991) asked the respondents to go back in time and report on the results over the last 2, 3 or 5 years. By doing so, the authors get an idea of the evolution of the indicators and they can correct for outlying figures. No researcher, however, discusses the point of how many years to go back. Moreover, these authors assume that past performance can be extrapolated into the future.

Asking whether the responsible manager is satisfied with the actual results, Louter et al. (1991), Cavusgil and Kirpalani (1993) and Cavusgil and Zou (1994) tried to capture the long range orientation of success in a more implicit way. Whether they succeeded in doing this is difficult to assess.

Only Diamantopoulos and Schlegelmilch (1994) deliberately projected one performance measure into the future. Asking for the management's projection of export involvement for the following three years, these scholars try to gain an insight into future success.

D. Measures

His research goal in mind, the researcher has to decide on the level of analysis, the frame of reference and the time frame he wants to adopt. As already discussed, the various options taken on each of these dimensions can have major implications on the operational measures to be implemented. In this paragraph the indicators presented in Table 1 will be weighed against each other and against the measures used in strategic marketing and new product development research.

Traditionally, only one indicator was used to measure export performance. However, Aaby and Slater's (1989) and Cooper and Kleinschmidt's (1985) plea to approximate long-term performance by *multiple indicators* seems to have been followed. In Table 1 only three authors measured one sole indicator: perceived profitability of export (Koh, 1991), export/sales-ratio (Chetty & Hamilton, 1993) and satisfaction with the company's export performance (Evangelista, 1994). Recognizing the multidimensional character of export performance, a measurement of success adopting multiple indicators is unavoidable.[2] As Thach and Axinn (1994) put it: "Conceptually, we must face up to the likelihood that different measures of performance capture different aspects of the strategic and operational phenomena which underlie them" (p. 14).

Both in strategic marketing and new product development research the use of multiple indicators is widely accepted. At the corporate export and the export venture level, various groups of people inside and outside the organization with their own objectives are involved (e.g., Ford & Schellenberg, 1982; Brown & Laverick, 1994). Nowadays the multidimensionality of performance is not under discussion (Griffin & Page, 1993), but rather *which* performance measures to use.

The various possible measures can be split up into two groups: *financial* measures and *non-financial* measures. As stated by Cavusgil and Zou (1994, p. 4) in strategic export research, "The most frequently used performance measures appear to be economic in nature."

Export intensity (export sales as a percentage of sales revenue) is probably the most widely used export performance measure (Diamantopoulos & Schlegelmilch, 1994). In Table 1, nine out of fifteen studies used it as sole indicator or in combination with other measures. However, Cooper and Kleinschmidt (1985) criticized this financial measure. Export intensity can not be used when the analysis is performed at the venture level. Furthermore, the validity of this indicator can be questioned. An extremely high export intensity is no guarantee for sustained profitability.

As can be read from Table 1, recent publications use a diversity of other economic yardsticks. Different types of profit, sales and growth measures are used simultaneously, often without regard to the options taken on other measurement dimensions of Figure 1. Using measures like ROI, ROA or corporate sales growth ignores the difference between corporate's overall performance and the corporate export performance. The application of measures like export profitability, overall export sales and overall export growth at the company level when the venture level was adopted, ignores the difference between the venture and the corporate export level. Furthermore, applying financial measures at the venture level in most cases is very difficult (Dess & Robinson, 1984).

In strategic marketing and new product development literature the use of financial measures is widely discussed. On the one hand, authors like Snow and Hrebeniak (1980) defend the use of financial indicators to measure performance in strategic marketing research. In their view, financial yardsticks are objective surrogates to overall organizational performance. Donaldson (1995, p. 104) considers financial criteria as the "central focus of the board oversight." He argues that standard financial indicators permit objective comparisons and facilitate discussion in terms all parties can understand. On the other hand, Eccles (1993) argues that financial measures carry such weight because they are *assumed* to be a uniform metric and hence a valid basis for future decision making and for comparative analysis. In practice, however, this assumption is wrong. Brown and Laverick (1994, p. 90) state that these figures "paint a facade of the company in the colors that the company desires." Published figures especially can be manipulated (e.g., profit figures of foreign affiliates are often more a reflection of tax policy than of marketing strength). Financial measures hardly refer to the strategic thrusts of the company: "Executives also understand that traditional financial accounting measures [...] can give misleading signals for continuous improvement and innovation ..." (Kaplan & Norton, 1992, p. 71).

Similarly, in new product development research, an evolution from the exclusive use of financial indicators to the combined application of both financial and non-financial indicators can be found (e.g., Cooper, 1979; Cooper & Kleinschmidt, 1993). Griffin and Page (1993) report on this evolution. They state that in this evolution the researcher is following the practitioner. When the practitioner would have the choice, all financial indicators would be eliminated. New product development projects would only be evaluated using customer acceptance measures.

Although it is less explicit, the same evolution can be observed in the field of export marketing research. Cavusgil and Zou (1994) combined economic and 'strategic' variables. Within a goal-related frame, the authors identified seven possible strategic goals. From a strategic point of view, a particular venture is successful when the goals were achieved within the first five years of the venture. As can be seen from Table 1, this attempt remains a rare one in the export marketing strategy literature. We encourage researchers to follow their track using both financial and strategic measures. Combined with financial measures, strategic indicators—the drivers for future performance—are a more valid proxy of sustained profitability, the ultimate goal (Aaby & Slater, 1989; Hart & Craig, 1993).

In most studies considering both success and failure cases, a binomial distribution is assumed: cases are considered as a complete success or as a complete failure (e.g., Madsen, 1989). Although this is a simplification of reality, selecting and studying clear-cut successes and failures can be valuable. Alternatively, different grades of success and failure can be implemented (e.g., Cavusgil & Zou, 1994). Whatever distribution is used, the cases have to get classified with respect to their scores on the performance measure(s). Being aware of the multidimensionality of performance, this is not an easy task. This multidimensionality leads to the possibility that measures conflict in nature. In one sole case some scores may indicate success while, at the same time, others may indicate failure.

To cope with the multidimensionality of performance, the researcher has two options: building a composite measure or doing the analysis of the success factors with respect to the different underlying dimensions of success independently.

Building a *composite performance measure* is far from trivial. In new product development literature some scarce attempts are reported (e.g., McGrath & Romeri, 1994). In strategic marketing research, Chakravarthy (1986) mentions the so-called Z-factor, an index combining various financial indicators. In export performance research at least four alternative techniques are possible.

A first alternative was applied by Evangelista (1994) and Koh (1989). Implementing a subjective frame of reference and using only one measure, Evangelista (1994) did not 'uncover' the multidimensionality of 'performance.' The scale used for this measure (in her case a 5-point scale) in fact represents the performance scale. The assessment of performance is exclusively done by the respondent who is free to project his relative perception into the judgement. The drawbacks of this method have been discussed in previous paragraphs.

A second alternative is reported by Cavusgil and Kirpalani (1993). In this study, the researchers themselves classified the cases *judgmentally* into one of 'limited or no success,' 'moderate success' or 'substantial success' categories. Unless the classification criteria are described in detail, reliability of this alternative can be very low.

Third, the researcher can adopt a *points system* (Craig & Hart, 1993). Cases have to score high on each of the performance indicators before they are considered successful. This system is probably the best alternative when, in the study, performance is assumed to be binomially distributed. However, in each study many cases will be classified neither as a complete success nor as a complete failure.

A fourth alternative is possible when all measures have been normalized. The researcher can add up all scores to an overall index per case (e.g., Cavusgil & Zou, 1994). The scores on each indicator can be weighted by the researcher or by the respondent. However, this system allows for poor results on one measure to be overshadowed by some good results on another measure. In fact, this system is not to be used when the researcher wants to study clear-cut success and failures. Moreover, the cutting-off point between success and failure is left untouched.

Most researchers in strategic export performance literature do not build a composite measure but consider all dimensions of performance independently. This option is taken by Madsen (1989), Lee and Yang (1991), Kaynak and Kuan (1993) and others. That way, they respect the multidimensionality of export performance. Indeed, as Venkatraman and Ramanujam (1986, p. 807) put it: "A unidimensional composite of a multidimensional concept such as business performance tends to mask the underlying relationships among the different subdimensions." Different indicators should not be combined because they might reflect distinct dimensions.

In most studies the *export sales*, the *export growth* and the *export profit* dimension are used (e.g., Madsen, 1989; Lee & Yang, 1991). Researchers refer to the application of these dimensions by previous authors. However, it can be questioned whether these three 'dimensions' are the 'real' dimensions underlying export performance. In new product development literature, Griffin and Page (1993) argue that most performance indicators are quite similar in nature but that some effort has to be made to 'uncover' the underlying dimensions. *Factor analysis* on the different indicators of export performance can be proposed (Venkatraman & Ramanujam, 1986) to discover some orthogonal dimensions underlying the various indicators. *Structural equation modeling* applied by Louter et al. (1991) and by Holzmüller and Kasper (1991) and *metric canonical analysis* applied by Diamantopoulos and Schlegelmilch (1994) can be proposed as two dependence methods that incorporate multiple dependent and independent variables.

E. Data Collection Method

Deciding on which data collection method to adopt and which source of data to consult is not an isolated problem. It depends on the primary goal of the empirical study (analytical or statistical generalization) and on the options taken on the four other dimensions of Figure 1.

Several *sources of data* are possible. On the one hand the researcher can consult secondary data sources: published (mostly financial) performance indicators or published case studies in which both financial and non-financial data are discussed. On the other hand, the researcher can consult primary data sources. In the latter case, (export) managers, industry experts, or managers of competing firms can be requested to assess the performance of a firm and / or an export venture. When the researcher adopts a primary data source, both mail questionnaires or in-depth interviews can be implemented as *data collection method.*

Besides the criticisms on the objectiveness of published financial performance indicators (e.g., Brown & Laverick, 1994), it can be argued that the exclusive use of published financial performance indicators can only be accepted when the researcher, adopting an objective frame of reference, is interested in the actual (and not the long-term) performance of the firm. Considering the relative assessment of future export performance, the researcher should complement these published financial indicators with 'strategic' indicators from primary data sources. Moreover, at the venture level, secondary data sources will mostly be unavoidable. In that case, the researcher has to choose a primary data selection method.

When building the data collection method, the researcher has to be aware about who is assessing the export performance of a particular firm or venture. Adopting an objective frame, the performance assessment can be fully controlled by the researcher. When the researcher wants to adopt a relative frame of reference (domestic, goal-related, industry-related or subjective frame) *self-assessment* by the respondent is necessary. This option makes interviewing or a mail-questionnaire unavoidable. Although criticized for its low reliability, for two reasons it can be argued that self-assessment by managers is a valuable approach. First, as mentioned before, in a managerial perspective, the *perceived* performance is more important than the actual performance. In the second place, Wong and Saunders (1993) in the strategy literature and Hart and Craig (1993) in the new product development literature, refer to empirical studies which label self-assessment a reliable alternative. Dess and Robinson (1984, p. 271) conclude that "subjective measures may be useful in attempting to operationalize broader, non-economic dimensions of organizational performance."

As can be read from Table 1, the most widely used data collection method in export marketing research is the *mail questionnaire* directed to the *manager* responsible for export or for a particular export venture. In none of the reported studies the mail questionnaire was directed to an external industry expert or to a manager of a competing firm. In a minority of the studies the data were gathered by in-depth interviewing of respondents. Only one study (Cavusgil & Kirpalani, 1993) reports on the exclusive use of published cases as data source.

The majority of studies with mail questionnaires included in Table 1 have a rather high response rate. A substantive contributor to this rather high response rate is the use of indirect, relative measures of performance. The use of scales instead of absolute measures avoids item non-response on delicate questions (e.g., profit or market share). Hart and Craig (1993) report high item non-response when absolute measures were used for financial items in the product innovation literature.

Finally, some researchers (Lee & Yang, 1991; Chetty & Hamilton, 1993 and Cavusgil & Zou, 1994) used the *personal in-depth interview* as primary data collection method. This method is energy and time consuming. However, interviewing is an appropriate way of data gathering when *analytical* (instead of statistical) *generalization* was set as primary goal of the empirical research. It can be argued that at this stage of knowledge of success factors in export, more exploratory studies based on interviews would contribute greatly to the formulation of more specific and concrete research hypotheses (Thach & Axinn, 1994; Grabner-Kräuter, 1992; Chetty & Hamilton, 1993).

IV. RECOMMENDATIONS FOR FUTURE RESEARCH

The measurement of export performance is one of the thorniest yet most fascinating issues in the export marketing research. A consistent and valid approach with respect to export performance measurement is of utmost importance to the further study of key success factors in export marketing (Aaby & Slater, 1989; Grabner-Kräuter, 1992). Incremental theory building in the field of export marketing requires replicable, valid and consistent measurement of export performance.

Ideally, export performance measurement incorporates a dynamic way of measuring long-term performance relative to the expectations of all stakeholders and decision-makers involved taking into account the competitive environment in which a venture or a company is engaged. To grasp the complexity of the export performance measurement, a five-dimensional model is proposed. Deciding on the level of analysis, the frame of reference, the time frame, the measures themselves and the data collection method, it is argued that the scholar will obtain a clear view on the operationalization of export performance measurement. The resulting scheme will help in making the measurement rationale explicit. That way, different measurement options implemented in various studies can be evaluated and compared. Ultimately, the comparison of various operationalizations resulting in different findings may lead to some generally accepted ways of operationalizing export performance measurement.

We argue that research explaining export performance at the *corporate export* and at the *venture* level are both important as contributions to marketing theory. Considering the actual imbalance between corporate and venture level studies illustrated in Table 1, it is argued that studies at the venture level should get priority. As shown by Madsen (1989), Cavusgil and Kirpalani (1993) and Cavusgil and Zou (1994), catching up on studying at the venture level could bring deeper insight into more concrete and manageable key success factors in export marketing. Corroborating the findings of these studies would contribute to this purpose.

Measuring export performance in a relative way, both an *internal* and an *external frame of reference* are necessary. Performance should be measured against the expectations of dominant decision-makers within the company or business-unit. However, in the long run the venture has to survive in a market and the company has to survive within a competitive environment. Hence an industry-related frame must be applied as well.

In previous studies, mostly past or actual export performance was measured. Considering the importance of the long-run viability of a business, more effort should be made measuring *future* performance. This urges a *dynamic* assessment of performance indicators relative to the internal and external goals. This can be done in an implicit way (e.g., Cavusgil & Zou, 1994) or, preferably, in an explicit way (e.g., Schlegelmilch & Diamantopoulos, 1995).

In order to grasp the multidimensionality of export performance, most scholars agree on a *multiple measurement* of performance. The various indicators should represent the measures of the decision-makers involved. Financial measures are to be complemented by strategic measures which are more future oriented. To cope with this multiple measurement, the researcher can build a composite measure or consider all underlying dimensions independently. We argue that, using multivariate analysis techniques, the performance dimensions underlying the indicators should be uncovered. These orthogonal dimensions could be combined in one overall index. That way, the empirical study can be strengthened doing the analysis both on each dimension independently and on the overall performance index.

Considering the need for more research at the venture level generating more concrete hypotheses concerning potential manageable key success factors, we argue it would be appropriate to apply more *case studies* based on in-depth interviewing the decision-makers involved. The quality of the operationalization of export performance will significantly improve when the relative assessment of performance of one venture is done by more than one respondent (Venkatraman & Ramunajam, 1986). Agreeing on an internal and external frame of reference, the assessment of the responsible manager could be complemented by an industry-expert assessment. The potential nonconvergence of both sources can be an opportunity for enriching the analysis.

We argue that the *construct validity* of the dependent variable 'export performance' might be improved when the future researcher implements the proposed five-dimension model. Attention paid to the construct validity of the dependent variable will largely contribute to the overall validity of the empirical study.

For academics fascinated by the issue of (export) performance measurement, three additional recommendations can be made. First, more attention can be paid to the hypothesis of a false *dichotomy* between success and failure. Are 'success' and 'failure' the extremes of a unidimensional performance scale? Are indicators built to measure 'success' able to measure 'failure'? Do 'success' and 'failure' have the same dimensions? Empirical studies to test these questions are welcomed.

Second, by analogy with the study reported by Griffin and Page (1993) in the field of new product development, scholars should take interest into how *practitioners* measure performance. An exploratory study examining the measures actually used and the measures desired by practitioners could bring new insights. The hypothesis is that academics use other measures that export managers.

Finally, it could be worth the effort trying to replicate the analysis of the studies listed in Table 1 considering various other ways of measuring export performance. More insight into the reliability, validity and manageability of the different ways of measuring performance would be gained.

Considering a recognized lack of attention paid to the export performance variable in export marketing research, this article intends to initiate a broader discussion that could lead to a more objective and manageable definition and operationalization of export performance in the future.

ACKNOWLEDGMENTS

The authors would like to thank the CIMaR members for some valuable comments on an earlier draft of this paper at the Third Annual CIMaR Meeting in Odense (Denmark). The authors are grateful to the editor and two anonymous reviewers for very valuable suggestions.

NOTES

1. An illustration of this resemblance is given by the publications by Cooper (1979, 1982) and Cooper and Kleinschmidt (1985, 1987, 1993) in both research streams.

2. Evangelista (1994) uses a sole indicator in which the variable performance is not specified. That way, she avoids using multiple indicators, leaving the problem of multidimensionality with the respondent.

REFERENCES

Aaby, N.-E., & S.F. Slater (1989). Management influences on export performance: A review of the empirical literature 1978-88. *International Marketing Review, 6*(4), 7-26.

Aaker, D.E. (1992). *Strategic marketing management*, 3rd Edition. New York: John Wiley & Sons Inc.

Anderson, C.R., & Paine, F.T. (1978). PIMS: A reexamination. *Academy of Management Review, 3*(July), 602-611.

Beamish, P.W., Craig, R., & McLellan, L. (1993). The performance characteristics of Canadian versus U.K. exporters in small and medium sized firms. *Management International Review, 33*(2), 121-137.

Biggadike, E.R. (1981). The contribution of marketing to strategic management. *Academy of Management Review, 6*(4), 621-632.

Bodur, M. (1994). Foreign market indicators, structural resources and marketing strategies as determinants of export performance. In S.T. Cavusgil & C.N. Axinn (Eds.), *Advances in international marketing* (Vol. 6, pp. 183-205). Greenwich, CT: JAI Press.

Brown, D.M., & Laverick, S. (1994). Measuring corporate performance. *Long Range Planning, 27*(4), 89-98.

Brown, S.L., & Eisenhardt, K.M. (1995). Product development: Past research, present findings, and future directions. *Academy of Management Review, 20*(2), 343-378.

Burton, F.N., & Schlegelmilch, B.B. (1987). Profile analysis of non-exporters versus exporters grouped by export involvement. *Management International Review, 27*(1), 38-49.

Cavusgil, S.T., & Kirpalani, P. H. (1993). Introducing products into export markets: Success factors. *Journal of Business Research, 27,* 1-15.

Cavusgil, S.T., & Zou, S. (1994). Marketing strategy-performance relationship: An investigation of the empirical link in export market ventures. *Journal of Marketing, 58*(January), 1-21.

Chakravarthy, B.S. (1986). Measuring strategic performance. *Strategic Management Journal, 7,* 437-458.

Chetty, S.K., & Hamilton, R.T. (1993). The export performance of smaller firms: A multi-case study approach. *Journal of Strategic Marketing, 1,* 247-256.

Cooper, R.G. (1979). The dimensions of industrial new product success and failure. *Journal of Marketing, 43,* 93-103.

Cooper, R.G. (1982). The dimensions of industrial firms' new product strategies. Working Paper, McGill University, April.

Cooper, R.G., & Kleinschmidt, E.J. (1985). The impact of export strategy on export sales performance. *Journal of International Business Studies, 16*(1), 37-55.

Cooper, R.G., & Kleinschmidt, E.J. (1987). Success factors in product innovation. *Industrial Marketing Management, 16*(3), 215-233.

Cooper, R.G., & Kleinschmidt, E.J. (1993). What distinguishes the winners in the chemical industry? *Journal of Product Innovation Management, 10,* 90-111.

Dess, G.G., & Robinson, R.B. (1984). Measuring organizational performance in the absence of objective measures: The case of the privately-held firm and conglomerate business unit. *Strategic Management Journal, 5,* 265-273.

Diamantopoulos, A., & Schlegelmilch, B.B. (1994). Linking export manpower to export performance: A canonical regression analysis of European and U.S. data. In S.T. Cavusgil & C.N. Axinn (Eds.), *Advances in international marketing* (Vol. 6, pp. 161-181). Greenwich, CT: JAI Press.

Donaldson, G. (1995). A new tool for boards: The strategic audit. *Harvard Business Review, 73*(July-August), 99-107.

Eccles, R.G. (1991). The performance measurement manifesto. *Harvard Business Review, 69*(January-February), 131-137.

Evangelista, F.U. (1994). Export performance and its determinants: Some empirical evidence from Australian manufacturing firms. In S.T. Cavusgil & C.N. Axinn

(Eds.), *Advances in international marketing* (Vol. 6, pp. 207-229). Greenwich, CT: JAI Press.

Ford, J.D., & Schellenberg, D.A. (1982). Conceptual issues of linkage in the assessmentof organizational performance. *Academy of Management Review,* 7(1), 49-58.

Fraser, C., & Hite, R.E. (1990). Impact of international marketing strategies on performance in diverse global markets. *Journal of Business Research, 20,* 249-262.

Frazier, G.L., & Howell, R.D. (1983). Business definition and performance. *Journal of Marketing, 47,* 59-67.

Grabner-Kräuter, S. (1992). Möglichkeiten und Grenzen der empirischen Bestimmung von Determinanten des Exporterfolges [Possibilities and limitations of empirical research in export success determinants]. *Zeitschrift für betriebswirtschafliche Forschung, 44*(12), 1080-1089.

Griffin, A., & Page, A.L. (1993). An interim report on measuring product development success and failure. *Journal of Product Innovation Management,* 10, 291-308.

Grunert, K.G., & Ellegaard, C. (1993). The concept of key success factors: Theory and method. In M.J. Baker (Ed.), *Perspectives on Marketing Management* (Vol. 3, pp. 245-274). Chichester: John Wiley & Sons Ltd.

Hart, S., & Craig, A. (1993). Dimensions of success in new-product development. In M.J. Baker (Ed.), *Perspectives on marketing management, 3,* 207-243., Chichester: John Wiley & Sons Ltd.

Holzmüller, H.H., & Kasper, H. (1991). On a theory of export performance: Personal and organizational determinants of export trade activities observed in small and medium-sized firms. *Management International Review, 31* (Special Issue), 45-70.

Jacobson, R. (1987). The validity of ROI as a measure of business performance. *The American Economic Review, 77*(3), 470-477.

Johne, F.A., & Snelson, P.A. (1988). Success factors in product innovation: A selective review of the literature. *Journal of Product Innovation Management,* 5, 114-128.

Kaplan, R.S., & Norton, D.P. (1992). The balanced scorecard—measures that drive performance. *Harvard Business Review, 70*(January-February), 71-79.

Kaynak, E., & Kang-yen Kuan, W. (1993). Environment, strategy, structure, and performance in the context of export activity: An empirical study of Taiwanese manufacturing firms. *Journal of Business Research, 27,* 33-49.

Kerin, R.A., Mahajan, V., & Varadarajan, P.R. (1990). *Contemporary perspectives on strategic market planning.* Boston: Allyn & Bacon.

Koh, A.C. (1991). Relationships among organisational characteristics, marketing strategy and export performance. *International Marketing Review, 8*(3), 46-60.

Lee, C.S., & Yang, Y.S. (1991). Impact of export market expansion strategy on export performance. *International Marketing Review,7*(4), 41-50.

Lim, J.-S., Sharkey, T.W., & Kim, K.I. (1993). Determinants of international marketing strategy. *Management International Review, 33*(2), 103-120.

Louter, P.J., Ouwerkerk, C., & Bakker, B.A. (1991). An inquiry into successful exporting. *European Journal of Marketing, 25*(6), 7-23.

Madsen, T.K. (1989). Successful export marketing management: Some empirical evidence. *International Marketing Review, 6*(4), 41-57.

McGrath, M.E., & Romeri, M.N. (1994). From experience the R&D effectiveness index: A metric for product development performance. *Journal of Product Innovation Management, 11,* 213-220.

Montoya-Weiss, M., & Calantone, R. (1994). Determinants of new product performance: A review and meta-analysis. *Journal of Product Innovation Management, 11,* 397-417.

Page, A.L. (1993). Assessing new product development practices and performance: Establishing crucial norms. *Journal of Product Innovation Management, 10,* 273-290.

Piëst, E. (1988). Dimensies van ondernemingssucces een overzicht [Dimensions of corporate success an overview]. *Maandblad voor Accountancy en Bedrijfshuishoudkunde, 62*(5), 177-187.

Samiee, S., & Roth, K. (1992). The influence of global marketing standardization on performance. *Journal of Marketing, 56*(8), 1-17.

Snow, C.C., & Hrebeniak, L. (1980). Strategy, distinctive competence, and organizational performance. *Administrative Science Quarterly, 25*(June), 317-336.

Thach, S.V., & Axinn, C.N. (1994). *Redefining export success: Not which measures, but why measure.* Paper presented at the Second Annual CIMaR Conference, COPPEAD, UFRJ, Brazil.

Varadarajan, P.R. (1986). Product diversity and firm performance: An empirical investigation. *Journal of Marketing, 50*(July), 43-57.

Venkatraman, N., & Ramanujam, V. (1986). Measurement of business performance in strategic research: A comparison of approaches. *Academy of Management Review, 11*(4), 801-814.

Wong, V., & Saunders, J. (1993). Business orientation and corporate success. *Journal of Strategic Management, 1,* 20-40.

Yang, Y.S., Leone, R.P., & Alden, D.L. (1992). A market expansion ability approach to identify potential exporters. *Journal of Marketing, 56,* 84-96.

Zeithaml, V.A., Varadarajan, V.R., & Zeithaml, C.P. (1988). The contingency approach: Its foundations and relevance to theory building and research in marketing. *European Journal of Marketing, 22*(7), 37-64.

Zwart, P.S., & Bijmolt, T.H.A. (1993). Invloed van interne factoren op exportsucces in het MKB [internal factors influencing export success in the SME]. *Small Business Research Memorandum,* Small Business Centre, University Groningen.

PART II

RESEARCHING AND ADAPTING TO EXPORT CONDITIONS

INSTRUMENTAL, CONCEPTUAL AND SYMBOLIC USE OF EXPORT INFORMATION:

AN EXPLORATORY STUDY OF U.K. FIRMS

Adamantios Diamantopoulos and Anne L. Souchon

ABSTRACT

Past research on information use is limited in the sense that most studies have been undertaken in a domestic setting and have taken a rather restricted view of information use. This exploratory study examines the extent and types of information use in an export context and links such use to export decisions. The results, based on interviews with export decision makers, indicate that different decisions are based on different types of information use, and that greater use of export information results in an increased level of confidence when making decisions.

Advances in International Marketing, Volume 8, pages 117-144.
Copyright © 1996 by JAI Press Inc.
ISBN: 0-7623-0164-3

I. INTRODUCTION

The role of information in securing competitive advantage and enhancing a firm's market orientation has long been recognized in the literature (Parsons, 1983; Porter & Millar, 1985; Turner, 1991; Glazer, 1991). However, nowadays, "essentially the same information is available to competing firms at about the same time. As a consequence, competitive advantage is to be found increasingly in what is done with information, that is, how it is used or employed rather than in who does or does not have it" (Zaltman & Moorman, 1988, p. 16).

Thus, although acquisition of information is necessary for decision making, it is the use of information that becomes the crucial link between information collection and the firm's performance (Feldman & March, 1981; Taylor, 1991; Goodman, 1993).

In an export setting, the importance of effective information use is highlighted by the fact that companies often claim that lack of export-specific knowledge is a main obstacle to their internationalization (Johanson & Vahlne, 1977; Walters, 1983; Reid, 1984; Cavusgil & Naor, 1987). Acquisition and use of export information helps reduce the uncertainty associated with export operations (Diamantopoulos et al., 1993; Koh et al., 1993; McAuley, 1993) and avoid mistakes and/or lost opportunities (Douglas & Craig, 1983; Ricks, 1983).

There is a well-established body of literature on information use in a domestic setting (for a review, see Menon & Varadarajan, 1992). A number of conceptualizations have been developed (e.g., Knorr, 1977; Weiss, 1981; Havelock, 1986), identifying different dimensions of knowledge utilization, and linking the various antecedent variables to the construct (e.g., Deshpandé & Zaltman, 1982, 1984, 1987; John & Martin, 1984; Lee et al., 1987). In contrast, the literature on export information has been very much concerned with issues surrounding the acquisition of export information. Among the issues that have been considered are the nature of export information needs (e.g., Cavusgil, 1985), their relative importance (e.g., Wood & Goolsby, 1987) and the factors moderating those needs (e.g., Culpan, 1989). Sources of export information have also been investigated, as various studies have sought to identify which export information sources firms are aware of (e.g., Walters, 1983), which sources are actually consulted/employed (e.g., Bodur & Cavusgil, 1985), and how useful/

effective alternative sources are perceived to be in terms of providing the required information (e.g., McAuley, 1993). Hardly any research has been conducted with regard to export information use; although Hart et al. (1994) touched upon the topic, their study was primarily concerned with export information acquisition rather than use issues.

The present study seeks to throw some light on the ways in which information is actually put to use in an export setting. Specifically, we approach information use as a multidimensional construct and explore, via qualitative research, its manifestation in export decision making. In doing so, we hope to provide preliminary insights into the role of information utilization in export operations and establish an initial platform for further research in this area.

We first draw from the literature on knowledge utilization and describe information use in terms of multiple dimensions. We then outline our research objectives and follow this with a discussion of data collection procedures, sample selection, and analytical methods. Finally, we discuss the results of our study, highlighting their exploratory nature and suggesting areas for future research; the study's limitations are also acknowledged in this section.

II. BACKGROUND AND RESEARCH OBJECTIVES

Information use is a concept that has been studied in many disciplines, including social science research and evaluation (e.g., Weiss, 1981; Patton, 1978), organizational behavior (e.g., Larsen, 1983), social policy decision making (e.g., Caplan et al., 1975; Knorr, 1977; Weiss, 1977), as well as marketing (e.g., Sinkula, 1990; Moorman et al., 1993). The construct of information utilization has been defined as "taking research into account" (Weiss & Bucavalas, 1977, p. 214) and "the extent to which the research influences the user's decision making" (Moorman et al., 1992, p. 316). The literature indicates that the construct is multidimensional in nature (e.g., Knorr, 1977; Deshpandé & Zaltman, 1982; Havelock, 1986; Weitzel, 1987; Taylor, 1991; Menon & Varadarajan, 1992). In this context, differences in terminology notwithstanding, three distinct dimensions of use can be identified: instrumental, conceptual and symbolic.

Using information instrumentally refers to applying knowledge directly, to solve a very specific problem; for example, "when a decision to introduce a new product is based on marketing research findings and recommendations, we have an instance of instrumental use of knowledge." (Menon & Varadarajan, 1992, p. 55). Conceptual use of information refers to the indirect application of knowledge, that is to "influence a policy-maker's thinking about an issue without putting information to any specific, documentable use. It also refers to planned uses of information 'in the future'" (Rich, 1977, p. 200). Finally, when a decision maker uses information symbolically, he/ she may either distort the information so that it may support an opinion (e.g., Piercy, 1983; Goodman, 1993), justify a decision already made with retrospectively-acquired information (e.g., Knorr, 1977), or simply pretend that he/she uses the information to keep superiors/subordinates happy (Cunningham & Clarke, 1975; Piercy, 1983; Goodman, 1993).

Note that most past studies of marketing information use have chosen to overlook conceptual and symbolic uses, focusing instead on instrumental use of information. For example, the well-known studies of Deshpandé and Zaltman (1982, 1984) were concerned with instrumental use of (domestic) marketing research information and it is only very recently that conceptual use was considered by Moorman (1995). In an export context, only Hart et al.'s (1994) study is relevant and is exclusively concerned with instrumental use.

In this exploratory investigation, we seek to provide insights into two interrelated issues. First, we examine how export information— however acquired—is used within exporting firms; the focus here is on the extent and types of information use. Second, we concentrate on the relationship between information use and export decisions, the aim being to link each dimension of use (i.e., instrumental, conceptual and symbolic) with specific export decisions. While fully rational decision making in light of all relevant information does not always characterize international marketing decisions (Cavusgil & Godiwalla, 1982), export information should nevertheless influence "managers' orientations toward priorities, the manner in which they formulate problems, the range of solutions they convey, and the criteria of choice they apply" (Menon & Varadarajan, 1992, p. 56). By examining the two issues mentioned above, the implications of information utilization in terms of its impact on export decision making should become clearer and so should potential benefits of effective export information usage.

III. METHODOLOGY

A. Research Design

A recent review of the literature has shown that the topic of export information use is as yet virtually unexplored (Souchon & Diamantopoulos, 1994). Past research on information use in a domestic context has tended to concentrate on information stemming exclusively from marketing research (e.g., Sinkula, 1990), ignoring other types of information sources. Furthermore, no comprehensive measurement instrument has yet been developed encapsulating all types of use; for example, Deshpandé and Zaltman's (1982) widely known measure of information use treats the construct as unidimensional, encompassing only instrumental elements. Lastly, no measure of information use has been developed/tested in an export context. Bearing in mind that a "reason for using qualitative measurement is that for particular outcomes no acceptable, valid, and reliable quantitative measurement exists" (Patton, 1980, p. 75), and that "if relatively little is known about the phenomenon to be investigated, exploratory research will be warranted" (Churchill, 1991, p. 70), it was decided to undertake a qualitative study of export information use.

An experience survey (i.e., key informant survey) of export managers was selected as the data collection method, given its applicability for studying decision makers (Robson & Foster, 1989). In implementing the research design, help was sought from local trade organizations, as their endorsement would enhance the project's credibility to the local business world upon whose cooperation the study depended (time and cost constraints rendered a study of exporters across the United Kingdom impossible). Thus, organizations such as the Overseas Trade Services Department of the local governmental Office, the Confederation of British Industry, and the local Exporters' Association were contacted and the research topic formally presented to them. All confirmed the high relevance of the research for exporters and provided support in the form of supplying lists of exporting firms and identifying potential respondents.

A total of 12 interviews in 11 companies were conducted; the firms were all located within a 20-mile radius of the university, proximity being important due to time and cost considerations. While no pretence is made that the firms contacted constitute anything but a

Table 1. Company Characteristics

Company Reference and Respondent Position	Number of Employees	Annual Turnover	Export Complexity (destinations)	Main Export Market	Export Experience	Sector of Activity	Export Intensity
1 Managing Director, and Business Processes Manager	68,000 (world) 580 (locally)	$12-14 billion	32 countries	Europe and the Middle East	14 years	Beverage Industry	50 to 60%
2 Sales Controller	730	£55 million	5 countries	Germany	1 year	Car Industry	5 to 10%
3 Administration Manager	35 (locally + Ireland) 10 (locally)	£5-6 million	1 country	Ireland	7 years	Freight Forwarder	17%
4 Managing Director	50	£2 million	15 countries	Europe	22 years	Highway Surveys	10 to 15%
5 Sales Director	180	£9.5 million	60 countries	France	20 or 30 years	Bakery Machinery	20%
6 General Director	500	£23 million	9 countries	USA	"always been exporting"	Carbon Products	50%
7 Director	75	£17.5 million	N/A	Middle East, West Africa Far East	124 years	Freight Forwarder	N/A
8 Technical Director	10	£1 million	N/A	N/A	N/A	Computer Industry	N/A
9 N/A	350	£40 million	3 regions	Holland, Belgium, France Italy. Spain	40 years	Strapping Systems	60%
10 Managing Director	400	£48 million	4 countries	Scandinavia	20 years	(or Industry)	10%
11 Plant Manager	88,000 (world) 5,000 (U.K.) 800 (locally)	$14,000 (world-wide)	30 countries	France	38 years	Diverse Industrial and Consumer Products	70 to 80%

Note: N/A: Not Available. These figures are unavailable due to the poor quality of the tape used during the recording of those question.

convenience sample, every effort was made at the selection stage to ensure substantial variability among the respondent firms in terms of size, industry sector, and export characteristics (see Table 1). With respect to size, the companies interviewed varied from 10 employees and a turnover of £1 million, to 730 employees and a turnover of £55 million. The number of export countries served ranged from 1 to 60, and their export experience, from 1 to 124 years. Four companies were highly dependent on export sales with 50 percent or more of their total turnover derived from exporting, while the remaining firms had an export intensity ranging from 5 to 20 percent. Lastly, the industries represented covered industrial sectors (such as carbon materials for the traction industry), consumer goods (such as beverages), and services (such as freight forwarding).

B. Research Instrument

Past literature on knowledge use in general and export information in particular was used to develop questions to be included in a semi-structured, undisguised interview guide. Available measures of information use (e.g., Weiss, 1981; Deshpandé & Zaltman, 1982) provided an initial basis for the formulation of questions, while the question sequence was kept flexible so that the instrument could be adapted to each respondent (e.g., Smith, 1975; Nachmias & Nachmias, 1976; Lyberg & Kasprzyk, 1991). The choice of a semi-structured versus a structured questionnaire was made due to the exploratory nature of the study as a standardized questionnaire would have proved impossible to develop from extant knowledge (e.g., Strauss & Corbin, 1994). The objectives of the study were never hidden from the informants and an undisguised approach to the interviews was adopted.

The length of the instrument was such that the interviews would last approximately half an hour each; shorter interviews would give no time to discuss the topic in depth, and thus accuracy of responses would be sacrificed. A longer instrument might, on the one hand, have rendered the appointments difficult to obtain or, on the other hand, made some interviewees impatient after a while (Miller, 1991). In this context, it is important to note that:

> there is an unfortunate tendency in the minds of many practitioners and buyers of qualitative research to equate time with quality. In relation to the

individual interview, the longer it takes is often assumed to be an indication of maximum depth. We contend that this is misconceived and naive... it is destructive to make the interview last longer than half an hour" (Gordon & Langmaid, 1988, p. 66).

The choice of half-hour interviews for our study is largely justified by the preliminary nature of the research. Given that only a first impression of export information use was sought, no in-depth knowledge about complex relationships between, for example, export information utilization and export performance was requested; thus the time needed to obtain the desired information was reasonably short. In this context, the reliance on a semi-structured instrument enables researchers to avoid superficial and unwarranted exchange of information, thus keeping the interview length to its optimal (e.g., Easterby-Smith et al., 1991).

C. Analytical Procedure

Each interview conducted was duly taped and the tapes transcribed. The analysis itself followed the sequence of steps described in Miles and Huberman (1994, p. 10), who "define *analysis* as consisting of three concurrent flows of activity: data reduction, data display, and conclusion drawing/verification" (Figure 1). These steps are necessary, as unreduced data in the form of original transcriptions can overload the analyst's data processing abilities (Faust, 1982).

Data reduction was undertaken for each of the 12 interviews, using mainly in-vivo codes, the latter being terms drawn from the respondents themselves (Strauss & Corbin, 1990). Such codes (as opposed to codes determined *prior* to the analysis) were chosen because of the exploratory nature of the study: the issues raised during the course of the interviews were specific to the construct of export information utilization on which very little is known. Rigid use of literature-based codes could have restricted the analysis to what was already known on information use in a domestic setting. At the time the interviews were conducted and analyzed, conceptual and symbolic uses of information had not been systematically examined and most terminology relating to knowledge utilization related to the instrumental dimension only. As our study was the first to be concerned with the investigation of *export* information use as a

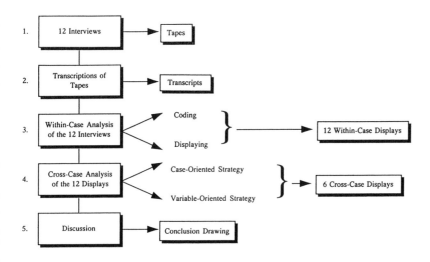

Figure 1.   Analytical Procedure

multidimensional construct encompassing conceptual and symbolic uses as well as instrumental use, it was important that these types of utilization be described in the decision makers' own words. Indeed, as will be shown later, while all three types of information use were encountered in the interviews, they were given different labels by the respondents.

The codes were arranged in the form of 12 within-case displays which took the form of a matrix or a network according to which was most appropriate to the interview being analyzed (Miles & Huberman, 1994).

Nine interviews needed to be organized along the network procedure because linkages between different activities were clearly depicted by the respondent, while three interviews best suited a matrix approach because no such links were readily observable. These twelve displays were then integrated and synthesized into fewer cross-case displays capturing the construct of export information use. Three types of approaches are relevant in a cross-case analysis: (a) case-oriented, (b) variable-oriented, and/or (c) mixed. A case-oriented approach considers the case as the unit of analysis and seeks patterns and associations within each case (Ragin, 1987). A variable-oriented approach is more focused and concentrates on key variables and relationships across several cases (Runkel, 1990). Finally, in a mixed strategy, a standard set of variables is used to write up each case (Miles & Huberman, 1994).

In the present analysis, a variable-oriented strategy was opted for, given that the study's objective was to explore the essential nature of information use in an export setting rather than provide detailed descriptions of specific companies (case-oriented strategy) or derive generalizations by contrasting cases on standard variables (mixed strategy).

IV. FINDINGS

A. Extent of Export Information Use

A key factor determining whether acquired information was put to any use was managers' perception of the quality and reliability of the source of the information; this is consistent with prior findings in the literature stating that decision makers' judgements upon information sources are likely to affect the extent to which they rely on that information (Jobber & Elliott, 1992). For example, information generated by commissioning research to external suppliers was considered to be reliable (and, thus, likely to be used) because it was a service the firm *paid for*. As the managing director of Company 1 said, "we actually pay to have the surveys done annually, so we get pretty reliable data." However, external export marketing research information was considered less reliable than information gathered by the company's own personnel (e.g., through visits to customers, trade show attendance etc.), because the former type of information does not come from people who are actual players (i.e., suppliers, competitors, etc.) within the industry they research. External researchers are generally mere observers who do not have an active role within the industry. This finding corroborates that of Garrett and Hart (1993) who found that international information stemming from internal sources carried more credibility than that collected by outside agencies. For example, as a sales director stated,

> I think the information we build up informally is probably better than the information we get through a formal market research ... When you approach

the market from a very formal basis and do marketing research and come up with a set of results, they could vary quite dramatically from the information that you can gather from people who are really, really on the ground and very close to what is happening. What we found was that information gathered within the company was far more accurate" (Company 6).

The second factor impinging upon the extent of use was the extent to which the information at hand was up-to-date and specific enough for the company's needs; for example, information provided by government export assistance organizations was hardly used because it was "too general" (Company 5), "irrelevant" (Company 3), and "outdated" (Companies 8 and 11). These findings are consistent with previous evidence on the effectiveness of export assistance bodies, the latter being often criticized for supplying information that is too general to suit the specific needs of exporters (see Diamantopoulos et al. [1993] for a review). Again, information generated in-house was considered to be superior in terms of both relevance and timeliness and, thus, more likely to be put to use.

B. Types of Export Information Use

Regarding the different types of use, it was found that companies did indeed use export information instrumentally, conceptually and/or symbolically, as the literature suggests; however, the terms employed by the respondents to describe alternative types of use were different.

Instrumental Use of Export Information

In many instances, export information was used on an immediate basis as soon as it had been collected, for specific decisions. This represents an instrumental use of knowledge. Such information was often obtained by commissioning specific research projects to specialists. For instance, "we commission people, such as notable marketing analysts and companies, marketing specialists and consultants such as Arthur Andersen, Robin Adams, and use the information for specific export projects" (Company 1).

However, before the information was actually considered in decision making, it was interpreted and evaluated. If such information came from external suppliers, it would be "corrected" if need be to make it consistent with the company's internal knowledge base. For example, "marketing research specialists tell what they *believe* is happening. The researcher will come to our company with his view and we will challenge the hell out of it, analyze it down and correct it. He will agree with the corrections if we have data" (Company 1).

The correction and agreement with information providers were intermediary stages to the process of using information only if the information came from external research suppliers. The findings here confirm previous evidence that there needs to be a high level of interaction and, indeed, trust between information providers and users for instrumental information utilization to be effective (e.g., Deshpandé & Zaltman, 1982; Moorman et al., 1992). If the information stemmed from internal/personal sources, the decision to use the information was made *directly* after the latter had been collected and/or analyzed/interpreted, based on its degree of perceived usefulness. Should it be considered useful, it would serve in the development of ideas and the formulation of opportunities on which certain export decisions would be based (e.g., which potential customers to target, foreign market entry strategies etc.). For instance, "if there is an opportunity or if we feel that there is an immediately exploitable opportunity, that a particular market is opening up for a particular product and we can meet that need very, very quickly, then obviously what we'll do is put together some sort of a crash team in order to go and exploit that market" (Company 5).

Information collected by company personnel as a by-product of day-to-day business was often used immediately because of its time relevance. An illustration of this is that, "anyone of us can come back in from a business trip with information that we've learned and we would use that information on an immediate basis." (Company 5).

Conceptual Use of Export Information

Several justifications for not using export information instrumentally were given. For example, "how many facts can anybody memorize at one time or a particular article at a particular time that you don't have a use for, so you log it, you memory it. And then six months later, you think, wait a minute, there was an article, and you go to the library, and usually they will pull it out" (Company 8).

When a company was part of a global organization, it often received unsolicited information from its "sister" firms abroad. Indeed, past research suggests that the company's own staff abroad is a vital source of information (e.g., Keegan, 1974; Higgins et al., 1991). Because such information was not always specific to a particular problem the company faced at the point in time when it was received, it was stored in a database. For instance, "we don't destroy anything. We get reports and what we do with them is extract the important parts and put that onto a database. Other information we just ignore. But normally, if we have a report on information which we feel would be of use to other people in our organization, we would pass it on to them" (Company 6).

When export information was acquired and had no direct relation to a current problem the organization was facing, or if the resources involved in reacting to that information were greater than what the company could afford, the information would be either kept in the form of reports in a company library, or stored on a computer database (to be used in the future). This represents a conceptual use of export information. As the sales director from Company 5 stated, "if an opportunity arises that is a wanton project, we'll put it on the back burner until we have the resources available ... It will be stored under 'M' for memory."

Export information was found to be continually updated by most companies, not for any specific decision at hand, but in order to be stored in a bank of knowledge, to keep track of the market. Maintaining regular contact with customers was unanimously the favored way of keeping a continuous update on the market. For example, "there is always an interchange of ideas. We can always talk about something that may have been of interest a year ago, 15 months ago, 18 months ago, and resurrect an idea, a particular market and discuss them again. There is no formal recall system" (Company 5).

Information bought on a subscription basis (e.g., from syndicated services) tended to be used more conceptually than instrumentally; as it is supplied to the company on a regular basis, it does not necessarily relate to a particular problem the exporter faces at the time. For example, industry-specific surveys bought annually provided what the managing director from Company 1 called "specialist information," which reflects the needs of entire industries; they were often kept for the sake of possessing up-to-date information for future decisions. Appendix 1 shows the variable-oriented display for instrumental and conceptual uses of information.

Symbolic Use of Export Information

Appendix 2 displays the process involved when making decisions based on intuition and instinct. In this case, information could be sought *after* having made the decision, but prior to implementing it. If the information confirmed the intuition, the decision would be implemented. If the information contradicted the instinct that led to making the decision, the project would abort. This is consistent with one manifestation of symbolic use, namely the use of knowledge merely to justify a decision already made (e.g., Knorr, 1977). Not surprisingly, no export decision maker admitted to distorting the information so that it might confirm their intuition (which is another manifestation of symbolic use), (Feldman & March, 1981). For instance, "it is difficult to change information to suit a decision because we are part of a group of companies. This tactic is probably easy if one owns one's own company. But in that case, you can probably react quickly to information that does not confirm the decision, anyway ..." (Company 10).

Sometimes, information was not used at all. Previous research undertaken on non-use of information has often assumed that the rationale underlying such a stance stems from a lack of fit between the information and the information need (Larsen, 1985). However, information non-use has also been said to occur when the surprising nature of the acquired knowledge would force the decision maker to reevaluate previously held assumptions and beliefs (e.g., Zaltman, 1986). In such a case, it is often easier for the decision maker to disregard the information entirely (e.g., Deshpandé & Kohli, 1989). After the implementation of a (usually tactical) decision based solely on instinct, the "retrospective" information that came back to the organization was one concerning the outcome (i.e., success or failure) of the decision (Company 2). Symbolic use of information thus took place when the export manager made a decision based on his/her intuition, backed his/her hunch with information that might confirm the instinct, and then implemented the decision. This finding supports Feldman's (1986) notion that the benefits of such use of information are enhanced by outcome feedback. For instance, the technical director of Company 8 stated that he "would back (his) instinct overall, against detailed market analysis."

Another instance of a lack of use of export information, was when a company did not have a particular strategy for a market. For instance, Company 1's business processes manager indicated that his company's marketing function was weak, and went on to illustrate his situation in the following way: "'where are you trying to get to,' asked the Cheshire Cat. 'I don't know,' replied Alice. 'So it does not matter which road you take, then.' This is it. Strategy is where you want to go to. And we get into this because sometimes, we are struggling with market strategy."

The more experience a decision maker had of his/her industry and exporting activity, the more he/she would tend to rely on intuition as a basis for making export decisions, because more familiarity with the market would have been acquired. This finding is consistent with past research on the effect of market/industry experience on knowledge utilization; it has been claimed that experience in itself is a source of information (e.g., Weiss & Bucavalas, 1977; Grønhaug & Graham, 1987) which breeds intuitive decision making (e.g., Shoemaker & Russo, 1993; Gittler, 1994). In the words of the technical director from Company 8, "the only way you acquire that know-how is a long experience of the industry and what's called a feel or a nose for something." The managing director from Company 9 also agreed that "instinct comes from experience, you can understand how the industry ticks. Only people who have been around can have it."

Small companies tended to use information to support decisions made because they often did not have the resources to commission a proper research study to a specialist. For instance, the technical director from Company 8 stated that "when I can, I will seek information to back up my instinct. I'm a great information gatherer in my own way. I'm a nosey individual. I read very avidly. There is nothing that isn't out there if you know where to read it. And if you read between the lines it will tell you what the competition is about to do, who is doing what, where ... "

Another element of a symbolic use of information was uncovered in the sense that information may be used as a diplomatic tool; some companies went to their information providers not because of particular information needs that may have arisen, but merely to ensure a good relationship with those providers. In the words of the business processes manager from Company 1, "any information we pick up, for instance as our sales manager is visiting companies, not necessarily to secure business, but to maintain regular contact with them."

No managers indicated the use of export information in all three different ways; for example, some interviewees appeared genuinely shocked when asked about the use of intuition when making a decision, others spontaneously approached the subject. Further, examination of the interview material revealed that the companies using export information instrumentally and/or conceptually were different firms from those relying on symbolic use of export information. For instance, the two companies using information purely symbolically with no mention of instrumental or conceptual uses whatsoever (Companies 2 and 10) were the two companies with the lowest export intensity (they also sold to few export markets). This finding is unsurprising as a company relying heavily on its export sales would be less likely to take the risk of basing its export decisions on instinct or intuition as opposed to objective information. Interestingly, export experience (as reflected by the number of years the firm had been exporting), appeared to have no effect on the way that export information was used. In this context, it was the *individual's* export experience rather than the *firm's* export experience that led to a heightened reliance on symbolic use of information. Indeed, intuition stems from a subconscious *personal* knowledge base, which is quite different from an easily accessible, concrete, *organizational* knowledge base (Parikh, 1994). While the use of the latter would legitimately constitute a conceptual use of information, reliance on the former is more consistent with a symbolic use.

C. Export Information Use in Relation to Decision Making

A number of export decisions were mentioned during the interviews, some short term and/or tactical (such as a rapid decision to fill the company's plant capacity), others longer term and/or strategic in nature (such as a standardization/adaptation dilemma); as Appendices 1 and 2 show, different types of export information use appeared to be associated with different types of decisions.

Foreign market entry and standardization/adaptation decisions were never associated with reliance on instinct or intuition. Indeed, where the former strategy is concerned, it was developed very specifically "in conjunction with clients" (Company 1); or with regards to both strategies, it probably again comes from travelling and networking. As I say, essentially, we are in a small industry. Most are family businesses, and therefore, networking is very, very strong, and you will then formulate an opinion or a desire to do something based on something you have learned on your travels: we will explore that avenue" (Company 5).

Finding the appropriate piggybacking partner was also a decision based heavily on objective export information, rather than subjective intuition. For instance, "information is never gathered by chance. Initially, all information is collected for the specific purpose of establishing a contact with a potential partner abroad" (Company 4).

Because the information was put to use immediately for a specific decision, decisions regarding foreign market entry, standardization/ adaptation and piggyback contracts appear to be made on the basis of export information being used instrumentally. Similarly, a decision involving the targeting of a potential export customer was likely to be based upon instrumental use of information; as stated by the managing director from Company 4, "names of potential customers cannot be guessed at." Pricing decisions, competitive positioning and the choice of a distributor also tended to require instrumental use of information. For instance, as the managing director from Company 1 said, "we like to know what the competition are doing. They are making investments and we are not. But we have the lowest price, and that's not an accident ... We track the metal rates daily on the London Metal Exchange."

The overall export strategy within the firms concerned was generally said to be developed on the basis of a continually up-dated information base. A team of company managers (such as the managing director, together with the sales and finance directors) would develop an export sales plan on the basis of information previously collected and regularly assembled. Thus, information was used conceptually. For example, "the flow of information is continuous. We actually collate that information, and, strategically, we would plan ahead for a long period of time: what's our strategy in the next five years" (Company 6).

Export information was never discarded or disposed of, and was often said to be kept either in a company library, on an on-line database, or filed as company internal reports to be used in future strategic decisions.

Short term, tactical decisions (such as the decision to accept an unsolicited order merely to fill plant capacity) would sometimes be implemented without relevant information (e.g., the potential customer's financial situation), because of time constraints. In the words of the business processes manager from Company 1, "we would simply justify the decision to ourselves in terms of the fact that we make fast money out of it."

Deciding on a production level may also be based on a guess when customers do not provide their orders sufficiently in advance or in sufficient detail. In the words of the sales controller from Company 2, "certain customers may give us a forecast for more than a year, but not split. So then we take the gamble of splitting it down by model."

New product development was sometimes said to be first based on an instinct that there could be a demand for a certain idea. This finding contradicts that of Moorman (1995) who found new product development decisions and new product performance to be positively correlated with a more conceptual use of information. Our results show that the decision to start developing a certain product was often virtually made before acquiring information to support it. The disparity between our findings and Moorman's (1995) could possibly be explained by the difference in environmental settings. Export information is not always as readily available as information concerning purely domestic markets (e.g., Douglas & Craig, 1983). Thus, decision makers may be faced with a necessity to rely on instinct for decisions involving a high degree of creativity, such as new product development before purposefully seeking information. For example, "you just say, come on, let's go, you just make the decision and you fly with it. You've got no real proof that it will work. So you do a small market research" (Company 11).

Other product decisions also often first arose because of an intuition, but did not get implemented on the basis of instinct alone. As the technical director from Company 8 said "I decide on which product to sell because people say I have an instinct, a bit of a feel, but I would not launch a new product based solely on intuition ... Well, I might, but the rest of the directors wouldn't let me!"

The level of a company's confidence in its export decision making activity was positively related to the extent to which it used information. This is consistent with previous findings on information use in a domestic setting (e.g., Lee et al., 1987). Those organizations relying to a great extent on instinct, with no use of export information

(Companies 1 and 2), tended to be firms without a clear marketing strategy, or a marketing function which was weak. For instance,

> we are not very good at developing a marketing strategy. We are good at developing a manufacturing strategy. We know what to do, manufacturing-wise, from an engineering stand point, for product improvement. Marketing ... no. I think that it's more difficult, somehow, to get your hands around other people's strategies, other people's direction (Company 1)

These companies never tended to be really certain about the accuracy of their decisions, and they were both unsatisfied regarding their export performance. For example, the business processes manager of Company 1 blamed his firm's marketing weakness for not being able to develop clearer strategies and improving export turnover. These results suggest that ineffective information use may result in a lack of confidence in export decisions as well as dissatisfaction with export performance.

V. CONCLUSIONS AND FUTURE RESEARCH DIRECTIONS

This study has uncovered rationales behind the different ways in which information is used in an export setting. In doing so, it confirmed the appropriateness of classifying export knowledge utilization under instrumental, conceptual and symbolic use, and highlighted the terminology used by decision makers to refer to these dimensions (i.e., immediate, future and instinctive use respectively).

Concerning the *extent* of information use, it was found that the latter was dependent on the decision makers' assessment of information sources. Specifically, information originating from internal/personal sources tended to be used much more extensively than that stemming from external sources, because it was trusted to a larger extent.

Different export decisions were found to be associated with different types of export information use; for instance, strategic decisions tended to be based primarily on conceptual use of information, while for tactical decisions, instrumental and/or symbolic uses tended to predominate. It was also found that exporters using information extensively were more confident in their decisions than companies who did not systematically rely on export knowledge.

The exploratory nature of the present study suggests that caution needs to be exercised in terms of overstating the salience of its findings. Given that the focus was explicitly on obtaining preliminary insights rather than testing strong theory, depth of understanding rather than generalization was the prime concern (Miles & Huberman, 1994). Indeed, the small sample size, the geographical location of the firms studied, and the non-probabilistic nature of respondent selection are all constraints upon generalizability and are openly acknowledged as such. Further research is needed to: (a) develop appropriate measures of different types of information use, (b) identify company-specific and environment-specific antecedents of such use, and (c) link the extent and types of information use to export performance.

More specifically, on the methodological front, appropriate adaptation and further development of information use measures originally derived in a domestic setting (Knorr, 1977; Weiss & Bucavalas, 1977; Dunn, 1980; Weiss, 1981; Deshpandé & Zaltman, 1982; John & Martin, 1984; Larsen, 1985; Shrivastava, 1987; Menon & Varadarajan, 1992; Moorman et al., 1992; Moorman, 1995) would be an important step forward in the study of export information use. Particular emphasis should be placed on investigating the convergent and discriminant validity of scales capturing the three types of use, in line with the theoretical distinction among instrumental, conceptual and symbolic use (Churchill, 1979; De Vellis, 1991; Spector, 1992).

On the substantive front, a systematic investigation of antecedent variables on the extent and types of export information use would help place the latter within the organizational and environmental context of the firm's export operations. There is domestic-based literature on the impact of such variables as company structure (e.g., John & Martin, 1984), market experience (e.g., Sinkula, 1994) and environmental turbulence (e.g., Glazer & Weiss, 1993), and this body of research can be used to develop and test propositions regarding antecedent factors affecting export information use. Moreover, the influence of the characteristics of the information itself in terms of perceived quality (e.g., O'Reilly, 1982), conformity with expectations (e.g., Lee et al., 1987), and credibility (e.g., Menon & Varadarajan, 1992) on the use of such information is open to investigation.

Finally and most importantly, the link between information use and performance needs addressing. While the present study has highlighted that information use results in increased confidence with export decisions, it did not explicitly link use with alternative indicators of export performance. There is, however, evidence that suggests that acquisition of export information contributes positively to export success (e.g., Koh, 1991; Koh et al., 1993; Crick et al., 1994); further, the domestic-based evidence indicates a link between information use and performance (e.g., Moorman, 1995). These observations suggest that the extent to, and ways in, which information is actually applied in export decisions may have important performance implications. In this context, it is imperative that a narrow view of export performance (e.g., as reflected in financial yardsticks only) is avoided given the multidimensional nature of the performance construct (e.g., Madsen, 1987; Buckley, 1988; Shoham, 1991; Cavusgil & Zou, 1994; Matthyssens & Pauwels, 1995); a narrow conceptualization of performance may mask the true benefits of effective information utilization and thus provide an inaccurate picture of the role of information as a competitive weapon in the export arena.

Appendixes to follow

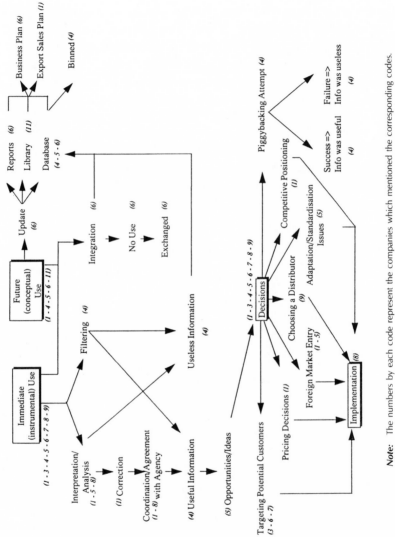

Note: The numbers by each code represent the companies which mentioned the corresponding codes.

Appendix 1. Instrumental and Conceptual Use of Export Information

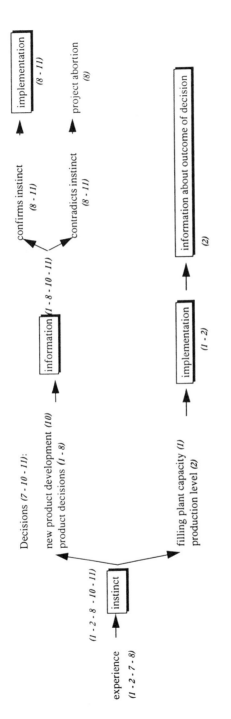

Appendix 2. Symbolic Use of Export Information

Note: The numbers by each code represent the companies which mentioned the corresponding codes.

ACKNOWLEDGMENT

The authors would like to thank Tage Koed Madsen and two anonymous reviewers for the helpful comments and suggestions to previous drafts of this paper.

REFERENCES

Bodur, M., & Cavusgil, S.T. (1985). Export market research orientations of Turkish firms. *European Journal of Marketing, 9*(2), 5-16.

Buckley, P.J., Pass, C.L., & Prescott, K. (1988). Measures of international competitiveness: A critical survey. *Journal of Marketing Management, 4*(2), 175-200.

Caplan, N., Morrison, A., & Stambaugh, R.J. (1975). *The use of social science knowledge in policy decisions at the national level.* Ann Arbor, MI: Institute for Social Research.

Cavusgil, S.T. (1985). Guidelines for EMR. *Business Horizons,* (November-December), 27-33.

Cavusgil, S.T., & Godiwalla, Y. M. (1982). Decision-making for international marketing: A comparative review. *Management Decision, 20*(4), 47-54.

Cavusgil, S.T., & Naor, J. 1987. Firm and management characteristics as discriminators of export marketing activity. *Journal of Business Research, 15*, 221-235.

Cavusgil, S.T., & Zou, S. (1994). Marketing strategy-performance relationship: An investigation of the empirical link in export market ventures. *Journal of Marketing, 58*(January), 1-21.

Crick, D., Jones, M., & Hart, S. (1994). International marketing research activities of UK exporters: An exploratory study. *Journal of Euromarketing, 3*(2), 7-26.

Churchill, G.A. (1979). A paradigm for developing better measures of marketing constructs. *Journal of Marketing Research, 16*(February), 64-73.

Churchill, G.A. Jr. (1991). *Marketing research: Methodological foundations.* Fort Worth: The Dryden Press International Edition.

Culpan, R. (1989). Export behavior of firms: Relevance of firm size. *Journal of Business Research, 18*(3), 207-218.

Cunningham, M.T., & Clarke, C. J. (1975). The product management function in marketing: Some behavioural aspects of decision taking. *European Journal of Marketing, 9*(2), 129-149.

De Vellis, R.F. (1991). *Scale development: Theory and applications.* London: Sage.

Deshpandé, R., & Kohli, A.K. (1989). Knowledge disavowal. *Knowledge: Creation, Diffusion, Utilization, 11*(2), 155-169.

Deshpandé, R., & Zaltman, G. (1982). Factors affecting the use of market research information: A path analysis. *Journal of Marketing Research, 19*, 14-31.

Deshpandé, R., & Zaltman, G. (1984). A comparison of factors affecting researcher and manager perceptions of market research use. *Journal of Marketing Research, 21*, 32-38.

Deshpandé, R., & Zaltman, G. (1987). A comparison of factors affecting use of marketing information in consumer and industrial firms. *Journal of Marketing Research, 24*, 114-118.

Diamantopoulos, A., Schlegelmilch, B.B., & Tse, K. (1993). Understanding the role of export marketing assistance: Empirical evidence and research needs. *European Journal of Marketing, 27*(4), 5-18.

Douglas, S. P., & Craig, C.S. (1983). *International marketing research.* Englewood Cliffs, NJ: Prentice Hall.

Dunn, W. (1980). The two community metaphor and models of knowledge utilization. *Knowledge: Creation, Diffusion, Utilization, 1*(4), 515-536.

Easterby-Smith, M., Thorpe, R., & Lowe, A. (1991). *Management research: An introduction.* Beverly Hills, CA: Sage Publications.

Faust, D. (1982). A needed component in prescriptions for science: Empirical knowledge of human cognitive limitations. *Knowledge: Creation, Diffusion, Utilization, 3*, 555-570.

Feldman, J. (1986). On the difficulty of learning from experience. In H.P. Simms Jr., D.A. Gioia & Associates (Eds.), *The thinking organization* (pp. 263-292). San Francisco: Jossey-Bass Publishers.

Feldman, M. S., & March, J.G. (1981). Information in organizations as signal and symbol. *Administrative Science Quarterly, 26*, 171-186.

Garrett, K., & Hart, S. (1993). An investigation of market research activities of multinational SBUs. *Proceedings of the 22nd Annual Conference of the European Marketing Academy*, Barcelona, 1, 519-542.

Gittler, H. (1994). Too many facts spoil the decision. *Industry Week, 3*(January), 46.

Glazer, R. (1991). Marketing in an information intensive environment: Strategic implications of knowledge as an asset. *Journal of Marketing, 55*(October), 1-19.

Glazer, R., & Weiss, A. M. (1994). Marketing in turbulent environments: Decision processes and the time-sensitivity of information. *Journal of Marketing Research, 30*(November), 509-521.

Goodman, S. K. (1993). Information needs for management decision-making. *Records Management Quarterly, 27*(4), 12-23.

Gordon, W., & Langmaid, R. (1988). *Qualitative market research: A practitioner's and buyers guide.* Aldershot: Gower.

Grønhaug, K., & Graham, J.L. (1987). International marketing research revisited. In S.T. Cavusgil (Ed.), *Advances in international marketing* (Vol. 2, pp. 121-137). Greenwich, CT: JAI Press.

Hart, S., Webb, J.R., & Jones, M.V. (1994). Export marketing research and the effect of export experience in industrial SMEs. *International Marketing Review, 11*(6), 4-22.

Havelock, R. G. (1986). The knowledge perspective: Definition and scope of a new study domain. In Beal, G.M., W. Dissanayake, & S. Konoshima (Eds.), *Knowledge generation, exchange and utilization* (pp. 11-34). Boulder: Westview Press Inc.

Higgins, L.F., McIntyre, S.C., & Raine, C.G. (1991). Design of global marketing information systems. *Journal of Business and Industrial Marketing, 6*(3-4), 49-58.

Jobber, D., & Elliott, R.H. (1992). The evaluation and use of marketing research information: A behavioural simulation. In J. Whitelock et al. (Eds.), *Proceedings of the marketing education group conference* (pp. 256-266).

Johanson, J., & Vahlne, J. (1977). Internationalization process of the firm-A model of knowledge development and increasing foreign market commitments. *Journal of International Business Studies, 8,* 23-32.

John, G., & Martin, J. (1984). Effects of organizational structure on marketing planning on credibility and utilization output. *Journal of Marketing Research, 21,* 170-183.

Keegan, W.J. (1974). Multinational scanning: A study of the information sources utilized by headquarters executives in multinational companies. *Administrative Science Quarterly, 9,* 411-421.

Koh, A C. (1991). An evaluation of international marketing research planning in United States export firms. *Journal of Global Marketing, 4*(3), 7-25.

Koh, A. C., Chow, J., & Smittivate, S. (1993). The practice of international marketing research by Thai exporters. *Journal of Global Marketing, 7*(2), 7-26.

Knorr, K. D. (1977). Policymakers' use of social science knowledge: Symbolic or instrumental? In C.H. Weiss (Ed.), *Using social research in public policy making* (pp. 165-182). Lexington, MA: D. C. Heath and Company.

Larsen, J. K. (1983). The nature of information utilization in local organizations. In B. Holzner et al. (Eds.), *Realizing social science knowledge* (pp. 311-326). Physica-Verlag, Wien-Würzburg.

Larsen, J. (1985). Effect of time on information utilization. *Knowledge: Creation, diffusion, utilization, 7*(2), 143-159.

Lee, H., Acito, F., & Day, R. (1987). Evaluation and use of marketing research by decision makers: A behavioral simulation. *Journal of Marketing Research, 24,* 187-196.

Lyberg, L.E., & Kasprzyk, D. (1991). Data collection methods and measurement error: An overview. In P.P. Biemer, R.M. Groves, L.E. Lyberg, N.A. Mathiowetz & S. Suman (Eds.), *Measurement errors in surveys* (pp. 237-258). New York: Wiley-Interscience Publication.

McAuley, A. (1993). The perceived usefulness of export information sources. *European Journal of Marketing 27,* 52-64.

Madsen, T. K. (1987). Empirical export performance studies: A review of conceptualizations and findings. In S. T. Cavusgil (Ed.), *Advances in International Marketing, 2,* (Vol. 2, pp. 177-198). Greenwich, CT: JAI Press.

Matthyssens, P., & Pauwels, P. (1995). Measuring success in export marketing strategy—a critical review. Paper presented at Third Annual CIMaR Symposium, Denmark.

Menon, A., & Varadarajan, R. (1992). A model of marketing knowledge use within firms. *Journal of Marketing, 56,* 53-71.

Miles, M. B., & Huberman, A. M. (1994). *An expanded sourcebook: qualitative data analysis.* Beverly Hills, CA: Sage Publications.

Miller, D.C. (1991). *Handbook of research design and social measurement,* Fifth Edition. Beverly Hills, CA: Sage Publications.

Moorman, C. (1995). Organizational market information processes: Cultural antecedents and new product outcomes. *Journal of Marketing Research, 32*(August), 318-335.

Moorman, C., Zaltman, G., & Deshpandé, R. (1992). Relationships between providers and users of market research: The dynamics of trust within and between organizations. *Journal of Marketing Research, 24*, 314-328.

Moorman, C., Deshpandé, R., & Zaltman, G. (1993). Factors affecting trust in market research relationships. *Journal of Marketing, 57*, 81-101.

Nachmias, D., & Nachmias, C. (1976). *Research methods in the social sciences.* London: St. Martin's Press

O'Reilly, C.A. (1982). Variations in decision makers' use of information sources: The impact of quality and accessibility of information. *Academy of Management Journal, 25*(4), 756-771.

Parikh, J. (1994). *Intuition.* Oxford: Blackwell Publishers.

Parsons, G. (1983). Information technology: A new competitive weapon. *Sloan Management Review, 25*(1), 3-14.

Patton, M. Q. (1978). *Utilization-focussed evaluation.* Beverly Hills, CA: Sage Publications.

Patton, M. Q. (1980). *Qualitative evaluation methods.* Beverly Hills, CA: Sage Publications.

Piercy, N. (1983). A social psychology of marketing information—learning to cope with the corporate battleground. *Journal of Market Research Society, 25*(2), 103-119.

Porter, M. E., & Millar, V.E. (1985). How information gives you competitive advantage. *Harvard Business Review*, (July/August), 149-160.

Ragin, C.C. (1987). *The comparative method: Moving beyond qualitative and quantitative strategies.* Berkeley: University of California Press.

Reid, S. (1984). Information acquisition and export entry decisions in small firms. *Journal of Business Research, 12*, 141-157.

Ricks, D. A. (1983). *Big business blunders.* Homewood, IL: Dow-Jones Irwin.

Rich, R. F. (1977). Uses of social science information by federal bureaucrats: Knowledge for action versus knowledge for understanding. In C. H. Weiss (Ed.), *Using social research in public policy making.* Lexington, MA: D.C. Heath and Company.

Robson, S. & Foster, A. (1989). *Qualitative research in action.* London: Edward Arnold.

Runkel, P.J. (1990). *Casting nets and testing specimens: Two grand methods of psychology.* New York: Praeger.

Shoemaker, P.J.H. & Russo, J.E. (1993). A pyramid of decision approaches. *California Management Review*, (Fall), 9-31.

Shoham, A. (1991). Performance in exporting: State-of-the-art literature review and synthesis and directions for future research. *Proceedings of the National Conference of the Academy of International Business*, Miami, Florida.

Shrivastava, P. (1987). Rigor and practical usefulness of research in strategic management. *Strategic Management Journal, 8*, 77-92.

Sinkula, J.M. (1990). Perceived characteristics, organizational factors, and the utilization of external market research suppliers. *Journal of Business Research*, (August), 1-17.

Sinkula, J.M. (1990). Perceived characteristics, organizational factors, and the utilization of external research suppliers. *Journal of Business Research*, (August), 1-17.

Smith, H.W. (1975). *Strategies of social research: The methodological imagination.* Englewood Cliffs, NJ: Prentice-Hall.

Souchon, A. L., & Diamantopoulos, A. (1994). Export marketing information use: A review of the literature and conceptual framework. *Marketing Education Group Conference Proceedings, 2*, 854-863.

Spector, P.E. (1992). Summated rating scale construction: An introduction. *Quantitative applications in the social sciences*, Series no. 07-082. Newbury Park, CA: Sage.

Strauss, A. & Corbin, J. (1990). *Basics of qualitative research: Grounded theory procedures and techniques.* Newbury Park, CA: Sage Publications.

Strauss, A., & Corbin, J. (1994). Grounded theory methodology: An overview. In N.K. Denzin & Y.S. Lincoln (Eds.), *Handbook of qualitative research* (pp. 273-285). Newbury Park, CA: Sage Publications.

Taylor, R. S. (1991). Information use environments. *Progress in Communication Sciences, 10*, 217-255.

Turner, P. (1991). Using information to enhance competitive advantage—the marketing options. *European Journal of Marketing, 25*(9), 55-64.

Walters, P. (1983). Export information sources—a study of their usage and utility. *International Marketing Review*, (Winter), 34-43.

Weiss, C. H. (1977). *Using social research in public policy making.* Lexington, MA: D.C. Heath and Company.

Weiss, C. H. (1981). Measuring the use of evaluation. In J. Ciarlo (Ed.). *Utilizing evaluation: Concepts and measurement techniques* (pp. 17-33). Beverly Hills, CA: Sage Publications.

Weiss, C. H., & Bucavalas, C.V. (1977). The challenge of social research to decision making. In C. H. Weiss (Ed.), *Using social research in public policy making* (pp. 213-233). Lexington, MA: D.C. Heath and Company.

Weitzel, J.R. (1987). Strategic information management: Targeting information for organizational performance. *Information Management Review, 3*(1), 9-19.

Wood, V., & Goolsby, J. (1987). Foreign market information preferences of established U.S. exporters. *International Marketing Review, 4*(4), 43-52.

Zaltman, G. (1986). *Knowledge utilization as planned social change.* In G. Beal, W. Dissanayake, & S. Konoshima (Eds.), Boulder, CA: The Westview Press.

Zaltman, G., & Moorman, C. (1988). The importance of personal trust in the use of research. *Journal of Advertising Research, 28*(3), 16-24.

DETERMINING CROSS-CULTURAL METRIC EQUIVALENCE IN SURVEY RESEARCH:

A NEW STATISTICAL TEST

Michael R. Mullen, George R. Milne, and
Nicholas M. Didow

ABSTRACT

Recent research (Mullen & Didow, 1991; Mullen, 1995) has
questioned the practice of comparing means cross-nationally without
diagnosing metric equivalence. Metric equivalence is an implicit
assumption made by managers who compare central tendency and
dispersion measures of survey data from one culture to another for
market analysis and informed managerial decision-making. Optimal
scaling was proposed as a technique for examining metric equivalence
by estimating and comparing the underlying metrics for the types of
rating scales often used in survey research. This paper extends this

Advances in International Marketing, Volume 8, pages 145-157.
ISBN: 0-7623-0164-3

line of research in two important ways. First, the issue of metric equivalence is addressed for cross-cultural comparative research in addition to cross-national research. Data from a cross-cultural study are optimally scaled to demonstrate the technique and the concerns of metric equivalence for cross-cultural comparisons, whether or not they are from the same country. Second, a statistical test for evaluating the results of the optimal scaling technique in relation to metric equivalence is developed and demonstrated. The results indicate that some survey items from distinct groups are comparable and others are not.

I. INTRODUCTION

It is common practice in business research to gather information with rating scales (i.e., Likert) and to compare the results across groups (e.g., Japanese vs. Americans, Hispanics vs. Blacks, etc.). For instance, managers looking to identify meaningful market segments might compare the means on an intention to purchase questionnaire item for Italians and Germans. In order to compare the groups, statistics (e.g., means) are often used which require the assumption of metric or higher quality data even though the data often do not measure up to that standard (Perreault & Young, 1980; Srinivasan & Basu, 1989). This practice normally results in little loss of information with well developed multi-item scales (Srinivasan & Basu, 1989). However, it is based on the implicit assumption that both groups have similar underlying metrics for the rating scales being compared.

The assumption that the underlying metric for an item is necessarily equivalent across groups has been challenged in the international marketing literature (Douglas & Craig, 1983; Mullen & Didow, 1991; Mullen, 1995; Zhang & Dadzie, 1991). For instance, Mullen and Didow (1991) demonstrated that Japanese and United States respondents do not always exhibit equivalent metrics on Likert scales. The issue of metric equivalence has been labeled as an area requiring urgent attention (Aulakh & Kotabe, 1993) for international business research. In recent research, Mullen and Didow (1991) and Mullen (1995) proposed a new approach called optimal scaling for diagnosing measurement equivalence in cross-national research. His empirical demonstration showed that some survey items were metrically equivalent cross-nationally and some from the same respondents were not. However, this research relied on heuristics to interpret and judge the results regarding metric equivalence or lack thereof. The issue of a statistical test to interpret the output of the optimal scaling procedure was left for future research.

Surprisingly, the issue of metric equivalence has not been addressed in the business literature for strictly cross-cultural academic research. Researchers continue to assume that intra-country groups react to scales in the same way and that the underlying metrics are equivalent. On the contrary, field research by at least one marketing research firm, Burke Inc., has demonstrated that population subgroups often use scales differently on intention to purchase items. Based on their experience with past purchases and stated intentions, they adjust reported mean purchase intentions (for further discussion, see Bhalla & Lin, 1987; Lin et al., 1980). We believe that it is necessary to demonstrate metric equivalence for all items being compared cross-culturally as well as in international research. If the underlying metrics are not equivalent, then it is clear that it is hazardous to rely on statistics such as means which rely on the assumption of metric or higher level data.

The purpose of this paper is to replicate and extend this stream of research in two important ways. First, we challenge the practice of comparing means and other statistics (which assume metric or higher level data) across culturally distinct groups without verifying the metric equivalence of the items being compared. Drawing on data from four distinct demographic groups, we demonstrate the necessity of establishing metric equivalence in cross-cultural research, whether domestic or international, before comparing means across groups. We use the optimal scaling approach for estimating the underlying metrics of the rating scales for each culturally distinct group. Second, we answer the call for future research by presenting a statistical test to determine whether the metrics are equivalent across the groups to be compared.

First, we introduce the data to be compared across the four subgroups. Second, we follow the approach recommended by Perreault and Young (1980) and used by Mullen and Didow (1991) of dividing the data into the mutually exclusive subgroups to be compared. Third, following Mullen (1995) we estimate the underlying metrics for the rating scales for each data set on an item by item basis with Alternating Least Squares Optimal Scaling. Fourth, we extend the work of Mullen (1995) by introducing a statistical test to determine if the metrics are equivalent across groups for each item. Finally, we discuss the implications of our findings and conclude with recommendation for future research.

II. METHOD

A. Data

The data used in this analysis are drawn from a 1991 Simmons Study of American Households. From the individual level response data of over 19,000 consumers, we extracted a random sample of 800 observations for each subgroup: black men, black women, white men, and white women. In this analysis we evaluated each subgroups responses to the following items which are measures of the brand loyalty construct:

1. I always look for the brand name on the package.
2. I do not buy unknown brands merely to save money.

Each question used a 5 point rating scale with the following categories: Agree a lot=1, Agree a little=2, Not Sure=3, Disagree a little=4, Disagree a lot=5.

The means and standard deviations for the subgroups using the raw data on these two items are shown in Table 1.

This data was of interest to us for many reasons. First, the a priori respondent classifications by race and sex are known to have high

Table 1.   Group Means and Standard Deviations on Scale Items[a]

Brand Loyalty Scale Items	Black Females	Black Males	White Females	White Males
Item 1	2.85	2.94	2.69	2.67
I always look for the	(1.42)	(1.39)	(1.45)	(1.39)
brand name on the package.				
Item 2	2.63	2.65	2.45	2.57
I do not buy unknown	(1.44)	(1.38)	(1.43)	(1.44)
brands merely to save money.				

Note: [a] Standard Deviations are shown 1 parentheses, 1=agrees a lot, 5 =disagrees a lot.

validity from the professional care of the Simmons research organization. Second, the brand loyalty construct frequently receives attention from marketing researchers and from marketing managers. Third, this data set provided a substantial number of respondents even for the most closely-defined analysis subcategory.

B. Optimal Scaling

The underlying metric for a non-metric rating scale may be determined by optimally scaling respondents answers to multi-item scales for a latent variable (Young, Takane, & de Leeuw, 1978; Young, 1981). Alternating Least Squares Optimal Scaling (ALSOS) has been used by a number of business researchers to estimate the underlying metrics of non-metric data for comparing metric equivalence cross-nationally (Mullen & Didow, 1991; Mullen, 1995) and for other non-comparative purposes (Perreault & Young, 1980; Didow, Keller, Barksdale, & Franke, 1985; Didow, Perreault, & Williamson, 1983).

PRINCIPALS (SAS, 1988), a data analysis procedure which is a member of the Alternating Least Squares Optimal Scaling family of statistical techniques is used here to estimate the underlying metric. It is a general extension of principal component analysis for use with non-metric data (Young, Takane, & de Leeuw, 1978). The PRINCIPALS analysis is done using Kruskal's (1964) secondary least squares monotonic transformation as recommended by Perreault and Young (1980) and Young (1981) for categorical, ordinal level data. The latent variable we consider is brand loyalty with the two items presented above as measures.

The optimally scaled value (OSV) for each of the five response categories of the two items are shown in Table 2 by subgroup. The raw or original ordinal categories are the column headings and the OSVs are reported in the cells of the table. The underlying metrics can now be compared across groups by examining the OSVs for each raw category. We can examine the OSVs by subgroup for the first item by looking at the top half of Table 2. For instance, the response category 4 was rescaled to 3.81 and category 5 to 5.28 for black males but to 3.58 and 5.12, respectively, for black females. The pattern exhibited by the OSVs for response categories 2 and 3 for black males were both rescaled to 2.37. The black males apparently did not discriminate between these response categories. On the other hand,

Table 2.   Optimally Scaled Values for Five Response
Categories by Group and Item

	Response Categories				
	1	*2*	*3*	*4*	*5*
Item 1					
Black Females	.91	2.10	3.58	3.58	5.12
Black Males	1.00	2.37	2.37	3.81	5.28
White Females	.98	2.33	2.33	3.64	5.37
White Males	.91	2.04	3.73	3.73	4.98
Item 2					
Black Females	1.07	2.00	3.38	3.38	5.31
Black Males	.91	2.34	2.34	4.00	5.04
White Females	1.02	2.21	2.21	3.68	5.35
White Males	1.00	2.07	3.52	3.52	5.32

the relative OSVs for black females were 2.10 and 3.58. More detailed descriptions of the general interpretation of OSVs from the PRINCIPALS procedure can be found in Didow et al. (1985) and Didow, Perreault and Williamson (1983).

To compare the underlying metrics for the four subgroups a researcher would examine the differences in OSVs. Previously, the only approach for determining meaningful differences in metric equivalence across groups was by "eyeballing" the patterns of OSV (see Mullen, 1995). In the next section, we present a statistical test for evaluating differences in metric equivalence across groups.

C. A Statistical Test To Determine Metric Equivalence

To evaluate differences in metric equivalence between two groups, we use the Kolmogorov-Smirnov test (Massey, 1951) to compare the pooled Cumulative Distribution Function (CDF) for the combined sample under different metric assumptions. This test investigates whether different demographic segments have statistically significant differences in metric equivalence for the response categories in a questionnaire item.

Our application of the Kolmogorov-Smirnov procedure is described with a short example. To begin, consider the second item which has 5 response categories for black females and black males. Table 3 shows the OSVs for these two separate demographic segments and reports the pooled frequency distribution of the answers to the item for the two groups.

Table 3.   Example of Comparing Two Groups on One Item

	Response Categories				
	1	*2*	*3*	*4*	*5*
Item 2					
Black Females (*N*=800)	1.07	2.00	3.38	3.38	5.31
Black Males (*N*=800)	.91	2.34	2.34	4.00	5.04
Pooled Frequency distribution	.259	.309	.078	.226	.129

The Kolmogorov-Smirnov test involves the comparison of one cumulative density function (CDF) with another (see Winkler & Hayes, 1975 for a more complete discussion). To compare the differences in OSVs between two groups, we examine the goodness of fit between the pooled CDF scaled with one group's metric to the pooled CDF scaled with the other group's metric. If the metrics between the groups are equivalent, we would expect the two CDFs to be very similar. Any differences would point out situations where the groups' metrics varied. The statistic used to measure the difference between the CDF's is:

$$D=maximum\ F1(x)\text{-}F2(x)\ | \qquad (1)$$

where $F1(x)$ and $F2(x)$ are the CDFs under metric assumptions of group 1 and 2, respectively. The test is one tailed and the maximum value between the CDFs is compared to a critical value. When n is 35, the critical value for D is 1.63 at the .01 level, 1.36 at the .05 level, and 1.22 at the .10 level (Massey, 1951, p. 70).

To use the Kolmogorov-Smirnov test, the first step involves calculating the CDFs for the groups being compared. The maximum difference between any two groups' CDFs is found by evaluating the differences in the CDFs at each OSV value reported. For example, when comparing the differences between black males and black females (see Table 3), the differences in their CDFs would be estimated for each distinct OSV. In this case there are 8 unique OSV between the two groups.

The densities $[F(x)]$ for the OSVs for black females and black males are reported in Table 4. The largest difference between the CDFs is the F(x) at the OSV for black females where x=3.38 which is .854 (see Table 3 above). The $F(x)$ for black males is .788, which is found by interpolating between the reported densities at x=2.34 and 4.

Table 4. Calculations for D-statistic Between Black
Females and Black Males

x	Black Females F(x)	Black Males F(x)	Difference
0.00	0.000	0.000	0.000
.91	.225[a]	.264	0.039
1.07	.264	.310[a]	0.046
2.00	.567	.578[a]	0.011
2.34	.638[a]	.676	0.038
3.38	.854	.788[a]	0.066
4.00	.901[a]	.854	0.047
5.04	.980[a]	1.000	0.020
5.31	1.000	1.000	0.000

Note: [a] Interpolated values.

For more complete discussion of the interpolation procedure see the
Appendix. Using Equation 1, D is the absolute maximum difference
in the densities where $x=3.38$: $|.854-.788|= 0.066$. Therefore, the
Kolmogorov-Smirnov D statistic is .066. In this case, D is statistically
significant at the .01 level.

III. EMPIRICAL RESULTS

The statistical test to determine metric equivalence was applied across
the four demographic segments resulting in six comparisons for each
item. We first examine whether each of the four groups OSVs are
different than the original 5 response categories for each item. To
make this comparison, the pooled CDF across the four groups are
used. Then, CDFs using each group's metric (OSV) are compared
to CDFs using the response categories. The results, reported in Table
5 show that all groups have OSVs which are statistically significantly

Table 5. Comparison of Groups' Metrics to
Original Response Categories[a]

	Kolmogorov-Smirnov D Statistic	
Group	Item 1	Item 2
Black Females	.104	.116
Black Males	.104	.074
White Females	.121	.110
White Males	.091	.090

Note: [a] The D Statistic is signficant at .01 level for each group.

Table 6.   Comparison of Optimally Scaled Values Between Groups

	Kolmogorov-Smirnov D Statistic	
Groups Compared	Item 1	Item 2
Black Female vs. Black Males	.053[a]	.066[b]
Black Female vs. White Females	.042	.040
Black Female vs. White Males	.029	.027
Black Males vs. White Females	.030	.035
Black Males vs. White Males	.043	.065[b]
White Females vs. White Males	.032	.050[a]

Notes: [a] $p < .05$
     [b] $p < .01$

different than the original 1-5 values for both items. Therefore, it is not reasonable to assume that the response categories represent metric scales with equally spaced intervals. This would not be an important problem if all of the groups have similar underlying metrics which we investigate next.

Six paired comparisons per item are made to assess the metric equivalence across groups. For each comparison, we use the pooled CDF for the two groups being examined. As shown in Table 6, there are statistically significant differences between black females vs. black males on both items and black males vs. white males and white females vs. white males on the second item.

IV. DISCUSSION

There are two important limitations which need to be acknowledged. First, optimal scaling based on the procedures used here require samples of at least 50 and preferably 100 observations to produce stable estimates of the OSVs (Didow & Mullen, 1992). Second, the Kolmogorov-Smirnov test may require large samples to be powerful enough to detect important differences in the relative underlying metrics because the denominator of the statistic consists of the square root of the sample size.

Nonetheless, the findings of this study demonstrate the usefulness of ALSOS and the PRINCIPALS procedure for exploring metric equivalence by allowing researchers to look at the underlying metrics of the same items for culturally distinct groups. The Kolmogorov-Smirnov test was introduced as a statistical test to determine whether or not the metrics are equivalent. If a researcher finds that the underlying metrics for rating scales are not equivalent across groups, then it would clearly be inappropriate to use statistics to compare results across groups which rely on the assumption of metric or higher level data. In our empirical study, we show that the items are metrically equivalent across groups in 8 of 12 paired comparisons. However, it would be very hazardous to compare the mean responses of black females vs. black males on either question or to compare means for black males vs. white males or white females vs. white males on the second question.

Unfortunately, we can at this point offer no post hoc solution where items fail the test of metric equivalence. A priori strategies and safeguards and post hoc statistical solutions, adjustments, and transformations are clearly directions for future research in this area.

Several possible solutions to measure inequivalence can be considered a priori and implemented. If metric equivalence is a potential problem, researchers can give extra attention to describing and anchoring the scales (Zhang & Dadzie, 1991). Examples may also help subjects respond to the scales in the same ways (Mullen, 1995). Response equivalence may be promoted by using the same data collection procedures for each group (Sekaran, 1983) and using the same researcher to collect the data (Sekaran & Martin, 1982). Bhalla and Lin (1987) recommend generating questionnaires with two or three times the required number of items. Then the traditional practice of purification by deletion of inequivalent items from the comparative analysis can be used.

There are several approaches for dealing with data already gathered where lack of metric equivalence remains a concern. The researcher may eliminate scaling as a consideration by standardizing the data and limiting the analysis to comparing measures of association. However, this remedy makes comparisons of mean differences meaningless. Kotabe, Duhan, Smith, and Wilson (1991) use a variation of this approach. They standardize the data by respondent rather than by variable which produces a relative mean for each group on each item. The authors use these standardized means for relative, rather than absolute comparison of means. Bhalla and Lin (1987) suggest adjusting scores based on experience.

Other future research is needed to assess the efficacy of our approaches in international marketing settings. A good study in this respect would have multi-item measures of well-developed marketing constructs obtained in similar settings and procedures from a large number of homogeneous respondents from different nations at the same general time period. The research should furthermore illustrate how the managerial implications drawn from the problematic data would be substantively different from implications drawn from data with metric equivalence. Large scale simulations, as well as survey data, may be appropriate strategies to pursue this line of research in the future.

V. CONCLUSION

In this paper we challenged the established practice of comparing data from culturally distinct groups with statistics which assume metric or higher level data without first establishing metric equivalence. We demonstrated a practical approach to estimate the underlying metrics and a statistical test for establishing metric equivalence. The robustness of our approach needs to be investigated with other a priori known groups. Further, statistical tests with greater power and post hoc statistical adjustments and transformations may also need to be developed to help researchers and managers who are faced with cross-cultural data that fails to meet the assumption of metric equivalence. Nonetheless, this paper makes an important contribution by raising cautions for cross-cultural, intra-national business researchers on this important issue, and by moving our ability to diagnose metric equivalence beyond the realm of subjective judgement.

APPENDIX

In this appendix we describe the procedure used to calculate the maximum absolute difference between CDFs that have different OSVs. The first step was to identify the possible points where maximum differences could occur. Since each CDF was comprised of line segments of varying slopes, the problem reduced to calculating the maximum differences between line segments across the two CDFS. It can be shown that the maximum difference only occurs for x values corresponding to the end points of a line segment associated with either of the CDFs. As can be see in the following equation, the smallest or largest difference in the line segments of the CDF being compared depends on the difference in slopes between the two groups.

$$y1-y2=(a1-a2) + (b1-b2)x. \qquad (2)$$

The second step involved estimating $F(x)$ for unobserved x values through linear interpolation.

In the third step we calculated the differences in $F(x)$ at all the x values where the slope in the CDFs changed for one of the two groups.

REFERENCES

Aulakh, P. S., & Kotabe, M. (1993). An assessment of theoretical and methodological developments in international marketing: 1980-1990. *Journal of International Marketing, 1*(2), 5-28.

Bhalla, G., & Lin, L.Y.S. (1987). Cross cultural marketing research: A discussion of equivalence issues and measurement strategies. *Psychology and Marketing, 4*(4), 275-285.

Didow, N. M., Keller, K. L., Barksdale, H.C., Jr., & Franke, G.R. (1985). Improving measure quality by alternating least squares optimal scaling. *Journal of Marketing Research, 22*(February), 30-40.

Didow, N. M., & Mullen, M.R. (1992). Sample size effects on the stability of optimal scaling estimates - a preliminary investigation. In R.P. Leone & V. Kumar (Eds.), *Enhancing knowledge development in marketing* (Vol. 3, pp. 290-295). AMA Educators' Proceedings.

Didow, N. M., Perreault Jr., W.D., & Williamson, N.C. (1983). A cross-sectional optimal scaling analysis of the index of consumer sentiment. *Journal of Consumer Research, 10*(December), 339-347.

Douglas, S.P., & Craig, S. (1983). *International marketing research.* Englewood Cliffs, NJ: Prentice Hall.

Kotabe, M., Duhan, D.F., Smith, D.K., & Wilson, D.R. (1991). The perceived veracity of PIMS strategy principles in Japan: An empirical enquiry. *Journal of Marketing, 55*(1), 26-41.

Kruskal, J.B. (1964). Multidimensional scaling by optimizing goodness of fit to a nonmetric hypothesis. *Psychometrika, 29*(1), 1-27.

Lin, L., McKenna, W., Rhodes, R., & Wilson, S. (1980). New product analysis and testing. In K.J. Albert (Ed.), *Handbook of business problem solving* (pp. 4-27). New York: McGraw-Hill.

Massey, F. J. (1951). The Kolmogorov-Smirnov Test for goodness of fit. *Journal of the American Statistical Association, 46.*

Mullen, M. R. (1995). Diagnosing measurement equivalence in cross-national research. *Journal of International Business Studies, 26*(3), 631-654.

Mullen, M. R., & Didow, N. M. (1991). Are cross cultural research data comparable? Optimal scaling provides useful evidence. In Gilly et al. (Eds.), *Enhancing knowledge development in marketing* (Vol. 2, pp. 608-609). AMA Educators' Proceedings.

Perreault, W. D. & Young, F.W. (1980). Alternating least squares optimal scaling: Analysis of nonmetric data in marketing research. *Journal of Marketing Research, 27*(February), 1-13.

SAS Institute, Inc. (1988). SAS Technical Report P-179: Additional SAS/Stat Procedures, release 6.03. Cary, NC: Sas Institute, Inc.

Sekaran, U. (1983). Methodological and theoretical issues and advancements in cross-cultural research. *Journal of International Business Studies*, (Fall), 61-73.

Sekaran, U. & Martin, H.J. (1982). An examination of the psychometric properties of some commonly researched variables in two cultures. *Journal of International Business Studies, 13*(Spring), 51-66.

Srinivasan, V. & Basu, A.K. (1989). The metric quality of ordered categorical data. *Marketing Science*, 8(3), 205-230.

Winkler, R. L. & Hays, W.L. (1975). *Statistics: Probability, inference, and decision.* New York: Holt, Rhinehart, and Winston.

Young, F. W. (1981). Quantitative analysis of qualitative data. *Psychometrika, 46*(4), 357-388.

Young, F. W., Takane, Y., & de Leeuw, J. (1978). The principal components of mixed measurement data: An alternating least squares method-with optimal scaling features. *Psychometrika, 43*(June), 279-282.

Zhang, L. & Dadzie, K.Q. (1991). Developing more meaningful and accurate measurement models in global marketing research: An empirical illustration. In Gilly et al. (Eds.), *Enhancing knowledge development in marketing* (Vol. 2, pp. 610-611)..MA Educators' Proceedings.

EXPORT PRICING STRATEGY-PERFORMANCE RELATIONSHIP:

A CONCEPTUAL FRAMEWORK

M.B. Myers and S. Tamer Cavusgil

ABSTRACT

Within the realm of international marketing management, pricing strategies and practices have often been identified as neglected areas of research when compared to other marketing variables such as products, promotion and advertising, and channels of distribution. The reason for the neglect can be attributed to the complex nature of the pricing issue, as well as the reluctance of managers to discuss their pricing strategies. Though the relationship between export marketing strategy and export performance has been addressed in past studies, the role of export pricing strategies in the success of export ventures is largely unexplored. This paper attempts to identify the factors that influence the export pricing process and why firms adopt the export pricing strategies that they do. A conceptual framework

Advances in International Marketing, Volume 8, pages 159-178.
Copyright © 1996 by JAI Press Inc.
All rights of reproduction in any form reserved.
ISBN: 0-7623-0164-3

for export pricing decisions is offered. The overall objective is to lay the conceptual foundation for subsequent empirical research that delves into the relationship between firm strategies in international pricing and performance.

I. INTRODUCTION

Over the past two decades the literature addressing the export behavior of firms has seen substantial growth. Much of this literature focuses on such issues as barriers to exporting, market entry strategies, and the impact of environmental factors on exporting. This literature has been reviewed by Bilkey (1978), Cavusgil and Nevin (1981), Li, and Cavusgil (1991), and Aaby and Slater (1989). While the increased research in these areas is reassuring, there has been relatively little work done regarding the export marketing decision variables and how they affect firms' export performance (Koh & Robicheaux, 1988).

Of all the marketing decision variables it is perhaps pricing which has been the most ignored by researchers (Graham & Gronhaug, 1989) despite being repeatedly identified as a problem area for international managers. Pricing was identified as a neglected area of international marketing management in 1981 (Cavusgil and Nevin) and again in 1991 (Li and Cavusgil). Empirical works to date have remained limited.

Businesses operating in a global environment must rely on a systematic procedure for pricing decisions. Pricing policies and objectives, both explicit and implicit, are an important part of the operation of these firms (Samiee, 1987). The purpose of this article is to address the issue of export pricing within the framework of the managerial decision making process. Based on a review of the existing literature, the article offers a conceptual framework for pricing. It also attempts to delineate constructs within this decision making framework.

II. EXISTING RESEARCH STREAMS IN PRICING

In addressing the issue of pricing, researchers have focused on four major topic areas covering a wide range of factors under the pricing umbrella: micro-economic literature on price, consumer perceptions and reactions to pricing, intra-corporate pricing, and company practice in international pricing. Neo-classical pricing research was based on the assumption of profit maximization as the firm's objective and the use of marginal analysis as the method to arrive at optimal price-output optimizations (Diamantopoulos & Mathews, 1995, p. 8). Both global and domestic economic environments have been linked to the pricing practices of the firm and, in turn, a wide range of pricing theories based upon the objectives of the firm have emerged. These include Williamson's (1964) managerial discretion theory, sales revenue maximization theory, and sales growth maximization theory (Baumol, 1958, 1962; Lynn, 1968), and conventional price theory (Ott, 1979). These studies and their relationship to the organizational behavior of the firm laid a groundwork for successive research in this area. Economic factors external to the firm have also resulted in a large body of literature, particularly that addressing the impact of foreign currency fluctuations on pricing. Research by Clague and Grossfield (1974), Choi (1986), Knetter (1994), Demirag (1988) and many others have addressed the pricing behavior resulting from operating in a dynamic currency environment.

According to Diamantopoulos and Mathews (1995), an imbalance in marketing literature exists in that a disproportionate amount of research has focused on the buyers' perceptions of and reactions to price. Consumer behaviorists have addressed at length such issues as price awareness, price as a proxy to quality, asymmetry of price information, price elasticity within markets, and price information processing among consumers. Comprehensive reviews of this literature are provided by Monroe (1990) and Nagle (1987), among others. This research show that, contrary to the assumptions of economists, buyers are not perfectly rational and do not have perfect information when purchasing products (Morris & Morris, 1990). The average consumer takes into consideration a wide variety of factors in every purchase-related decision, and over the decades researchers have focused extensively on these decision making processes, as well as the emotional and psychological variables that are involved in those decisions, not only in the marketing literature, but also in psychology and sociology.

Intra-corporate pricing, or transfer pricing, has received increased attention consistently over the years due to the prevalence of multinational operations, and the rising number of cooperative arrangements and multiple-location facilities found throughout the world. In order to successfully compete in the global marketplace, the multinational firm must confront a complex set of political factors, tax regulations, import-export restrictions, and fund transfer restrictions, as well as other challenges associated with operating in multiple international markets (Al-Eryani, Alam, & Akhter, 1990). Concurrently, transfer pricing policy must reward the management of overseas subsidiaries and cooperative ventures.

Studies have shown that firms have often developed an international transfer pricing policy based on conventional pricing practices such as cost-plus (Tang, 1979, Greene & Duerr, 1970), market pricing (Arpan, 1971), or negotiated pricing (Greene & Duerr, 1970), and that these practices often differ according to the home country of the firm. Studies by Lecraw (1985) and Schulman (1969) have also addressed the use of transfer prices to circumvent custom duties and taxes as well as profit repatriation restrictions.

The foundations laid by these research streams have led to an increased interest in the role of pricing in overall market performance of the firm. The micro-economic, consumer behavior, and intra-corporate pricing literature have contributed greatly to the understanding of the pricing of goods and services in the marketplace. However, a significant gap remains between these research streams and research regarding international pricing strategy and its role in export performance, or the specific challenges faced by exporting firms in pricing their products. It is our goal to address the role of the international pricing practices of the firm and their relationship to export performance, and to identify the factors that influence the export pricing process.

A. Company Practices in International Pricing

Given the critical nature of pricing decisions, one would expect a wide range of studies concerning company practices in international pricing. As noted, however, relatively few studies have been conducted on this issue. According to Walters (1989), most of the work that has been done in this area concerns the transfer pricing problem in multinational corporations (Al-Eryani, Alam, & Akhter, 1990; Arpan, 1972). The affect of overseas market environment on pricing has also received attention, and studies have included pricing in developing countries, pricing in specific markets, and price controls overseas (Walters, 1989). Several pricing decision models have resulted from the studies on fluctuating exchange rates, including Grossfield and Clague (1974). Contingency models of the international pricing decision process have been developed by several authors (Walters, 1990; Rao, 1984), and the literature includes an application of a descriptive modeling approach in an overseas pricing situation (Farley, Hulbert, & Weinstein, 1980). Samiee (1987) discovered that firms outside the United States considered the pricing of their products to be significantly less important than U.S. firms, with a greater degree of autonomy afforded to the local managers. In a study in 1988 Lancioni states that international price setting should be done on two different levels: the external level (customers, competition, governmental regulations), and internal levels (cost reduction, ROI levels, and sales volume requirements), and that both environments must be taken into account when setting prices in international marketing.

Within the field of international pricing, company practices in *export* pricing have received even less attention than other topics, and the role of this important element in export performance remains largely unexplored.

III. THE ROLE OF PRICING STRATEGY IN EXPORT PERFORMANCE

Exporting can be conceptualized as a strategic response by management to the interplay of internal and external forces (Cavusgil & Zou, 1994, p. 3). Internal forces relate to organizational characteristics such as the firm and product, and external forces include industry and export market characteristics. The degree of coalignment of these forces with the marketing strategy of the firm determines the results of the export performance, in line with the strategy-environment coalignment principle (Porter, 1980; Aldrich, 1979).

Aaby and Slater (1989) suggest that export performance is directly influenced by a firm's business strategy. Historically, exporting has been seen as a means of realizing the economic goals of the firm, such as sales and profits, and variety of measures have been used in past studies to evaluate export performance (e.g.,

Axinn, 1988; Evangalista, 1994). Performance viewed in this manner fails to relate the firm's attempt to attain its *strategic* and *competitive* goals in the overseas market (Cavusgil & Zou, 1994). The majority of past studies have addressed the direct relationship between firm, product, industry, and international market factors, ignoring the role of export market strategy in firm performance. With increasing competition in international markets, the strategic benefits of exporting will become as important as the economic aspects, and therefore export marketing strategy should be emphasized in future research as a critical determinant of firm performance.

Since export performance is directly influenced by strategy, the individual variables within export strategy need be addressed in order to better ascertain their effect on the decision making process of the firm. Cavusgil (1983) has identified four variables which influence successful export marketing: (1) basic company offering, (2) Contractual links with foreign distributors and agents, (3) promotion, and (4) *pricing*. It is the influence of the firm's export pricing strategies on export market performance which we seek to understand, that is, the statistical explanatory power of the linkage between these two critical constructs.

A variety of studies focusing on the role of marketing variables in exporting success have found that pricing plays a critical role in export performance. Kirpalani and Macintosh (1980) found that a firm's pricing strategy is significantly associated with export performance. Bilkey (1982) also found that export prices played an important role in exporting success in a study that explored variables associated with export profitability. Koh and Robicheaux (1988) conducted a study similar to Bilkey and concluded that export pricing is one of three variables related to export performance.

In a study of 24 midwestern companies, Cavusgil (1988) identifies six variables that influence export pricing: (1) the nature of the product or industry, (2) the location of the production facility, (3) the system of distribution, (4) the location and environment of the foreign market, (5) U.S. government regulations, and (6) the attitude of the firm's management. A review of the literature reveals that most of the existing studies that focus strictly on pricing have addressed the characteristics of the firm and the managerial environment in pricing strategies and practices, and that these studies have been relatively infrequent.

IV. A CONCEPTUAL FRAMEWORK FOR PRICING DECISIONS

By focusing on established export pricing strategy and practices as well as past research regarding the relationships of the major determinants with these strategies, we may formulate a conceptual framework designed to provide directions for future research in determining best practices for international marketing managers. Through the introduction of the key constructs within this framework (see Figure 1), we can address the relationships between the internal and external forces described by Cavusgil and Zou (1994) and export pricing strategy and practices, this to better understand the relationship between these strategies and export performance. Concurrently, this framework identifies specific factors within the constructs of past export performance models (e.g., Axinn, 1994), and is the first step toward the development of research hypotheses that will enable future research to empirically explore the export pricing strategy-export performance relationship.

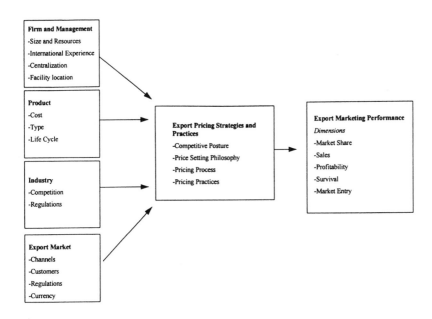

Figure 1. A Conceptual Framework for Export Pricing Decisions

V. EXPORT MARKETING PERFORMANCE

Over the years there has been an assortment of definitions of export performance used in international marketing research. Export sales level (Madsen, 1989; Cooper & Kleinschmidt, 1985; Bilkey, 1985), export sales growth (Kirpalani & Macintosh, 1980; Madsen, 1989), ratio of export sales to total sales (Axinn, 1988), and propensity to export (Kaynak & Kothari, 1984, Reid, 1986; Cavusgil, 1984) have all been used as benchmarks to evaluate the performance of firms export related activities. Most measures have focused on the economic goals of the firm, (e.g., sales and profits), rather than the strategic goals (e.g., competitive response, market expansion). Here, export marketing performance is defined as the extent to which a firm's objectives, with respect to exporting a product into a foreign market, are achieved through the planning and execution of export marketing strategy (Cavusgil & Zou, 1994). Both economic objectives and strategic objectives are included in this definition.

VI. EXPORT PRICING STRATEGY AND PRACTICES

Firms venturing abroad must rely on a systematic procedure for their pricing decisions; pricing policies, whether explicit or implicit, are very much a part of the operation of the firm (Samiee, 1987). Export pricing strategy is viewed as a systematic attempt to meet the firm's objectives through the response of the interplay of internal and external forces, and is seen as a function of product, industry, firm, market, and environmental characteristics. The types of export pricing strategies conducted by firms are extensive, and vary according to the factors associated with these determinants. Strategies range from hedging and currency choice during the transaction (exporter's, importer's, or third country), to rigid versus flexible pricing and full-cost versus predatory pricing. Figure 1 provides a conceptual framework depicting the relationship between export pricing strategies, firm performance, and various determinants of these two central constructs. This conceptualization views firm management in a proactive role; through various choices with respect to pricing for international customers, it can influence outcomes in firm performance. Some of these choices may be imposed by external factors such as export market or industry considerations. Others are entirely within the discretion of management.

A. Competitive Posture

The degree to which importance is attached to price as a competitive tool is reliant in part on whether the firm seeks competitive advantage by offering its customers a less expensive product than its competitors or by offering a differentiated product (Nagle, 1987). A firm that can offer an equal-quality product at lower cost can increase sales via opportunistic pricing, yet this advantage can only be maintained if costs can be controlled. Those firms that emphasize non-price benefits to the customer may not perceive price as a competitive tool, and a superior product often enables the firm to profit from premium prices.

Whether or not a firm perceives export pricing as a competitive tool will often be determined by the firms experience in the international markets and its emphasis on price vs. non-price benefits. International experience has been shown to be positively related to export performance (Kirpalani & Macintosh, 1980). In addressing the characteristics of the firm, Katsikeas and Morgan (1994) found that more experienced firms perceived export pricing activities more problematic than less experienced firms, and that firms of all experience levels found pricing problems to factor very highly in their export decisions. This is perhaps indicative of the realization by more experienced firms of the complex nature of export pricing and their willingness to address the issue through a comprehensive pricing strategy. Firm size advantage, including resources, will also allow the exporter to implement and execute successful pricing strategies. Larger firms tend to possess the resources that allow them to absorb initial losses incurred by pricing below full costs (Lecraw, 1984), this in order to increase market share at the expense of an "overpriced" competition.

B. Price Setting Philosophy

The philosophy adopted by the firm in setting its export prices includes such issues as pricing objectives, pricing drivers (costs, demand, competition, margins, etc.), full vs. marginal costing, and the centralization of the pricing decision.

In pricing their products, studies have shown that most exporting companies focus on a cost-centered pricing strategy, particularly that of full-cost and cost-plus (Hunt, 1969). According to Cavusgil (1988) product and resource costs influence the pricing strategies of the firm: Costs are frequently used as a basis for price determination largely because they are easily measured and provide a "bottom line" under which prices cannot go in the long term. Inputs such as resources, labor, and technology will vary across products and influence export price.

Naturally the nature and type of product will effect exporting decisions. One product characteristic which has been shown to effect pricing strategies is age. Where the product is located in its life cycle within the individual markets often determines whether the firm will use a full-cost or predatory pricing approach (Lecraw, 1984). In order to capture market share with new products in overseas markets the firm may need to price the product at less than full cost, particularly where competitive national brands are already established. .

Along with product cost, the degree and caliber of industry-wide competition is perhaps the most important factor in the firm's export pricing decision (Abratt & Pitt, 1985). Most companies will adjust price or other elements of their total offer in order to meet competitive situations (Farley, Hulbert, & Weinstein, 1980; Lecraw, 1984); this means that flexibility in product price and customer satisfaction regarding issues such as currency choices during the transaction are critical to remaining competitive within an industry. In many competitive situations the exporter will have no choice but to offer comparable currency choices as those of competitors (Piercy, 1983), whereas in industries where there is little competition the currency choice is generally the exporter's.

The location of the pricing decision within the organizational structure of the firm plays a critical role in pricing procedures (Abratt & Pitt, 1985; Clague & Grossfield, 1974). Who is responsible for the pricing decision and the degree of price-setting autonomy outside of upper-level management will determine in part whether the firm prices its products based on costs or on competition (Baker & Ryans, 1973). Sales-force personnel tend to concentrate on competitive factors that effect sales volume, while management tends to be concerned with profit margins above the total costs of the product.

C. Pricing Process

A firm's pricing process includes the frequency of the pricing review and the adjustments to the process, and flexible versus rigid export pricing.

Traditionally, the policy of an annual pricing review has been consistent with the literature (Diamantopoulos & Mathews, 1995), which posits that prices should be changed no more than once a year, enabling customers to lock in prices for their own costing and pricing purposes (Garda, 1984). This policy, however, can bring problems to the firm in two distinct ways: (1) forward buying by distributors who are aware of the price-review schedule of the firm, and (2) in a volatile international market, losses are often incurred due to the rapidly changing variables which dictate profitable pricing policies.

Farley, Hulbert, and Weinstein (1980) analyzed industrial marketing decision systems within two European firms to price and plan volumes in their production facilities. Here the authors argue that prices and volumes of each product are under continuous review since conditions constantly change in many end-use markets. Firms develop ongoing systems for volume planning; this via a forecasting system; and pricing systems, which are feedback systems triggered by perceived changes in market conditions. As competitive levels fluctuate within an industry, exporters must constantly monitor their prices in relation to the changing prices and offerings of competitive products. Concurrently, exchange rate volatility also affects the frequency of export pricing review (Cavusgil, 1988). Those firms exporting to markets with widely fluctuating currencies will by necessity increase the frequency of their review process over more stable currency situations.

Due to the complex nature of export pricing many managers have adopted the rigid cost-plus pricing strategy that is simple to follow and insures margins (Cavusgil, 1990). With the increase in global competition and the need to export to multiple markets in order to cover costs, managers are becoming increasingly aware that in order to compete they must be more flexible in pricing their products. While the adaptation of products may indeed increase the costs to the firm, *specialized* products or products with a technological edge allow the company to adopt a flexible pricing policy, since in many markets there is little or no competition and government barriers are minimal (Cavusgil, 1990).

Location of the firm's resources and subsidiaries will factor heavily into the pricing strategy (Demirag, 1988). Production facilities established in locations other than the home country will introduce logistical, labor, and regulatory concerns into the decision making process. Firms that produce overseas seeking inexpensive wage rates may incur other costs that effect final prices. However, multiple production facilities will enable the firm to produce in markets where production costs are cheapest, allowing more leeway and flexibility in the pricing of exports to its customers. By rotating production to the facility where inputs are cheapest, managers can reduce costs and modify their prices as the transaction warrants.

D. Pricing Practices

The pricing practices of the firm include pricing strategies for adapted or adopted products, pricing within the channel of distribution, uniform pricing for all markets and customers vs. pricing to local differences, choice of currency, and price escalation.

Customer satisfaction can be better met by adapting the product to the individual markets (Douglass & Craig, 1989), however the adaptability of the product to those markets (and the costs incurred during the adaptation process), along with the advantages gained by adaptation will influence the export price of the product. The standardization/adaptation issue has long been debated regarding the perceived benefits of market coverage, capacity utilization, specialty products, and market niches (Samiee & Roth, 1992). Product adaptation incurs costs in developing alternative product variations (Cavusgil, Zou, & Naidu, 1993), and these costs in turn must be reflected in the export price. Managing a series of adapted products in multiple markets calls for pricing decisions to be made closer to those markets, away from the exporter's home-base. Concurrently, sophisticated customers familiar with competitive prices and experienced in purchasing decisions will demand quick pricing decisions at the market, not at upper-level management.

Within domestic marketing literature the effect of channels and distribution processes on pricing decisions have received extensive focus. In the international environment, however, relatively little work has been done on this issue. An exception is that of Williamson and Bello (1992), who presented an empirical study of export management companies (EMCs) and the pricing methods used in transactions between EMCs and domestic producers. The study suggested that the nature of the promotional function and the type of product sold by the producer to the EMC impacts the pricing method, the services offered within the channels in overseas markets, as well as the complexity and development of those channels, will influence pricing strategy. Often control over the final price of a product is decreased as the product travels though the distribution channel, this depending on the relationships between the channel members and the exporter.

Related to traditional research regarding the influence of distribution channels on pricing decisions is the issue of uniform pricing and gray market (parallel) imports. Defined as the practice which involves the selling of trademarked products through channels of distribution that are not authorized by the trademark holder (Duhan & Sheffet, 1988), gray marketing is in effect a type of arbitrage brought about by the inflexibility of pricing in response to price and exchange rate fluctuations across markets.

The volume of gray market imports is significant, particularly in premium products and brands (Cavusgil & Sikora, 1988), and while gray markets sometimes result from unavailability of products in certain markets and ease of product movement across borders, most often substantial price differences between national markets are the cause of this phenomenon.

There are several pro-active and re-active strategies available to combat gray market effects (Cavusgil & Sikora, 1988, Cespedes, Corey, & Rangan, 1988), as prices rise and fall within individual markets (due to factors such as changing demand conditions of the consumer) the exporter may need to change prices in other markets in order to avoid parallel imports. This problem is enhanced as the firms' presence in economically diverse markets increases.

What currency a firm chooses to use in its export transactions is determined by a variety of factors. In order to meet customer demand, larger, resource-rich firms can accept more foreign currency risk than their smaller counterparts, this from to their ability to absorb potential losses due to fluctuations in the currency markets. As a firm increases its international involvement, its experience in the exporting process also increases in an incremental manner (Johansson & Vahlne, 1977; Bilkey & Tesar, 1977). As a firm gains this experience its familiarity and expertise with the complex nature of exchange rates also increases, allowing it to price exports in various currencies as dictated by regulations or the consumer. Perhaps more importantly, the ability to source products from multiple-country locations gives the firm a tremendous advantage in responding to changes in exchange rates. When, for example, the home currency is appreciating, it can choose to export from a production base where the exchange rate is more favorable.

Import policies and trade barriers in international markets have a significant effect on export pricing decisions (Johannson & Erickson, 1985). In markets where price escalation results from import barriers, firms may not be able to experience large profit margins due to the already inflated price of their product. Price-quality relationships in overseas markets will vary significantly since all imported products may suffer from price escalation effects. The strategy options open to the firm may be limited in order to maintain affordable products for the customer. With the increased tension between nations over trading policies, intellectual property rights, and non-tariff barriers, anti-dumping legislation has become an highly important topic with an obvious tie to export pricing. Anti-dumping laws regarding specific products will affect the pricing decisions of the firm, and although Joelson and Wilson (1992) offer answers to commonly asked questions regarding this topic more in-depth studies that focus on these regulations are called for.

The characteristics of the international market provide firms with both opportunities and dangers. Export pricing strategies must take into account these characteristics if the firm is to operate in this dichotomous environment. While managers often price their exports according to a cost-based strategy, Piercy (1981) found that certain firms base their pricing strategy on the individual target markets. In his study of British exporters, Piercy found that almost two-thirds of industrial exporters emphasized a market based approach rather than a cost-based strategy.

VII. PROPOSITIONS AND DIRECTIONS FOR FUTURE RESEARCH

Future research ought to investigate the complex set of interrelationships implied by this conceptualization. To what extent are management strategy choices and pricing practices responsible for firm performance? What are "best" practices in international pricing? What role do firm, product, industry, international market, and other environmental variables play in setting export pricing strategies? How do managers make decisions about international pricing? How much information is utilized in this process? How systematic is the process? These and similar questions require empirical verification through future studies.

Several general propositions can assist in the future development of research hypotheses and empirical study. The relationship between export pricing practices and strategies and export marketing performance need be the goal of subsequent research:

Proposition 1. The export marketing performance of the firm is expected to be significantly influenced by the export pricing strategies of the firm.

Concurrently, within each of the four major constructs, a variety of factors is expected to have an effect on firm pricing strategies. Similar to the export performance model of Axinn (1994) and the internal/external influences discussed by Cavusgil and Zou (1994), these factors can be categorized as firm and product specific factors (internal), and industry and market specific factors (external). Addressing firm specific internal factors first:

Proposition 2. The export pricing strategies adopted by the firm are expected to be significantly influenced by:

a. the international experience of the firm
b. the size of the firm
c. the degree of centralized decision making in the firm
d. the location of the firm's facilities

Similarly, product specific factors will influence pricing strategies:

Proposition 3.   The export pricing strategies adopted by the firm are expected to be significantly influence by:

a. the type of product exported
b. the costs related to the product exported
c. whether the firm is exporting a product line or a single product

External factors affecting exporting decisions are well documented, yet how these factors affect export pricing decisions is yet to be determined:

Proposition 4.   The export pricing strategies adopted by the firm are expected to be significantly influenced by:

a. the degree of competition within the industry
b. exchange-rate volatility
c. channel complexity within the export market
d. governmental regulations
c. gray market activity and parallel imports

In order to succeed in overseas markets, managers must develop pricing strategies which address a variety of factors that are not found in domestic markets. What is considered best practices, however, may vary widely according to the type of firm participating in the markets, the location of that firm's assets, the product type, industry type, level of competition, industry and market regulations, structure of distribution channels, and consumer. The impact of these influencing variables on the pricing strategy of the firm is still largely unexplored; and future research is necessary in order to determine the relationships between these issues and productive export pricing strategies, as well as with the overall performance of the export ventures of the firm.

REFERENCES

Aaby, N., & Slater, S.F. (1989). Management influences on export performance: A review of empirical literature 1978-88. *International Marketing Review, 6*(4), 7-26.

Abratt, R., & Pitt, L.F. (1985). Pricing practices in two industries. *Industrial Marketing Management, 14*, 301-306.

Aldrich, H. (1979). *Organizations and environments.* Englewood Cliffs, NJ: Prentice-Hall.

Al-Eryani, M. F., Alam, P., & Akhter, S.H. (1990). Transfer pricing determinants of U.S. multi-nationals. *Journal of International Business Studies, 21*(3), 409-425.

Anderson, C., & Zeithaml, C.P. (1984). Stage of product life cycle, business strategy, and business performance. *Academy of Management Journal, 27*, 5-24.

Arpan, J. (1973). Multi-national firm pricing in international markets. *Sloan Management Review, 15*(Winter), 1-9.

Axinn, C.N. (1994). International perspectives on export marketing. In S.T. Cavusgil (Ed.), *Advances in International Marketing* (Vol. 6, pp. xi-xvi). Greenwich, CT: JAI Press.

Axinn, C.N. (1988). Export performance: Do managerial perceptions make a difference? *International Marketing Review, 5*(Summer), 61-71.

Baker, J.C., & Ryans, J.K. (1973). Some aspects of international pricing: A neglected area of management policy. *Management Decisions,* (Summer), 177-182.

Baumol, W.J. (1958). On the theory of the oligopoly. *Economica, 25*(August), 187-198.

Bilkey, W.J. (1982). Variables associated with export profitability. *Journal of International Business Studies, 13*(2), 39-55.

Bilkey, W.J. (1978). An attempted integration of literature on the export behavior of firms. *Journal of International Business Studies, 9*, 33-46.

Bilkey, W.J., & Tesar, G. (1977). The export behaviour of smaller-sized Wisconsin manufacturing firms. *Journal of International Business Studies, 8*(1), 93-98.

Buzzell, R.D. (1968). Can you standardize multinational marketing? *Harvard Business Review, 49*(November-December), 102-113.

Cavusgil, S. T., & Nevin, J.R. (1981). State-of-the-art in international marketing. In *Review of Marketing* (pp. 309-312). Chicago: American Marketing Association.

Cavusgil, S. T. (1983). Success factors in export marketing: An empirical analysis. *Journal of International Marketing and Marketing Research, 8*(2), 63-73.

Cavusgil, S. T. (1984). Organizational characteristics associated with export activity. *Journal of Management Studies, 21*(1), 3-22.

Cavusgil, S. T. (1988). Unravelling the mystique of export pricing. *Business Horizons, 31*(3), 54-63.

Cavusgil, S. T. (1990). Pricing for global markets. In *Marketing strategies for global growth and competitiveness* (pp. 57-90). New York: Business International Corp.

Cavusgil, S. T., & Sikora, E. (1988). How multinationals can counter gray-market imports. *Columbia Journal of World Business*, (November/December), 27-33.

Cavusgil, S. T., Zou, S., & Naidu, G.M. (1993). Product and promotion adaptation in export ventures: An empirical investigation. *Journal of International Business Studies, 24*(3), 479-506.

Cavusgil, S. T. (1994). Marketing strategy-performance relationship: An investigation of the empirical link in export market ventures. *Journal of Marketing, 58*(January), 1-21.

Cespedes, F. V., Corey, R.E., & Rangan, K.V. (1988). Gray markets: Causes and cures. *Harvard Business Review, 66*(4), 75-82.

Choi, J.J. (1986). A model of firm valuation with exchange exposure. *Journal of International Business Studies, 17*(2), 153-160.

Clague, L., & Grossfield, R. (1974). Export pricing in a floating rate world. *Columbia Journal of World Business*, (Winter), 17-22.

Cooper, R.G., & Kleinschmidt, E.J. (1985). The impact of export strategy on export sales performance. *Journal of International Business Studies, 16*(Spring), 37-55.

Demirag, I. (1988). Assessing foreign subsidiary performance: The currency choice of U.K. MNCs. *Journal of International Business Studies, 17*(2), 257-275.

Diamantopoulos, A., & Mathews, B. (1995). *Making pricing decisions: A study of managerial practice*. London: Chapman and Hall.

Douglass, S.P., & Craig, C.S. (1989). Evolution of global marketing strategy: Scale, scope, and synergy. *Columbia Journal of World Business*, (Fall), 47-58.

Duhan, D., & Sheffet, M.J. (1988). Gray markets and the legal status of parallel importation. *Journal of Marketing, 52*(3), 75-83.

Evangalista, F. (1994). Export performance and its determinants: Some empirical evidence from Australian manufacturing firms. In S.T. Cavusgil (Ed.), *Advances in International Marketing* (Vol. 6, pp. 207-229). Greenwich, CT: JAI Press.

Farley, J.U., Hulbert, J.M., & Weinstein, D. (1980). Price setting and volume planning by two European industrial companies: A study and comparison of decision processes. *Journal of Marketing, 44*(Winter), 46-54.

Garda, R.A. (1984). Strategy vs. tactics in industrial pricing. *The McKinsey Quarterly*, (Winter), 49-64.

Greene, J., & Duerr, M.G. (1970). *Intercompany transactions in the multinational firm*. New York, NY: Conference Board.

Gronhaug, K., & Graham, J.L. (1987). International marketing research revisited. In S.T. Cavusgil (Ed.), *Advances in International Marketing* (Vol. 2, pp. 121-137). Greenwich, CT: JAI Press.

Hunt, H. G. (1969). Export management in medium sized engineering firms. *Journal of Management Studies, 6*(1), 33-44.

Joelson, M., & Wilson, R. (1992). An international antidumping primer: Know the rules before an antidumping complaint arrives. *Journal of European Business, 3*(4), 53-65.

Johansson, J.K., & Erickson, G. (1985). Price-quality relationship and trade barriers. *International Marketing Review, 2*(3), 52-63.

Johanson, J., & Vahlne, J. (1977). The internationalization process of the firm: A model of knowledge development and increasing foreign market commitments. *Journal of International Business Studies, 8*(Spring/Summer), 23-32.

Karikari, J. (1988). International competitiveness and industry pricing in Canadian manufacturing. *Canadian Journal of Economics, 21*(2), 411-427.

Katsikeas, C., & Morgan, R.E. (1994). Differences in perceptions of exporting problems based on firm size and export market experience. *European Journal of Marketing, 28*(5), 17-35.

Kaynak, E., & Kothari, V. (1984). Export behavior of small and medium sized manufacturers: Some policy guidelines for international marketers. *Management International Review, 24*(2), 61-69.

Kirpalani, V.H., & Macintosh, N.B. (1980). International marketing effectiveness of technology oriented small firms. *Journal of International Business Studies, 112*(Winter), 81-90.

Knetter, M. M. (1994). Is export price adjustment asymmetric?: Evaluating the market share and marketing bottleneck hypothesis. *Journal of International Money and Finance, 13*(1), February, 13-68.

Knetter, M. M. (1989). Price discrimination by U.S. and German exporters. *American Economic Review, 79*(1), 198-210.

Koh, A., & Robicheaux, R.A. (1988). Variations in export performance due to differences in export marketing strategy: Implications for industrial marketers. *Journal of Business Research, 17*(3), 249-258.

Lancioni, R. A. (1988). The importance of price in international business development. *Asia Pacific Journal of Business Logistics, 1*(1).

Lecraw, D. J. (1984). Pricing strategies of transnational corporations. *Asia Pacific Journal of Management,* (January), 112-119.

Li, T., & Cavusgil, S.T. (1991). International marketing: A classification of research streams and assessment of their development since 1982. *American Marketing Association Summer Educator's Conference Proceedings,* 592-607.

Lynn, R.A. (1968). Unit volume as a goal for pricing. *Journal of Marketing, 32*(October), 34-39.

Madsen, T. K. (1989). Successful export marketing management: Some empirical evidence. *International Marketing Review, 6*(4), 41-57.

Monroe, K. B. (1990). *Pricing: Making profitable decisions.* New York: McGraw-Hill.

Morris, M.H., & Morris, G. (1990). *Market oriented pricing.* New York: Quorum.

Nagle, T. (1987). *The strategy and tactics of pricing.* Englewood Cliffs, NJ: Prentice-Hall.

Ott, A.E. (1979). *Grundzuege der preistheorie.* Vandenhoeck und Ruprecht: Goettingen.

Piercy, N. (1981). British export market selection and pricing. *Industrial Marketing Management,* (October), 287-297.

Porter, M. E. (1980). *Competitive strategy. techniques for analyzing industries and competitions.* New York: The Free Press.

Rao, V.R. (1984). Pricing research in marketing: The state of the art. *Journal of Business, 57*(1), 39-60.

Reid, S.D. (1986). Is technology linked with export performance in small firms? In Hubner (Ed.), *The art and science of innovation management.* Amsterdam: Elsevier Science Publication.

Samiee, S. (1987). Pricing in marketing strategies of U.S. and foreign based companies. *Journal of Business Research, 15,*(March), 17-30.

Samiee, S., & Roth, K. (1992). The influence of global marketing standardization on performance. *Journal of Marketing, 56*(2), 1-17.

Schulman, J. (1967). When the price is wrong-by design. *Columbia Journal of World Business, 4*(May-June), 69-76.

Tang, R.Y.W. (1979). *Transfer Pricing Practices in the United States and Japan.* New York: Praeger Publishers.

Walters, P.G.P. (1989). A framework for export pricing decisions. *Journal of Global Marketing, 2*(3), 95-111.

Williamson, N.C., & Bello, D.C. (1992). Product, promotion and "free market" pricing in the indirect export channel. *Journal of Global Marketing, 6*(1/2), 31-54.

Williamson, O.E. (1964). *The economics of discretionary behavior: Managerial objectives in the theory of the firm.* Englewood Cliffs, NJ: Prentice-Hall.

THE HARMONIZATION OF EXPORT CONTROLS IN THE EUROPEAN UNION

Lothar Weinland

ABSTRACT

First of all, changes in the political, economic and technological environment that have fundamentally altered the general framework for export controls are discussed. Subsequently, the necessity for an international harmonization of export controls will be demonstrated. After that, we develop a harmonization-matrix which is useful to identify fields prone to harmonization of export controls. Following, the harmonization process in the European Union (EU) will be analyzed and its results will be assessed. We then discuss its implications for the European Union and for European exporters. Finally, future research directions are briefly mentioned.

Advances in International Marketing, Volume 8, pages 179-205.
Copyright © 1996 by JAI Press Inc.
All rights of reproduction in any form reserved.
ISBN: 0-7623-0164-3

I. THE NEW INTERNATIONAL GENERAL
FRAMEWORK FOR EXPORT CONTROLS

The export opportunities of corporations and nations are inter alia determined by many legal requirements. Particularly, export control regulations exert a strong influence on the attainable export performance of national economies. Consequently, there is an urgent necessity to analyze the export control regulations of nations, the environment in which they are applied, and their effects on export performance. An important field of research in this context is the international harmonization of export controls.

Recently, a great number of changes have occurred in the political, economic, and technological environment in which export controls are being applied. These alterations have essentially modified the traditional conditions of export controls. As a result, both the focus and the principle objective of export controls have been fundamentally influenced. The two most important changes in the political environment have been the following:

- the fall of the Iron Curtain and the subsequent collapse and disappearance of the Soviet Union and the Eastern Bloc, and
- the attempt of a lot of Third World countries to get access to nuclear, biological and chemical weapons of mass destruction and missile systems to deliver them.

In spite of the breakdown of the Warsaw Pact, the military threat posed by the former Soviet allies has not disappeared. It has changed and has become qualitatively different. On the one hand, the threat has diminished, because of the changes in the political structures that led to the relaxation of the West-East relationship. But although democratic forces in Eastern Europe have strengthened their position, the depth of the political and economic crises continues to make any further progress uncertain. The member states of the EU would have to seize all opportunities to support democratic forces in Eastern Europe. It appears to be in the interest of the member states to increase investment and technology transfer to the Eastern European nations in order to accelerate their integration into the Western political and economic system (Panel, 1991, p. 13).

On the other hand, for the simple reason that there have not been significant reductions in the number or capability of weapons possessed by the Eastern European countries the subliminal military threat remains nearly unchanged. In addition, there is the new threat of arms export and technology transfer from the former Soviet allies to proliferator regimes that exacerbates the export control dilemma of the Western nations. Besides, proliferator regimes also try to lure former Soviet scientists and engineers with extraordinary financial enticements to their countries (Rudney, 1993, p. 16).

For a few years a great number of countries and political organizations have been trying to gain access to advanced conventional weapon systems, nuclear, biological, and chemical weapons of mass destruction and the missile systems to deliver them. Commonly, there are growing concerns in the EU about the intentions underlying these acquisition activities because the proliferation of this kind of activity could be a decisive factor in the expansion of global conflicts initiated by regional powers, the exacerbation of regional instabilities, and the spread of extremist violence and state-sponsored terrorism (Panel, 1991, p. 2).

The proliferation of weapons of mass destruction and of the technical know-how and process equipment necessary to manufacture these types of goods has already increased the danger of regional conflicts in the Middle East, the Indian subcontinent, Southeast Asia, and South America. It is absolutely conceivable that the EU will be involved in these regional collisions, probably to prevent the deployment of weapons of mass destruction or to protect their foreign nationals and financial investments.

Concurrently, the spread of capabilities to produce biological and chemical weapons of mass destruction has increased the threat many regional states pose to their neighbors. A few countries in the Third World and in the Middle East have regional power aspirations based on their weapons of mass destruction. The tragic incidents in the Gulf war have dramaticially drawn world attention to the dangers posed by such proliferation (Sloniewsky & DeVaughn, 1993, p. 115; Stillman & Connaughton, 1991, p. 4). "The prospects of the emerging threat are unclear since power ambitions in this area run parallel with Islamic fundamentalism and explicit anti-Western impetus" (Rode, 1993, p. 102). Assuming that the proliferation regimes are able to procure longer-range missile delivery systems, they could endanger the entire world. Therefore, regional conflicts and arms races are now the main sources of instability within the evolving multilateral security structure of the world (Rudney, 1993, p. 15). Consequently, the EU is searching for effective export control policy options to oppose these new regional threats.

The rapid diffusion of weapons of mass destruction and the related technical know-how has also enlarged the danger that the EU faces from violence by terrorist or extremist organizations. Some of these groups are operating with the direct or indirect support of governments. There is an increasing danger that terrorists could acquire weapons of mass destruction either from countries that do not have well-developed export control systems or from nations that support the goals and objectives of terrorist violence (Panel, 1991, p. 54).

The outlined global political situation makes a reassessment of export control policies necessary. The events in Eastern Europe require a reappraisal of the strategic threat posed by the former Soviet allies, while the increasing proliferation of nuclear, biological, and chemical weapons in a great number of Third World countries demands an appropriate response (Haendel & Rothstein, 1991, p. 275). In former times the key issue in the export control field was how to prevent the procuring of strategic technology through the members of the Warsaw Pact. Nowadays the principal export control activities must be concentrated on the proliferation activities of several Third World countries and organizations (Bailey, 1993, p. 53; Czinkota, 1995, p. 4). Inevitably, the export control focus must shift from West-East to North-South controls (Stillman & Connaughton, 1991, p. 4) and the export control approach must move from a strategic balance to a tactical balance approach.

In addition to the political changes, a few alterations in the economic and technological environment have influenced the traditional conditions of export controls. First of all, one must consider that the acceleration of technical progress and the power and dissemination of information technologies around the world have enormously increased. In the past decade, information technologies have become "more powerful, more diverse, more plentiful, more dispersed, and more affordable than almost any observer might have imagined" (Goodman, Blumenthal, & Geipel, 1989, p. 59). The consequences of these alterations for export controls are evident. On the one hand, the acceleration of innovation in information technology is far greater than the speed with which the control bureaucracy can respond. Therefore, a lot of outdated and common technologies remain controlled, while new probably threatening technologies receive insufficient attention. On the other hand, the globalization of manufacture leads to the situation in which a great number of sales of computer components and systems takes place outside any multilateral export control agreements, especially when the newly industrialized Southeast Asian and South American countries, which are not subject to self-imposed export controls, are involved (Goodman, Blumenthal, & Geipel, 1989, pp. 58-59).

The incessant shift to global production has resulted in the emergence of a new type of product, the so-called world product. Such goods are composed of a great number of parts that are produced in two or even more countries. The components mostly have crossed national borders a number of times during the production. This kind of manufacture also has increased greatly the number of countries that are capable of producing high-technology goods. As a result, such goods have become technological commodities (Panel, 1987, p. 55). Many global products—for example personal computers—are produced in large quantities in an even greater number of countries without effective export control systems. In consequence, many high-technology products are problem-free and available world-wide from many sources.

The foreign availability of high-technology items shows clearly the futility of unilateral export control attempts. If sufficient quantities of the unilaterally controlled goods or technologies could be obtained from uncontrolled sources for shipment to the proscribed destinations or if the items could be produced in the denied destinations, export controls would be almost ineffective.

Besides, more and more high-technology goods and technologies can be used for civilian and military purposes. Consequently, goods and technologies increasingly are of "dual-use" nature, and the export of such items should be controlled. An example for such a dual-use item is a pesticide factory, which can also be used to produce poison gas (Hucko, 1993, p. 15). Unfortunately, the classification of civilian-use products, dual-use products, and military-use products, and the achievement of a multilateral agreement on such a classification is extremely problematic.

Accordingly, the export control standard in the dual-use area is extraordinarily different.

The expanded foreign availability of a great number of dual-use goods and technologies from countries without an export control mechanism illustrates that export controls applied by the Western nations "at present are to an important degree ineffective, superfluous, and above all harmful to the export capacity of industry in Western countries in relation to the position of industry in countries not applying similar export control mechanisms" (ERT, 1990, p. 9).

In addition, there is the issue of equipment size to consider. In former times, due to their size, high-technology products used to be difficult to hide. Any movement of such high-technology equipment was easily detectible. Nowadays, the components needed for state of the art technology have been miniaturized. Much leading edge technological equipment is so small that it has become nearly impossible to closely supervise the transfer of such products. In this way, advances in miniaturization support unavoidably the possibilities of smuggling and diversion (Parkhe, 1992, p. 56).

The revolutionary progress of telecommunication technologies (Panel, 1987, p. 55) has facilitated the development of integrated multinational corporations and simultaneously fundamentally effected the conditions of multilateral export controls. The multinational firms now have a much wider range of choices when selecting sites for research and development and manufacturing facilities (Panel, 1991, p. 40). As a consequence, corporations grow more independent and often maintain hundreds of establishments operating around the globe. Furthermore, new trading alliances and global operations are being established through mergers and acquisitions and joint ventures (TBR, 1990, p. 1). Therefore, corporations are increasingly less likely to be affected by prohibitive export control laws, which are only imposed by individual countries. Frequently, they are able to circumvent the unfavorable export controls and the resulting burden to their activities. Many firms are doing so already in order to avoid restrictions on corporate activities such as genetic research or tax rates. Often, overly stringent local export impediments can simply be overcome by transferring activities to a country that offers a comparatively more advantageous export platform. In the EU, every exporting corporation knows that it is comparatively easy to fulfill delivery obligations out of Greece or Portugal. As long as the essential export control regulations are not totally harmonized, every person who wants to can, by founding a subsidiary, shift export activities into a member state with less restrictive export rules (Dichtl, 1994a, pp. 5-6, 1994b, p. 1727).

II. THE NECESSITY FOR AN INTERNATIONAL HARMONIZATION OF EXPORT CONTROLS

The outlined developments, especially the expanding international integration of world trade and, consequently, of corporations, the increasing speed of global diffusion of innovation and of technology, the growing technological and manufacturing capabilities in Third World countries, and the enlarging threats emerging from proliferation and terrorism strengthen the need to apply effective multilateral export controls.

At this time, only a few sophisticated multilateral export control regimes exist in the area of weapons of mass destruction: the Missile Technology Control Regime [MTCR] (Shuey, 1992), the Nuclear Suppliers Group [NSG] (Fischer, 1992), and the Australian Group [AustG] (Robinson, 1992), which are responsible for chemical weapons-related exports (Bauer & Greene, 1992, pp. 13-17). In the conventional weapons and the dual-use items sector, multilateral export controls have been discontinued since the dissolution of the Coordinating Committee for Multilateral Export Controls (COCOM). This organization was established in 1949 by the countries of the North Atlantic Treaty Organization (NATO) and Japan in order to coordinate Western efforts to prevent products and technology of military relevance from falling into the hands of the former Union of Soviet Socialist Republics (USSR) or of its allies (Bauer & Greene, 1992, p. 18). As a result of the disappearance of the Soviet Union, the COCOM regime disbanded in the spring of 1994. Negotiations about the successor organization to COCOM—"New Forum"—which in future must integrate the export control policies of the Western nations, are just beginning.

This situation is extremely alarming. On the one hand there is a lack of effective export control systems in a few countries, and on the other hand there are essential divergences in the existing unilateral arms and dual-use items export control systems of the important industrial nations. The lack of and the discrepancies in export control systems lead to inequality in competition conditions, and the diversion of exports.

Inequalities in competition conditions are emerging from the fact that exporters in countries with less restrictive export control systems have greater sales potentials for a wide range of products, in particular for dual-use items. As more and more goods and technologies are dual-use items, exporters operating in countries with strict dual-use controls, like Germany and the United States, are at an extreme disadvantage in world-wide competition.

The diversion of controlled goods and technologies is possible, either with or without the direct knowledge of the exporter. In the first case, an item is exported legally to a recipient in a nonproscribed country and then re-exported—often through some other nonproscribed destinations—to a proscribed country. The exporters and their accomplices in other countries participate in these diversions, normally by constructing networks of front companies and accommodation addresses in order to obscure the export trail and to cover the illegal activities. In the second instance, the exporter delivers the items to a trustworthy recipient in a third country, who immediately re-exports it to a proscribed destination. A further possibility is that the recipient incorporates the controlled item as a component in another product or in a system and re-exports the end-product.

The lack of controls and the possibility to circumvent controls lead to an extremely low export control level that poses extraordinarily great problems to the security of the international community. Consequently, there is an urgent necessity for international harmonization of export controls.

III. THE FIELDS OF AN
INTERNATIONAL HARMONIZATION
OF EXPORT CONTROLS

The harmonization of different export control policies is a complex phenomenon with many facets to consider. In a wealth of exploratory interviews with representatives of multinational companies and officials of responsible ministries and export control authorities, it turned out that it is advisable to structure the tasks emerging within the framework of international harmonization of export controls by differentiating harmonization levels and harmonization areas.

The integration of the assessments of the experts in export controls led to the result that a complete harmonization of export control systems has to be executed on the following four levels:

- legal basis of export controls,
- licensing (permission) criteria,
- licensing (permission) procedures, and
- punishment procedures.

Until today, most export control standardization efforts have only included one harmonization level, the legal basis of export controls. Such a harmonization mode is completely insufficient, because the export control practice is extensively determined by the licensing criteria. Frequently, dual-use items that require official license in many countries get an export permission in countries with less restictive licensing criteria, while countries with strict licensing criteria totally prohibit the export of controlled items. In the same way, the divergences in permission practice lead to the situation in which a number of countries allow the export of items to certain countries, whereas others forbid the export of the same goods to these destinations. In addition, the licensing procedures are very important, because the period of time to get needed export permission has an enormous influence on the sales opportunities of most exporting corporations. Therefore, different permission times cause distortions of competitive positions. Finally, there is the necessity to harmonize punishment procedures, because penalty differences initiate the shift of export activities to countries with low penalties.

Futhermore, following the judgment of the specialists in export controls an extensive harmonization of export control approaches must include the following five areas:

- weapons of mass destruction,
- conventional arms,

HARMONIZATION-AREA				
Weapons of Mass Destruction	Conventional Arms	Dual-Use Items	Armament-Related Services	Transfer of Sensitive Knowledge

HARMONIZATION-LEVEL	Weapons of Mass Destruction	Conventional Arms	Dual-Use Items	Armament-Related Services	Transfer of Sensitive Knowledge
Legal Basis					
Licensing Criteria					
Licensing Procedures					
Punishment Procedures					

Figure 1.   Harmonization-Matrix

- dual-use items,
- armament-related services, and
- transfer of sensitive knowledge.

The result of the combination of harmonization levels and harmonization areas is a "harmonization matrix" that elucidates the entire spectrum of an international harmonization of export controls (see Figure 1) (Weinland, 1995, p. 28). A few institutions could constitute starting-points on the way to a comprehensive international harmonization of export control approaches—the existing multilateral export control regimes like the AustG, the MTCR, and the NSG, on the one hand, and trade blocs and international organizations like the EU, the Organization for Economic Cooperation and Development (OECD), and the United

Nations on the other hand. The following section analyzes the efforts to harmonize divergent export control systems of the member states of the EU.

IV. THE HARMONIZATION OF EXPORT CONTROLS IN THE EUROPEAN UNION

A. The Necessity for an European Harmonization Initiative

The EU has a wealth of good reasons to develop a common supranational export control system (Eavis & Greene, 1992, pp. 283-285; Saverworld, 1992, pp. 1-2). First, a few member states of the EU are deeply involved in the international arms trade, in particular the United Kingdom, France, and Germany (SIPRI, 1994). Recently, the enormous potential risks of uncoordinated EU arms exports have been dramatically demonstrated by the fact that EU suppliers contributed to the build-up of Saddam Hussein's military strength before his invasion of Kuwait.

Second, the EU is becoming more and more a principal actor on the political and economic world stage. In addition, other dominant nations increasingly perceive the Community as considerably more than the sum of its parts and mark it as Fortress Europe (Berg, 1990, p. 79; Dichtl, 1990, p. 32). Consequently, a coordinated EU export control approach to other major participants in world trade is to a much higher degree credible and acceptable than initiatives by single member states.

Third, during the past decades great differences existed in the export control policies of the member states, because each of them applied its own export controls on an important range of goods to a number of proscribed destinations. Divergences in export control policies had seriously undermined the practices of those member states enacting strict controls. Therefore, for example, the refusal of arms exports to Iraq by some member states had insufficient consequences given the arms export practices of other member states.

The fourth and most important reason for the construction of a common EU export control approach has been the introduction of the internal market. Since the beginning of 1993, the EU has abolished most trade barriers and implemented a single market which in principle guarantees the unrestricted flow of goods, services, capital, and people among the member states. Export controls are in principle restricted to the external frontiers of the EU. An undesirable but probable result of the internal trade liberalization of the EU is the circulation of previously controlled items from one country with strict export controls—for example Germany—to another member state with a less stringent control policy (Rudney, 1993, p. 15). As a result, EU manufacturers and dealers who want to export strategic goods to problematic destinations could theoretically move their products problem-free across the Union to an export point of their choice where border controls are the least efficient. Therefore, the elimination of intracommunity controls will increase integration but also create "opportunities to divert trade to the countries with the weakest controls, where sensitive goods may travel more easily to the most undesirable destinations" (Mueller, 1993, p. 10).

The enormous security risks involved in that kind of detour exporting have been demonstrated several times by illegal exports in earlier years. In spite of the problems associated with crossing a few borders of EU member states, criminal exporters have carefully chosen the export platforms for their illicit export activities. Thus, arms destined for Iran went out through Lisbon with forged Guatemalan and Honduran end-user certificates, and grenades from the French company Luchaire made their way to Iran through Greek ports. To eliminate or minimize the risk of diversion, many different types of export controls in the Community were applied among the member states themselves. Consequently, both extra-EU and intra-EU export controls are an extremely important area of concern for the EU.

B. Article 223 of the Treaty of Rome as a Legal Restraint for a Common Export Control Approach

In principle, the EU would have been well advised to create a single export control regime for weapons and for sensitive dual-use goods and technologies. Unfortunately, this approach is presently not available. Article 223 of the Treaty of Rome, the constituent document of the European Community, states that "each member state may take measures which it deems necessary for the protection of interests which are vital to its security and which concern the production of or trade in weapons, ammunition or war materials." Therefore, in this area the Community is not responsible, and the member states are able to derogate from the basic provisions of the EU Treaty. But article 223 also stipulates that in the internal market these measures should not aggravate the competitiveness of goods that are not specially designed for military purposes. Furthermore, article 223 placed the European Council under the obligation to draw up a list of products to which the derogation would be applicable.

In the opinion of the Commission, the EU Treaty must be applied to all goods that are not part of the article 223 list, especially to dual-use goods and technologies. In addition, the Commission believes that dual-use goods and technologies should move as freely between the member states as they do within each of them. Consequently, the Commission is convinced, that intra-EU trade export controls on dual-use items must be eliminated (Wenzel, 1993, p. 95).

The member states did not share the Commission's view on this point. Their judgment contrasted sharply with the assessment of the Commission. Because dual-use items undoubtedly allow military use, nearly all member states except Germany took the view that they must be defined as defense-related items and excluded from a common EU export control approach. They traditionally regarded export controls on dual-use items as a concern of national security and considered all control questions to be outside the competence of the Community (Kauzlarich, 1993, p. 88; Wenzel, 1993, p. 97).

The member states have been interpreting article 223 in accordance with their position on the construction of a common export control approach in the Community. France and the United Kingdom especially, were in favor of an extremely broad interpretation that would allow them to maintain national controls on sensitive dual-use products and technologies. They were afraid of the effect on their industry that the submission of a wide range of dual-use goods to common EU export control regulations may have. In addition, they feared that the EU Commission will be allowed a greater involvement in export controls, because Commission activities will unavoidably lead to the imposition of tighter controls.

In contrast, Germany and the Netherlands, which preferred tighter export controls and a common EU approach, have opted for a narrow interpretation, which would limit the opportunity for unilateral national controls (Prouvez, 1992, p. 88). In their opinion, a correct interpretation of article 223 must take the following considerations into account. The provisions of article 223 derogate from the essential provisions of the EU Treaty. Therefore, they must be interpreted in the most restrictive manner. This is confirmed by the wording of paragraph 2 of the article, which states very clearly that the measures must be necessary, not only useful, and must be justified by the protection of essential security interests of the member states, and should not adversely affect the conditions of competition in the Common Market regarding products which are not intended for special military purposes. The three points indicate that article 223 does not apply to dual-use goods which are not intended for special military purposes (Prouvez, 1992, p. 88).

C. The Harmonization Process

As explained above, it is not possible at this time for the EU to construct a single export control regime for arms and dual-use items. Therefore, the Commission was forced to initiate separate harmonization efforts in both areas. The development of strong and effective EU arms export control regulations is an extraordinarily complex issue, because the trade in and consequently the export of weapons are exempted from the competence of the Community (Prouvez, 1992, p. 87), and the attitudes toward arms trade are contrasting between the member states because of cultural differences, so that the arms export control laws of the member states are excessively inconsistent.

For France and Britain, arms exports are indispensably necessary to achieve economies of scale in the arms industry. In their opinion the arms industry otherwise would not be viable because domestic market demand would never be sufficient to sustain the production capability, which is necessary to stay close to the cutting edge of defense technology. In both countries arms export is seen as a legitimate instrument of foreign policy, an attitude left over from the era when both nations were world powers (Mueller, 1993, p. 10). The French philosophy is based on national autonomy and independent nuclear capability. In the United Kingdom arms exports have always been seen as a political tool to increase the security of non-EU-allied former overseas possessions. On the contrary, Belgium, Denmark, Germany, Italy and the Netherlands have distanced themselves from applying weapons exports as an instrument of foreign policy and taken a position in favor of restraint (Bauer & Greene, 1992, pp. 5-6).

Although the member states agreed that the coordination of arms trade policies is an important area of concern that could not be entirely exempted from a common security policy approach of the EU, most of them were not willing to relinquish their national export controls on conventional arms to the supranational authority of the Community. Nevertheless, the member states of the EU drafted common guidelines that are to apply in licensing the transfer of conventional arms to third parties. In accordance with the guidelines, the member states in arms trade are obliged to take several aspects into account (Mueller, 1993, p. 11; Rusman, 1992, p. 274; Weller, 1992, pp. 45-46):

- respect for the international commitments of the member states of the Community, in particular sanctions decreed by the Security Council of the United Nations or by the Community, agreements on non-proliferation and other subjects, and other international obligations,
- respect of human rights in the country of final destination,
- internal situation in the country of final destination (e.g., existence of tensions or internal armed conflicts),
- preservation of regional peace, security and stability,
- national security of the member states, of territories whose external relations are the responsibility of the member states, and of friendly and allied countries,
- behavior of the buyer country toward the international community, regarding particularly its attitude to terrorism, the nature of its alliances, and respect for international law,
- existence of a risk that equipment will be diverted within the buyer country or re-exported under undesirable conditions,
- compatibility of arms exports with the technical and economic capacity of the recipient country, taking into account the desirability that states should achieve their legitimate needs of security and defence.

Despite the announcement of these common arms export criteria there have been, up to now, remarkable differences in the arms export practice because the criteria—for example, insufficient respect for human rights—are interpreted differently in the member states (Bauer & Greene, 1992, pp. 5-6). As long as these discrepancies in the arms export practice of the member states continue to exist, the abolishment of article 223 of the Treaty of Rome, and consequently of the exemption of military goods from EU export control regulations remains unlikely (Mueller, 1993, p. 11). Recently, discussions on the design of a "Common Foreign and Security Policy" of the EU have shown that the member states agree on the basic principle that there should be an even tighter cooperation in the coordination of their arms export policies. But right now the future shape and content of an EU Arms Export Policy is still completely unclear (Prouvez, 1992, p. 87).

Since the member states came to the understanding that dual-use items are subject to the Treaty of Rome, there has been no legal obstacle to the construction of a common dual-use items export control approach. Consequently, since 1991 several project teams, composed of participants of the member states and of the Commission, have been trying to develop an EU Dual-Use Items Export Policy (European Commission, 1992a). First, the groups analyzed the export control systems of the member states to identify differencies, strengths, and weaknesses. They ascertained the most important discrepancies in the following areas:

- lists of restricted goods and technologies,
- lists of restricted countries/ destinations,
- licensing criteria and licensing procedures, and
- penalties for violation of export control laws.

Second, the teams worked out a draft for an EU regulation. They considered that the following key elements have to be addressed to ensure an operational and effective export control approach on the Community level (Jestaedt, 1992, pp. 55-56):

- a common list of dual-use goods and technologies that are subject to EU controls,
- a common list of proscribed destinations,

- a forum to coordinate licensing and enforcement policies in the Community,
- standard licenses for extra-EU exports and the conditions for granting them throughout the Community,
- explicit procedures for administrative cooperation between licensing and customs authorities throughout the Community, including an information system.

In August 1992 the Commission presented the temporary results of the efforts of the project groups as a proposed regulation on the control of dual-use items (European Commission, 1992b). Unfortunately, it took nearly three years to align the divergent interests of the member states with regard to a wealth of rules of the proposed regulation (Pietsch, 1994, p. 305). Finally, the EU Dual-Use Items Regulation could come into force in July 1995.

The harmonization of dual-use items export controls in the European Union is characterized by several results (Hahn, 1995; Jestaedt & Behr, 1995; Reuter, 1995). In particular, the member states agreed on a common dual-use regulation and on common licensing guidelines. The EU Dual-Use Items Regulation comprises the following elements:

- a common dual-use items list,
- a common special facilities country list enclosing Australia, Canada, Japan, Norway, Switzerland, and the United States,
- license requirements for the extra-EU export of all dual-use items contained in the common dual-use items list,
- license requirements for the intra-EU export of a few special sensitive dual-use items,
- a catch-all-clause that makes non-listed dual-use items subject to an export authorization when the exporter has been informed by his government that the goods in question are or could be, in their entirety or in part, intended for use in connection with the development, production, transfer, handling, maintenance, storage, detection, identification, or dissemination of chemical, biological or nuclear weapons and the development, production, maintenance, or storage of missiles capable of delivering such weapons,

- a safeguard-clause that authorizes member states to retain existing or to enact new legal requirements to prohibit the export of non-listed dual-use items.

In accordance with the common licensing guidelines member states are obliged to take several aspects into account:

- their commitment within the framework of international agreements on nonproliferation and control of items sensitive to security,
- their commitment within the framework of sanctions imposed by the Security Council of the United Nations or other international organizations,
- considerations of national foreign and security policy, and
- considerations of end-use and the danger of diversion.

D. An Assessment of the Results of the Harmonization Efforts

An assessment of the results of the harmonization efforts of the export control approaches in the European Union leads to the following three main critique points:

- several important export control areas were not included in the harmonization efforts,
- the harmonization results in the arms area are insufficient, and
- the harmonization results in the dual-use items sector are not satisfactory.

First of all, it is disturbing that three very important export control areas—in particular weapons of mass destruction, armament-related services, and transfer of sensitive knowledge— have not been included in the negotiations in the Community. As a result, an alarming lack of control exists in the future EU export control approach.

Besides, the outcome of the harmonization of weapons export controls is not sufficient. On the one hand, because of the absence of common arrangements on three harmonization levels—namely the legal basis, the licensing procedures, and the punishment procedures—on the other hand on account of the deviating interpretation of the common arms export criteria by the member states. Consequently, there are substantial discrepancies in the arms export practice in the Community.

Finally, for four reasons the harmonization effort in the dual-use items area is not satisfactory. In the first place, with regard to the inadequacy of the construction of the EU Dual-Use Items Regulation:

- The regulation lays down intra-EU export controls on a few sensitive dual-use items. Consequently, the EU is not a license-free zone, and the internal market is not totally completed.
- The catch-all-clause is not applicable to exports determined for the conventional arms sector. Therefore, the future EU export control regime neglects an important control purpose.
- The safeguard clause authorizes member states to retain existing and to enact new legal requirements to prohibit the export of non-listed dual-use items. Thus, the degree of harmonization depends on the extent of application of this option through the member states. Unfortunately, it is very likely that member states will retain and enact a great number of extremely differing additional national legal requirements, so that the export control practice will inevitably differ in the Community. As a result, detour exports and a distortion of competition are to be expected.

In the second place, it is extraordinarily problematic that the member states have not been able to reach an agreement on a common negative list of proscribed countries/ destinations or, alternatively, on a list of proscribed suspect projects. Consequently, in the future every member state draws up its own national negative list of proscribed destinations. These lists are likely to differ widely. This fact leads to the situation wherein every member state continues to decide independently to which destinations they are willing or not willing to export goods and technologies itemized in the EU dual-use items list. The logical consequence of the individual permission practice is a divergence in competition conditions and a diversion of controlled goods and technologies. Therefore, the problem of preventing manufacturers and dealers from exporting their goods via other member states to problematic destinations continues to exist.

Third, the licensing guidelines of the Community are to a high degree non-committal, and there is a lack of notices regarding the interpretation of the guidelines. Consequently, the existing divergence on interpretation between member states causes a different permission practice and the distortion of competition. In the future, the licensing guidelines have to be put in a more concrete form (Greene, 1992) so as to guarantee a nearly identical permission practice in each country of the Community.

Fourth, it is alarming that two very important export control levels have been neglected in the dual-use items harmonization approach of the Community: the licensing procedures and the punishment procedures. The absence of common licensing procedures is alarming, because the real effectiveness of export controls lies in the enforcement of the legal basis in the daily practice of agencies in member states charged with licensing, customs, and investigation (Mueller, 1993, p. 14). It is astonishing that member states were not able to install an EU Export Control Agency that coordinates and supervises the control practices in the Community. Consequently, a different control behavior of the member states that facilitates trade diversion is to be expected.

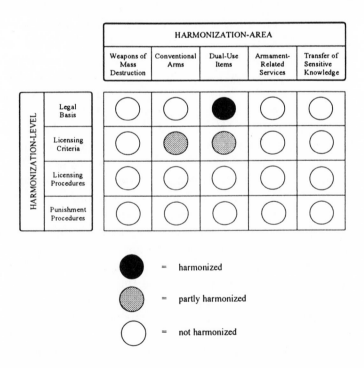

Figure 2. Harmonization-Matrix of the European Union

The lack of common punishment procedures or rather of the establishment of an EU Export Control Criminal Law leads to the situation that violators will be differently punished for an identical offence in individual member states. As long as such divergences in punishment of violators exist in the EU, there will be incentives for diverting trade.

Finally, the result of the harmonization of export controls in the Community can be illustrated by means of an Harmonization Matrix of the European Union (see Figure 2).

The Matrix shows clearly that previous harmonization efforts in the European Union have only been a first step on the way to an extensive EU export control approach, because there are a great number of fields left to be harmonized.

V. CONCLUSIONS AND FUTURE RESEARCH DIRECTIONS

A. Implications for the European Union

Due to insufficient harmonization of export controls in the EU, the Community is confronted with:

- enormous export control gaps,
- threatening security risks,
- a distortion in competition conditions, and
- non-observance of the aims underlying export controls.

These issues will impose enormous problems on the EU. Therefore, the Commission has to enhance the harmonization process within the Community. It must within the bounds of feasibility attempt to reach the highest possible export control standard.

Fortunately, there are two points of departure for a continued harmonization of export controls in the EU. First, a clause contained in article 19 of the EU Dual-Use Regulation stipulates that member states in 1998 have to decide whether several legal requirements of the EU Dual-Use Regulation are retained or not. According to article 19, member states are forced to discuss further harmonization activities at that time.

Second, the revision of the Maastricht Treaty in 1996 gives the Community the chance to make further progress with regard to the harmonization of export controls in line with the structuring of the Common Foreign and Security Policy. In this context, it appears to be possible to conceive an European Arms Export Control Policy.

Harmonization of the divergent arms export control policies of the member states of EU in all probability would have a positive impact on the alignment of control policies in other harmonization areas. As soon as the Community is able to reach an agreement concerning a Common Arms Export Control Policy accepted by all EU countries, ideally on all harmonization levels, divergences regarding the export of dual-use items and armament-related services and the transfer of sensitive knowledge will inevitably disappear.

In this case, it seems possible to install a "license-free zone" in the EU. Within such a zone every kind of good could be moved without export permission. The license-free zone could be expanded by the inclusion of countries that are willing to adapt their own export control system to that of the EU.

Finally, the establishment of "European Export Control Agency" responsible for the coordination and supervision of the export control practice in the Community would complete an extensive European export control system.

B. Implications for European Exporters

The EU was not able to eliminate many existing divergences in the export control systems of their member states in the course of the export control harmonization process. Therefore, it seems necessary to distinguish exporters from member states with restrictive export control laws and exporters from such countries with less restrictive export control systems in order to analyze the implications of insufficient harmonization of export controls for European exporters.

Corporations from member states with lax export control laws still have a competitive advantage based on the remaining divergences in export control policy. For instance, they have greater sales potentials resulting from a generous licensing policy. Consequently, they are able to adhere to their well-established strategies and profit from their competitive advantages.

On the other hand, exporters from member states with strict export control systems still have to cope with competitive disadvantages. Unfortunately, the result of the harmonization of export controls in the EU has not come up to their expectations. The divergences in the export control policies of the member states have been reduced but not eliminated. Consequently, inequality in competition conditions within the European Union is likely to exist for years. Handicapped exporters are forced to intensify their efforts to compensate for their competitive disadvantage.

First, they must exert pressure on their governments, the European Parliament and the European Commission with a view to harmonizing export controls in the EU. They need to seek support from professional associations, for example, the "Worldwide Industry" and the "European Roundtable of Industrialists."

Nevertheless, exporters have to put their main emphasis on the evolution of legal business management strategies to diminish competitive disadvantages. In this connection, exporting corporations in particular should take the following activities into consideration:

- spin off operations in member states with low export control standard,
- establish subsidiaries in member states with generous regulations in the export control area,
- cooperate with exporting companies from less restricted member states, and
- give up business units where competive disadvantages caused by export control divergences continue to exist.

In particular, European conglomerates are in a position to foster such legal activities with a view to lessening the negative implications of insufficient harmonization of export controls in the EU, while small and medium-sized firms can do no more than adapt to any prevailing situation.

C. Future Research Directions

Given a great number of unsolved problems concerning the multilateral harmonization of export controls, one must realize that much research needs be done. First, it seems necessary to develop a step-by-step plan for a continued international harmonization of export control systems. One must find ways, which for the first time, guarantee sufficient involvement of the business sector in the harmonization process.

Furthermore, the evolution of a method to determine the costs imposed on the national economies and on the companies concerned by the enforcement of export controls is pressing task. Richardson's technique (Richardson, 1993) could serve as a fundamental basis for the development of a complete cost-finding system. In addition, an approach to ascertain the extent and the implications of the distortion of competitive positions caused by the divergent export control standards of nations has to be developed. On the basis of the two required approaches, it would be possible to conduct empirical studies to determine the effects of the existing differences in the export control systems of exporting countries.

It is imperative to develop an approach to detect problem areas of companies caused by export controls and to elaborate a program to reduce the resulting burden on corporations. The simplification of the corpus of law and the improvement of administration proceedings represent two main elements of such a program.

Finally, it seems essential to generate measures to improve the enforcement of export controls within companies. In particular, activities concerning the organization of export controls have to be developed. The evolution of an EDP-based export control system should be a further main target.

REFERENCES

Bailey, K. (1993). Nonproliferation export controls. problems and alternatives. In K. Bailey, & R. Rudney (Eds.), *Proliferation and export controls* (pp. 49-55). Lanham/London: University Press of America.

Bauer, H., & Greene, O. (1992). The present state of export controls within the EC and its member states. In Saferworld (Ed.), *Arms and dual-use exports from the EC: A common policy for regulation and control* (pp. 5-24). Bristol: Saderworld.

Berg, H. (1990). European integration: Aims, methodsm experiences, perpectives. Yu H. Berg, H. G. Mcioourc, & W. B. Schüuemann (Eds.)., *Markets in Europe strategies for marketing* (pp. 1-97). Stuttgart: Poeschel-Verlag.

Czinkota, M. R. (1995). *A new export control regime. security in a volatile environment, world business policy brief.* Washington, DC: Georgetown University Center for International Business Education and Research.

Dichtl, E. (1994a). Defacto limits of export controls: The need for international harmonization. Paper presented at the Second Annual Consortium for International Marketing Research (CIMaR) Conference, Rio de Janeiro.

Dichtl, E. (1994b). Dejacto limits of export controls the need for international harmonization of export controls. In *BetriebsBerater, 49*(25), 1726-1730.

Dichtl, E. (1990). The elimination of border clearances and technical impediments. In E. Dichtl (Ed.), Steps to the European market, (pp. 13-34). München: Beck-Verlag.

Eavis, P., & Greene, O. (1992). Regulating arms exports. a programme for the European community. In H.G. Brauch, H.J. Van der Graaf, J. Grin, & W. Smit (Eds.), *Controlling the development and spread of military technology: Lessons from the past and challenges for the 1990s* (pp. 283-299). Amsterdam: VU University Press.

European Commission. (1992a). *Export controls on dual-use goods and technologies and the completion of the internal market.* Brussels.

European Commission. (1992b). *Proposal for a council regulation on the control of exports of certain dual-use goods and technologies and of certain nuclear products and technologies.* Brussels.

European Round Table of Industrialists [ERT]. (1990). *European industry and COCOM.* Brussels.

Fischer, D. (1992). The effectiveness and shortcomings of the NPT control regime. IAEA, EURATOM and the London suppliers club. In H.G. Brauch, H.J. Van der Graaf, J. Grin, & W.A. Smit (Eds.), *Controlling the development and spread of military technology: Lessons from the past and challenges for the 1990s* (pp. 141-155). Amsterdam: VU University Press.

Goodman, S.E., Blumenthal M.S., & Geipel, G.L. (1989). Export control reconsidered. *Issues in science and technology*, (Winter), 58-62.

Greene, O. (1992). Developing and implementing export control guidelines. In Saferworld (Ed.), *Arms and dual-use exports from the EC: A common policy for regulation and control* (pp. 69-86). Bristol: Sajerworld.

Haendel, D., & Rothstein, A. L. (1991). The shifting focus of dual use export controls. An overview of recent developments and a forecast for the future. *The International Lawer, 25*(Spring), 267-276.

Hahn, V. (1995). The neue EU dual-use items regulations. *Außenwirtschaftliche praxis, 1*(1), 5-10.

Hucko, E. M. (1993). Foreign Trade Law-War Weapons Control Law, Fourth Edition. Cologne: Bundesanzeiger Verlagsgesellschaft.

Jestaedt, T. (1992). European harmonization of export control, on dual-use items the initiative of the European commission. *Europäisches Wirtschafts-und Steuerrecht, 3*(3), 53-56.

Jestaedt, T., & Behr, N. (1995). The Eu dual-use items regulation. *Europäische Zeitung für Wirtschaftsrecht, 6*(5), 137-141.

Kauzlarich, R. (1993). US-EC nonproliferation cooperation. an American view. In K. Bailey & R. Rudney (Eds.), *Proliferation and export controls* (pp. 87-90). Lanham/London: University Press of America.

Mueller, H. (1993). The export controls debate in the "new" European community. *Arms control today,* 10-14.

Panel on the Future Design and Implementation of U.S. National Security Export Controls. (1991). Finding common ground: U.S. export controls in a changed global environment. Washington, DC: National Academy Press.

Panel on the Impact of National Security Controls on International Technology Transfer. (1987). *Balancing the national interest. U.S. national security export controls and global economic competition.* Washington, DC: National Academy Press.

Parkhe, A. (1992). U.S. national security export controls. implications for global competitiveness of U.S. high-tech firms. *Strategic Management Journal, 13,* 47-66.

Pietsch, D. (1994). Limitation and control of exports of dual-use goods in the market the present state of negotiations. *Europäisches Wirtschafts-und Steuerrecht, 5,(9),* 298-305.

Prouvez, N. (1992). Implementation and enforcement of an EC arms and dual-use goods export policy. In Saferworld (Ed.), *Arms and dual-use exports from the EC. A common policy for regulation and control* (pp. 87-112). Bristol: Saferworld.

Reuter, A. (1995). Dual-use goods export controls the new EU dual-use items regulations. *Neue Juristische Wochenschrift, 48*(34), 2190-2192.

Richardson, J. D. (1993). *Sizing up U.S. export disincentives.* Washington DC: Institute for International Economics.

Robinson, J. P. P. (1992). The Australia group. A description and assessment. In H.G. Brauch, H.J. Van der Graaf, J. Grin, & W.A. Smit (Eds.), *Controlling the development and spread of military technology. lessons from the past and challenges for the 1990s* (pp. 157-176). Amsterdam: VU University Press.

Rode, R. (1993). Improving nonproliferation export controls. In K. Bailey & R. Rudney (Eds.), *Proliferation and export controls* (pp. 102-105). Lanham/ London: University Press of America.

Rudney, R. (1993). Introduction. In K. Bailey & R. Rudney (Eds.), *Proliferation and export controls* (pp. 15-20). Lanham/London: University Press of America.

Rusman, P. (1992). A conventional arms transfer regime in the European community. In H.G. Brauch, H.J. Van der Graaf, J. Grin, & W.A. Smit (Eds.), *Controlling the development and spread of military technology. lessons from the past and challenges for the 1990s* (pp. 271-281). Amsterdam: VU University Press.

Saferworld. (Ed.) (1992). *Arms and dual-use exports from the EC. A common policy for regulation and control.* Bristol: Saferworld.

Shuey, R. (1992). Assessment of the missile technology control regime. In H.G. Brauch, H.J. Van der Graaf,J. Grin, & W.A. Smit (Eds.), *Controlling the development and spread of military technology: Lessons from the past and challenges for the 1990s.* Amsterdam: VU University Press.

Sloniewsky, R. W., & DeVaughn, M. (1993). Developments in export controls. the non-proliferation initiatives. In H. E. Moyer, R.C. Cassidy, M.T. Buckley, & J.C. Frazier (Eds.), *Law and policy of export controls: recent essays on key export issues* (pp. 115-135). Washington, DC: American Bar Association, Section of International Law and Practice.

Stillman, T. H., & Connaughton, A. Q. (1991). Export controls in a changing world. *Business America*, 3-4.

Stockholm International Peace Research Institute [SIPRI]. (1994). *SIPRI-yearbook*. Oxford: Oxford University Press.

The Business Roundtable [TBR]. (1990). *Focus on the future: A global export control framework*. Brussels.

Weinland, L. (1995). Limited harmony. *EUmagazin, 4*, 28-29.

Weller, M. (1992). The guidelines governing export controls. In Saferworld (Ed.), *Arms and dual-use exports from the EC: A common policy for regulation and control* (pp. 45-68). Bristol: Saferworld.

Wenzel, J. (1993). The european community's approach to export controls. In K. Bailey, & R. Rudney (Eds.), *Proliferation and export controls* (pp. 95-99). Lanham/London: University Press of America.

Advances in International Marketing

Edited by **S. Tamer Cavusgil,**
The Eli Broad Graduate School of
Management, Michigan State University

Volume 7, Marketing in Asia Pacific and Beyond
1996, 255 pp. $78.50
ISBN 1-55938-839-0

Edited by **Charles R. Taylor,** *Department*
of Marketing, Villanova University

CONTENTS: Preface, *S. Tamer Cavusgil.* Introduction, *Charles R. Taylor.* PART I. CORPORATE STRATEGY IN THE 1990s. Global Comparisons of Channel Integration Strategies and Strategic Alliances, *Heon Deok Yoon, Edward A. Morash, M. Bixby Cooper and Steven R. Clinton.* Strategic Alliances: Contrasting Korean and U.S. Preferences, *Seoil Chaiy and David B. Montgomery.* Marketing, Open Markets and Political Democracy: The Experience of the Pacrim Countries, *Hans B. Thorelli.* A Comparison of the Perceptions of Clients and Design Consultants Toward Corporate Identity Programs, *Dae Ryun Chang, Don Ryun Chang and Kwoon Soo Lee.* PART II. ISSUES IN GLOBAL DISTRIBUTION AND THE MARKETING OF SERVICES. Competitive Intensity and Channel Structure in Korean Consumer Goods Industries, *Changhoon Shin, Minhi Hahn and Sehoon Park.* International Marketing and the Role of Logistics: Logistics Strategies and the Implications for Management and Government, *John C. Taylor.* Negotiation Processes and Outcomes in Intenational Technology Transfer, *Sejo Oh and Sungil Kim.* Evaluation and Management of Professional Services in Korea, *Mary Anne Raymond and William Rylance.* PART III. INTERNATIONAL ADVERTISING. The Changing Information Content of Advertising: A Longitudinal Analysis of Korean Magazine Ads, *Young Sook Moon and George R. Franke.* Environmental Influence on U.S. Multinational Advertising Agencies: A Market Development Perspective, *Alan T. Shao.* Advertising Presentations of the Independent vs. Interdependent Self to Korean and U.S. College Students, *Julie Scott Wilcox, Gyungtai Ko, James W. Gentry, Michael Stricklin and Sunkyu Jun.* Foreign Elements in Korean and U.S. Television Advertising, *Charles R. Taylor and Gordon E. Miracle.* PART IV. METHODOLOGICAL CONTRIBUTIONS TO THE INTERNATIONAL MARKETING LITERATURE. Dimensions of Global Strategy and Their Utilization by European and Japanese MNCs: An Exploratory Study, *Shaoming Zou and Jay L. Laughlin.* Evaluating the CYMC Cosmopolitanism Scale on Korean Consumers, *Sung-Joon Yoon, Hugh M. Cannon and Attila Yaprak.* Country of Production/Assembly as a New Country Image Construct: A Conceptual Application to Global Transplant Decisions, *Dong Hwan Lee and Charles M. Schaninger.* An Investigation of the Optimum Number of Response Categories for Korean Consumers, *Kyung Hoon Kim.*

Also Available:
Volumes 1-6 (1986-1993) $78.50 each